Computa

KU-350-889

ARNE RYDE
8 December 1944–1 April 1968

Computable Economics

The Arne Ryde Memorial Lectures

Kumaraswamy Velupillai

OXFORD
UNIVERSITY PRESS

1004291
330.0151
VEL

OXFORD

UNIVERSITY PRESS

Great Clarendon Street, Oxford OX2 6DP

Oxford University Press is a department of the University of Oxford.
It furthers the University's objective of excellence in research, scholarship,
and education by publishing worldwide in

Oxford New York

Athens Auckland Bangkok Bogotá Buenos Aires Calcutta
Cape Town Chennai Dar es Salaam Delhi Florence Hong Kong Istanbul
Karachi Kuala Lumpur Madrid Melbourne Mexico City Mumbai
Nairobi Paris São Paulo Singapore Taipei Tokyo Toronto Warsaw

and associated companies in Berlin Ibadan

Oxford is a registered trade mark of Oxford University Press
in the UK and in certain other countries

Published in the United States
by Oxford University Press Inc., New York

© Kumaraswamy Velupillai 2000

The moral rights of the author have been asserted

Database right Oxford University Press (maker)

First published 2000

All rights reserved. No part of this publication may be reproduced,
stored in a retrieval system, or transmitted, in any form or by any means,
without the prior permission in writing of Oxford University Press,
or as expressly permitted by law, or under terms agreed with the appropriate
reprographics rights organization. Enquiries concerning reproduction
outside the scope of the above should be sent to the Rights Department,
Oxford University Press, at the address above

You must not circulate this book in any other binding or cover
and you must impose this same condition on any acquirer

British Library Cataloguing in Publication Data

Data available

Library of Congress Cataloging in Publication Data

Velupillai, Kumaraswamy, 1947–
Computable economics : the Arne Ryde memorial lectures /
Kumaraswamy Velupillai.
p. cm.
Includes bibliographical references (p.).
1. Economics, Mathematical. 2. Induction (Mathematics)
3. Recursive theory. I. Title.
HB135.V42 1999 330'.01'51—dc21 99–24070

ISBN 0–19–829527–8

1 3 5 7 9 10 8 6 4 2

Printed in Great Britain
on acid-free paper by
T. J. International Ltd
Padstow, Cornwall

Arangu inri vaddu ādiyatre – nirambiya
nūl inrik kōttik kolal

Thirukkural, no. 401

[To try to address an audience without first equip-
ping oneself with the necessary knowledge is like
trying to play chess without the chessboard.
My translation]

Dedicated to my mother
and to the memory of my father

The Arne Ryde Foundation

ARNE RYDE was an exceptionally promising young student on the doctorate programme at the Department of Economics at the University of Lund. He died after an automobile accident in 1968 when only twenty-three years old. In his memory his parents Valborg Ryde and pharmacist Sven Ryde established the Arne Ryde Foundation for the advancement of research at our department. We are most grateful to them. The Foundation has made possible important activities which our ordinary resources could not have afforded.

In agreement with Valborg and Sven Ryde, we have decided to use the funds made available by the Foundation to finance major initiatives. Since 1973 we have arranged a series of symposia in various fields of theoretical and applied economics. In 1990 we published 'Seven Schools of Macroeconomic Thought' by Edmund S. Phelps, the first issue in a series of Arne Ryde Memorial Lectures. Thomas J. Sargent's 'Bounded Rationality in Macroeconomics' followed in 1993, 'High Inflation' by Professors Daniel Heymann and Axel Leijonhufvud in 1995, and 'Rational Risk Policy' by Professor W. Kip Viscusi in 1998. The present book by Professor Kumaraswamy Velupillai, based on lectures held at Lund University in May 1994, is the fifth issue in this series. We are very glad and grateful that Professor Velupillai agreed to come to Lund to give his Arne Ryde Memorial Lectures.

Bjørn Thalberg

Preface and Acknowledgments

Just as in the uprooting of wild grasses;
If not grabbed properly, they cut the hand.
In ethical training, if there be no proper restrain,
One is picked for hell through one's own making.

(Chinese version of) *Dharmapada*, ch. 30, no. 6

The contents of this essay incorporate the substance of the lectures delivered as the fourth Arne Ryde Lectures on May 24/5 1994, at Trolleholm Castle in Scania, Sweden. I have gone into greater detail in some cases, particularly in Chapters 4, 6, 7, 8, and 9, than I was able to do in the delivered lectures because of the obvious time constraints during their actual delivery, although the planned program was substantially the same as the structure of this printed text.

I am greatly indebted to Professor Björn Thalberg for having invited me to give this prestigious series of lectures. My indebtedness to him, however, extends far beyond the acknowledgment of gratitude for this particular invitation. I began life as an academic economist twenty-seven years ago under his teaching, supervision, and guidance. Whether the work reported here is an adequate partial compensation for his initial faith and investment I do not know. But none of my work would have been possible without his consistent personal and professional support during the whole of the period I have known him.

I was taught by Richard Goodwin that the problems of dynamics, optimization, and computation are inextricably intertwined in the economic sphere. The full significance of his message began to dawn on me only after I understood his idea of computation universality for dynamical systems and the recursion-theoretic underpinnings of induction. He followed my faltering attempts at synthesizing his vision with sympathy, and even enthusiasm, to almost his last days. I hope something of that great man's teaching comes through in the unspoken message of this book.

I have worked in the general area of computable economics for over two decades. During this period the collaboration with my friend Berc Rustem has meant a great deal to me. He introduced me to the weird and wonderful world of computational complexity theory long before it was fashionable to think about the efficiency of algorithms, using recursion-theoretic mathematics, in economic contexts.

Bob Clower, Axel Leijonhufvud, Francesco Luna, John McCall, and Stefano Zambelli have also been instrumental in guiding me and helping me to focus on computability issues in economic hypothesis. Their inspired friendship, advice, and help as the written text evolved turned out to be decisive in ways that cannot easily be described.

Almost all the material that has gone into this text was conceived, if not also finalized, during my tenure as associate director of the Centre for Computable Economics (CCE), in the Department of Economics at UCLA. The director, Professor Axel Leijonhufvud, and the CCE's chief benefactor, Dr Spiro Latsis, deserve special thanks for the freedom and facilities they made available to me, through the CCE, for extended periods of time. The challenge of being associated with the establishment and nurturing a research institution was indescribably exciting.

The final version of this text was prepared during my tenure as a member of the Department of Economics at the Queen's University of Belfast. I am grateful to the director of the School of Social Sciences, Professor John Spencer, for having given me unusual latitude to schedule my lectures in ways that made it possible for me to devote extended and continuous periods of time to the preparation of this manuscript.

Viveka, Sumithra, and Aruna, my three daughters, played their usual background music that has sustained my sanity and peace of mind for almost a quarter of a century. Viveka's interest in the music of Bartok, Sumithra's in the history of film, and Aruna's in that of photography gave me perspectives that were, at times, decisive in breaking conceptual and methodological dead-ends that blocked progress.

Maria Johansson, friend and companion, nursed me through a sequence of personal and professional catastrophes that impinged upon my life from almost the day I began to conceive and pen the thoughts that were to become this book. She was also instrumental in making the final text available for print. She did it with love and care.

Growing up in old Colombo gave me the privilege of basing my ethical training on the twin wisdoms of the *Thirukkural* and the

Dharmapada. I have chosen, therefore, as an epigraph for this work a verse from the ancient Tamil collection of couplets, the *Thirukkural*, attributed to the sage Thiruvalluvar. My father instructed me on its interpretations and its wise ambiguities. This work is, in a way, an attempt to extol the virtues of ambiguities in a domain of economic theory replete with pseudo-formal uncertainties. I hope, however, that the chessmen are not bereft of the chessboard.

More important than that, as taught in the wisdom of the *Dharmapada*, I hope that I have not extolled the virtues of ambiguities without appropriate restraint.

K.V.

Dervio, Lago di Como
April 1998

Contents

1 Introduction and Overview 1

2 Ideas, Pioneers, and Precursors 10

3 Computable Rationality 28

4 Adaptive Behavior 44

5 The Modern Theory of Induction 66

6 Learning in a Computable Setting 89

7 Effective Playability in Arithmetical Games 107

8 Notes on Computational Complexity 134

9 Explorations in Computable Economics 146

10 Conclusions: Reflections and Hopes 178

Appendix: A Child's Guide to Elementary Aspects of Computability Theory 185

References 201

Author Index 213

Subject Index 217

1
Introduction and Overview

I have long been considering the purchase of an electric drill, and I am sure that when I finally buy one I will drill dozens of holes I do not really need. But triviality is a universal failing; . . . The remedy against it is strength of character, not technological backwardness. *Problems must dictate methods, not vice versa.*

Solow (1954: 374; emphasis added)

[T]here are games in which the player who in theory can always win cannot do so in practice because it is impossible to supply him with *effective instructions* regarding how he should play in order to win.

Rabin (1957: 148; emphasis added)

The above is a statement of the first important result in what I have come to call *computable economics*. The key word is "effective," referring to a procedure whose execution is specified in a finite series of instructions, each of which is finite in length and where all the details of the execution are specified exactly, thereby leaving no room for magic, miracles, or other such metaphysical entities. The exact meaning of "effectivity" is mathematically equivalent, under the Church–Turing thesis,[1] to "computability."

[1] Many different, independent attempts were made in the formative years of recursive function theory to formalize the intuitive notion of effectively calculable or computable function, number, object, etc. Thus, there was Turing's device of a machine, constructed on principles obtained by abstracting that which human beings with particular physiological architectures would do when indulging in computing activities as it is commonly understood; there was the Gödel–Herbrand notion of general recursiveness coming down from Dedekind, Peano, and others who used mathematical induction and iteration to build up the number system; there was Church's attempt at abstracting the imperative content of the functional notation leading to the λ-calculus; and so on. Church's thesis is a statement encapsulating the phenomenological fact – or, as Emil Post called it, a natural law – that all of these independent attempts ultimately yielded one and the same class of functions, numbers, and objects as effectively calculable or computable.

I was taught by my teacher, mentor, and, subsequently, valued friend, Richard Goodwin, to view economists and the economic system itself as problem-solvers.[2] This meant, of course, that problems of the economic sphere had to be identified. Methods to solve the identified problems had to be devised. The epistemological status and nature of the solution sought had to be defined. Finally, and most importantly, the problem-solver had to be formally characterized.

Many different mathematical formalisms can be used to frame problems and problem-solvers. Alternative formalisms for problems and problem-solvers lead, often, to methods for their solution, and to procedures to be adopted by the problem-solvers, that depend on the particular mathematical framework chosen for their representation. That there is no given, *a priori*, single formal framework that is natural, in any sense, for the formalization of economies and economists as problem-solvers was the main message that Goodwin, among others, tried to suggest. In this work I have chosen a recursion-theoretic formalism in the hope that it may lead to some interesting insights into economic problems and problem-solvers. In other words, "problems must dictate methods," but there is no evidence that the mapping between them is bijective.[3]

Mathematical logic itself is divided into set theory, proof theory, model theory, and recursion theory. The study of computable objects and domains is the subject matter of recursion theory. The formalisms of economic analysis are, in general, based on mathematical foundations relying on set theory or model theory (e.g. nonstandard analysis). Computable economics, as I see it, is about basing economic formalisms on recursion-theoretic fundamentals.[4] This means we will have to view economic entities, economic actions, and economic institutions as computable objects or algorithms (cf. Scarf 1989).[5]

---

[2] Perhaps in the same sense in which mathematics and mathematicians were viewed by Polya (cf. Velupillai and Punzo 1996).

[3] I have in mind the kind of suggestions made, and questions posed, by David Ruelle in his fascinating Gibbs Lecture (Ruelle 1988). His main theme was circumscribed by the question, how natural is our human 20th-century mathematics? His conclusions were that there was nothing natural about it. It is in this sense that I assert that there is no evidence for a bijection between problems and methods.

[4] Recursion theory did not exist at the time mathematical economics was rigorously codified in the early 1930s. Had it existed, there is no doubt, in my mind, that the computable numbers would have been the natural domain, computable analysis and combinatorial optimization the natural framework, for economic analysis.

[5] Analogously, as Debreu (1984: 268) points out, "one can describe the action of an economic agent by a vector in the commodity space R^l. The fact that the commodity space has the structure of a real vector space is a basic reason for the success of the

For the moment these broad indications must suffice. In this book I will try to draw my picture with a broad brush on a rough canvas with selected problems and classes of problem-solvers pertaining to: rationality, learning, (arithmetical) games, dynamics and optimization. I give them recursion-theoretic interpretations and content and draw the ensuing economic implications. These examples, I hope, will create the image I want to convey, about the nature and scope of computable economics.

The book is structured as follows. In the second half of this general introduction and synopsis and in the concluding Chapter 10 there are brief excursions into general methodological and epistemological issues that have arisen as a result of the new ontology implied by the philosophies underlying recursion theory – incompleteness, undecidability, and uncomputability being the prime examples. The other chapters, apart from the second, are discussions of examples from standard economic theory. In each example, roughly speaking, the implicit question I pose is: what is the effective or computable content of these examples?[6] or, what is the computational complexity of a particular operator? or, again, how does the computable characterization of a problem constrain the methods of solution for it? and, yet again, what are the implications of characterizing problem-solvers' recursion theoretically? And so on. Each example or operator is chosen in such a way that it enables me to introduce selected fundamental concepts and tools of recursion theory and to show their workings in an economic setting.

In Chapter 2 I have attempted to outline the work of the pioneers and precursors of computable economics. At least until the late 1980s and early 1990s, the work by Rabin, Putnam, Kramer, Futia, Lewis, Spear, and Rustem remained isolated and scattered without the kind of unifying umbrella provided by computable economics.

mathematization of economic theory. In particular convexity properties of sets in R^l, a recurring theme in the theory of general economic equilibrium, can be fully exploited." As we will see in what follows, "one can also describe the action of an economic agent" as if "it" were a Turing machine; in this case the commodity space would have an appropriate recursive structure in which computable and combinatorial properties would be exploited. This would have been no less a reason "for the success of the mathematization of economic theory" – if we were allowed the luxury of speculating in counterfactuals.

[6] It is like asking, what is the constructive content of standard mathematics? Then one would try to eliminate, for example, the indiscriminate use of the law of the excluded middle in existential statements (cf. e.g. Beeson 1978 for a lucid discussion of these matters).

Mercifully, this fate did not have to be shared by Simon and Scarf. This is partly because some aspects of their important contributions spawned wholly new research programs in behavioral economics and computable general equilibrium (CGE) theory. I try to tell a unified story, albeit briefly, and to extract a theme that I believe to be of some importance also in the mathematization of economics.

In Chapter 3, I take rationality, classically conceived, and show that the implicit procedural content in standard definitions enables one to show an equivalence between the rational economic agent of orthodox theory and a *Turing machine* (TM). With this equivalence, I investigate, in Chapter 4, some recursion-theoretic implications of adaptive behavior. In Chapter 5 I take up the issue of induction, its modern recursion-theoretic formalization, and, by reinterpreting learning-as-induction, use it in a simple application to a standard problem in economics in Chapter 6. This is an eclectic chapter in that I fuse elements of computable analysis with applied classical recursion theory to generate overwhelmingly positive results on the computable identifiability of a rational expectations equilibrium (REE). This chapter also gives formal content to some of the epistemological speculations in the introduction, particularly on induction, simplicity, complexity, and a few other classic and much maligned concepts. Moreover, the nature of the example gives me the chance to introduce the basics of algorithmic complexity theory – that part of applied recursion theory lying at the basis of the modern theory of induction.

In Chapter 7 I discuss Rabin's pioneering paper and the way in which he imposed recursion-theoretic contents into a standard model of games, and I introduce the extensions to this model that Jones has suggested in a series of fundamental contributions. This whole line of thought seems to have escaped the notice of economists interested in applying recursion-theoretic ideas to standard problems in game theory.

In Chapter 8 I try to tackle the problem of the computational complexity of a procedural decision maker. One particular algorithm is constructed and discussed in some detail, and Khachiyan's algorithm is applied to show the polynomial-time complexity of the procedurally rational agent.

In Chapter 9 I move from the "bread-and-butter" issues to "cheese-and-cakes". In speculating about the frontiers of computable economics, in this chapter, I look at some fundamental economic tools, concepts and methodologies from tentative recursion-theoretic formalisms. Economic dynamics – such as growth and business cycle theories – poses intriguing questions about the paradoxes of multiple equilibria, and about the advantages of linear stochastic formalisms over nonlinear deterministic formalisms to model growth and fluctuations in the economy. I suggest that recursion-theoretic tools could provide elegant resolutions of some of the paradoxes and disagreements – not always in directions that I would have felt like approving *a priori*. The mathematical underpinnings of the Second Fundamental Theorem of welfare economics, *tâtonnement*, interpreted recursion-theoretically rather than topologically, and computable reflections on the socialist calculation debate are some of the other topics discussed in this chapter.

Finally, I return once again to methodological and epistemological issues in the concluding chapter. This is probably best viewed as counterfactual speculation, trying to chart a course for the future of computable economics, as if it were in the past.

The mathematical appendix is an attempt at providing a "child's guide to classical recursion theory." It is neither comprehensive nor self-contained; the field is too vast, and the tools I harness somewhat opportunistic, so that it would be impossible to be either one or the other. It is, instead, a catalogue of building-blocks and rules and a few lessons on structures that could be built with them. I had in mind the Meccano sets of my childhood – the box containing the basic elements and a book of instructions on some of the possible constructions, but leaving the more interesting possible constructions to the fertile imagination of a child.

I should like to add a minor caveat, without sounding pompous or imputing unnecessary originality due to ignorance of other and parallel work.[7] To the best of my knowledge, the results I have stated in Chapters 3, 4, 6, 8, and 9, as theorems and propositions seem to be "new"; the rest tend to be adaptations and expositions of known results in somewhat newer contexts – but not always so.

At this point some additional technical background remarks – at a general level – may be useful, to set the methodological backdrop

---

[7] I am reminded of Myrdal's acid remark about "the attractive Anglo-Saxon kind of unnecessary originality, which has its roots in certain systematic gaps in the knowledge of the German language on the part of the majority of English economists" (Myrdal 1939: 8–9). I do not know the exact nature and extent of the "systematic gaps" in my knowledge; hence the caveat.

against which the contents of this book should be viewed. Recursion theory has an applied wing,[8] which in turn has at least three subdivisions: computational complexity theory, diophantine complexity theory, and algorithmic complexity theory. The latter has its own applied wing: stochastic complexity theory.

In a rigorously quantitative sense, computational complexity theory can be called the economic theory of computations – in any field. This is because computational complexity theory is about the *efficiency* of algorithms, and the efficiency is, in general, quantified and measured in terms of the cost of computation in time, space, and other related dimensions.[9]

Induction and information have been at the heart of economic reasoning ever since the subject was codified into an independent discipline.[10] Algorithmic complexity, based on classical recursion theory, provides the foundations for a rigorous modern theory of induction and randomness; the latter, in turn, lie at the basis of a theory of information content in finite objects, be they finite sequences or individual objects. On the other hand, induction as learning from finite objects – extracting universals from particulars – and learning as estimation is based on the empirics of algorithmic complexity: for example stochastic complexity theory, or the *minimum description length principle* of Rissanen (1989). Diophantine complexity theory, on the other hand, is a direct outgrowth of the methods and results associated with the negative solution to Hilbert's Tenth Problem.

Finally, straddling constructive and computable analysis, there is the fascinatingly intractable world of combinatorial optimization. Harnessing, in particular, the unifying concepts and tools of computational complexity theory and classical recursion theory, combina-

---

[8] In the same sense in which there is applied mathematics, which used to be called "methods of mathematical physics."

[9] There is also the fascinating area of measuring efficiency in terms of the thermodynamics of computation where, also, computational complexity theory acts as one of the theoretical frameworks (cf. e.g. Bennett 1982).

[10] Indeed, from the outset: Petty via Smith and Hume, through Jevons and Mill down to Keynes, Leontief, and Simon. It was, in my opinion, Ricardo who subverted economics toward a deductive discipline, and then the various mathematizations of the subject remained faithful to the axiomatic-deductive method – this in spite of profound changes in mathematics, the foundations of mathematics and logic. These changes – the "renascence of empiricism in the recent philosophy of mathematics," in the characteristically pungent and colourful view of Lakatos (1978: ch. 2) – have seen a movement away from axiomatic–deductive rigidities to a more experimental vision of mathematical philosophy. Anything experimental must always have a large inductive component.

torial optimization almost defines the frontiers of *modern* operations research. A generation or two ago, economists were trained in the tools of *classical* operations research: linear programming and the simplex algorithm, nonlinear programming, dynamic programming, the maximum principle, and much else. Developments in computational complexity theory and combinatorial optimization have completely changed the nature of the questions posed: optimization problems are now posed as *decision problems*, as defined in logic and recursion theory. Such a fundamental transformation gives immediate content to Simon's fertile concepts of bounded rationality and satisficing. Moreover, these new tools and concepts show that even some of the most widely used algorithms and operators – simplex, dynamic programming, optimal control, etc. – are theoretically intractable (i.e. computationally complex). That they seem to work in practice – especially simplex – and are used by purists in economics must only mean that Simon has always been right and, moreover, that the purists have, in fact, been speaking prose[11] all their optimizing lives, whenever they tried to compute a solution to their problem. One of the implicit messages of this book is that such schizophrenia is neither necessary nor desirable, with emphasis on the former.

I conclude this chapter with the following broad, epistemological, remarks. Ian Hacking has characterized the period 1800–1936 as a time when chance was tamed only to give rise to indeterminism – the taming of chance and the rise of indeterminism, in Hacking's felicitous terminology:

> The taming of chance and the erosion of determinism constitute one of the most revolutionary changes in the history of the human mind. I use the word "revolutionary" not as a scholar but as a speaker of common English. If that change is not revolutionary, nothing is. That is the real justification for talk of a Probabilistic revolution, 1800–1930. (Hacking 1987: 54)

The afterglow of this probabilistic revolution and the "changed vision of the world in which we live" (Hacking 1987: 54) brought forth, for example, Haavelmo's "Probability Approach to Economics," decades of Cowles Foundation methodology, and the

---

[11] I am, of course, referring to Monsieur Jourdain's famous remark in Molière:

Par ma foi! il y a plus de quarante ans que je dis de la prose sans que j'en susse rien, et je vous suis le plus obligé du monde de m'avoir appris cela.

["Well, my goodness! Here I've been talking prose for forty years and never known it, and mighty grateful I am to you for telling me!" This translation is by John Wood in the Penguin Classics version of Molière's plays.]

more recent stochastic modelling approaches in economic theory and econometrics. All of this was consciously, even deliberately, woven into the fabric of the theoretical technology of modern analytical economics.

The confluence of events that led to the fundamental results of Gödel, Kleene, Church, Post, and Turing – the fashioning of recursion theory – in the 1930s heralded a new period and a new characterization: the taming of indeterminism and the rise of undecidability. This is the fundamental epistemological background thesis on the basis of which this book is written.

Confluences linking logic, mathematics, philosophy of science, and economics have characterized earlier turning points in the development of economic analysis: from Petty and his Baconian convictions on induction and political arithmetic through Adam Smith's remarkable early work on the history of astronomy, where his philosophy of science was a clear anticipation of Kuhn's sociological theory of growth of knowledge (Kuhn 1977), and then down the British line[12] of Ricardo, Mill, Jevons, and Keynes, who each in his own way was part of such an interdisciplinary confluence. And this interdisciplinary linkage had influences on the development of quantitative methods, bolstered by logic and mathematics, which in turn made decisive differences to the structure and scope of economic theorizing.

These are the broad senses in which I believe that a reasonable, philosophical, epistemological, and methodological[13] case can be made for the *computable approach to economics* – paralleling the mathematization (or the mathematical approach to) economics (of 1830–80 and 1926–56) and the probability approach to economics (of 1920–50) – especially because of the changes in ontology, or, as Hacking more succinctly states it, "changes in our vision of the world in which we live." We accepted a non-deterministic ontology and theorized about it and within it. The rise of incompleteness, uncomputability, and undecidability will bring forth an inductive ontology and the need to theorize within it and within a vision of the world implied by it. It should not be forgotten that advances in recursion

[12] But not only the "British line": it was true of many of the other great traditions too: the Austrians, the Swedes, and some of the American Institutionalist pioneers.

[13] "Methodological" in the sense of the new methods of recursion theory for gaining knowledge about the (economic) world; "epistemological" in the sense of what that knowledge should or might be; "philosophical" in the sense of our notions about the world about which we seek knowledge.

theory – and its sub-branches – have been instrumental in the renascence of empiricism in mathematics and logic, and hence in the formalisms underlying reasoning processes. The new methodologies demonstrate the inherent and intrinsic incompleteness of reasoning processes, and so a subject like economics, which has its whole analytical edifice based on the rationality principle, cannot avoid being influenced by these developments. The new ontology brings with it, therefore, new and enhanced modes of thinking and hence, possibly, modes of behavior untameable by unadapted theoretical technologies. I shall return to these broad themes, once again, at the end of this book.

2
Ideas, Pioneers, and Precursors

What must be achieved is in fact this: That every paralogism be recognized as an *error of calculation*, and that every *sophism* when expressed in this new kind of notation ... be corrected easily by the laws of this philosophic grammar. ... Once this is done, then when a controversy arises, disputation will no more be needed between two philosophers than between two computers. It will suffice that, pen in hand, they sit down ... and say to each other: *Let us calculate.*

Leibniz (1686/1965: xiv; final emphasis added).

2.1 INTRODUCTION

I do think there are some very worthwhile and interesting analogies between complexity issues in computer science and in economics. For example, economics traditionally assumes that the agents within an economy have universal computing power ... Computer scientists deny that an algorithm can have infinite computing power.

Karp (1987: 464)

I have tried, in the opening paragraphs of the previous chapter, to delineate the nature of computable economics by suggesting that recursion-theoretic formalisms of economic fundamentals, broadly conceived, are the key features of the subject. This does not, of course, restrict the scope of computable economics to the "pure" aspects of recursion theory. The "applied" wings of recursion theory, in particular the varieties of *complexity theories* – computational, algorithmic, stochastic, and diophantine – have an equally important role to play in redirecting the formalization of economic fundamentals. By this I mean a redirection away from the dominant set-theoretic and model-theoretic formalisms of economic fundamentals. The hope is that the new insights that "a re-examination of several of the primitive concepts" of economic analysis will entail might make the subject intrinsically numerical and computational, with strong foundations in computability theory. The alternative route, tried and tested for over half a century, via the set-theoretic, Bourbakian path, for example, has a less direct link with the numerical content and computational constraints of the formalized entities. There is also the deductive and declarative bias of the standard formalism. The most vivid illustration of this thesis is the way computable general equilibrium models have developed from their initial, formal – even Bourbakian – structures.

In this chapter I begin, in the following section, with an attempt to define, in less general terms than in the previous chapter, the nature and scope of what I mean by "computable economics." The ideas underlying a more focused definition for computable economics are based on a study of the way in which economics was mathematized in the "modern era." By "modern era" I mean, on the one hand, the era that had its origins in the debates on the proper formalism for economic analysis to pose, and answer, questions of the existence, uniqueness, and stability of general economic equilibrium, and, on the other hand, the post-von Neumann–Morgenstern era. I have told my version of these stories in greater detail in other, related, writings (cf. Velupillai 1996 and 1998*b*); what is reported in the following section is a summary of these companion pieces, modified to provide the context in which it is possible to highlight the relevance of the contributions of the pioneers and precursors of computable economics.

With the possible exception of Alain Lewis, none of the pioneers and precursors seems to have envisaged a sustained research program in computable economics (as I have defined it). In certain specific ways, the work of the two most famous pioneers (the two Herberts: Simon and Scarf) did spawn research programs of breadth, intensity, and vision. But these programs, in the end, substantiate the case for computable economics without quite being confined by it or to it. I think that Simon and Scarf had broader scope and vision than the narrower one of computable economics according to my definition. In Section 3.3 below this aspect of computable economics, and speculative thoughts on mild counterfactual themes on the "roads not taken"[1] in the mathematization of economics, are given some positive considerations.

[1] I have in mind the last three lines of Robert Frost's exquisite "The Road Not Taken": *over/*

2.2 IDEAS

> To use the past for present purposes, we should see the history
> of the field as sequences of decisions, of choices, leading up to
> the present. Imagine a huge decision-tree. . . . I wish to maintain
> that knowledge of the past, when the past is understood as such
> a decision-tree, can be quite useful to the economist working on
> present questions at today's frontier.
>
> Leijonhufvud (1991: 4–5)

The mathematization of economic analysis in the "modern era,"
when viewed as "sequences of decisions" along the nodes of an
"imagined decision-tree," can be seen to have based the formalism
of economic entities (institutions, agents, etc.) and behavior (for
example rationality – individual and collective) in set theory and
model theory. As mentioned in the previous chapter, these are two
of the four branches of modern logic, the other two being recursion
theory and proof theory. There are no compelling doctrine-historical, analytical, or descriptive reasons for preferring a formalism of
economics on the basis of set theory and model theory rather than,
say, recursion theory. It is my contention that it was entirely an
accident of the history of ideas that the mathematization of economics took the path that led to a basis in set theory and model
theory (cf. Velupillai 1996, 1998b). Some of the pioneers of mathematical economics have claimed otherwise, i.e. deliberate design
rather than fortuitous events and accidents. Thus, Frank Hahn has
claimed:[2]

> Two roads diverged in a wood, and I –
> I took the one less travelled by,
> And that has made all the difference.

[2] Surely Hahn's conclusion that we have "almost completed the task we set ourselves after the war to deduce all that was required from a number of axioms" must
rank with Mill's famous conclusion that all that had to be said on the theory of value
had been said by Ricardo (on the eve of the marginal revolution); with Lord Kelvin's
audacious statement, in 1898 (on the eve of the quantum mechanical and relativity
revolution), that all the problems of theoretical physics had been solved, except for the
little matter of black-body radiation and the Michaelson–Morley experiment; with
Solow's assertion, in 1965 (on the eve of the rational expectations–New Classical revolutions), that all that remained to be resolved in short-run macroeconomic theory
was "the trivial job of filling in the empty boxes and that will not take more than 50
years of concentrated effort at a maximum . . . "!

But the task we set ourselves after the last war, to deduce all that was required from a number of axioms, has almost been completed, and while not worthless has only made a small contribution to our understanding. (Hahn 1994: 258)

Couple this to the following series of clear and defining statements by Debreu:

The theory of value is treated here with the standards of rigour of the contemporary formalist school of mathematics. (Debreu 1959: viii)

Especially relevant to my narrative is the fact that the restatement of welfare economics *in set-theoretical terms* forced a re-examination of several of the primitive concepts of the theory of general economic equilibrium. (Debreu 1984: 269; emphasis added)

Walras and his successors for six decades perceived that his theory would be vacuous without an argument in support of the existence of at least one equilibrium, and noted that in his model the number of equations equals the number of unknowns, *an argument that cannot convince a mathematician.* One must, however, immediately add that the mathematical tools that later made the solution of the existence problem possible did not exist when Walras wrote one of the greatest classics, if not the greatest, of our science. It was Abraham Wald . . . who eventually in Vienna in 1935–36 provided the first solution in a series of papers that attracted so little attention that the problem was not attacked again until the early 50s. (Debreu 1984: 268; emphasis added)

The fundamental methodological statements by two of the pioneers of contemporary mathematical economics suggest, I claim, the following ideas:

- The early attempts at formalizing economic entities and behavior were based on the available theoretical technology, i.e., essentially, set theory.
- Hence the economic questions posed, and the answers sought and obtained, had to be confined to those that could have been framed in set-theoretic formalisms.
- The development of model-theoretic tools, e.g. nonstandard analysis, and the resurgence of interest in constructive analysis had immediate impact in the mathematization of economics – the former in the contribution of Abraham Robinson himself, but more particularly through the work of Aumann and others, who pointed out that the economic significance of price-taking behavior in perfectly competitive markets required the use of

infinitesimals that were not part of the standard number system. The latter – i.e. constructive methods and their impact on mathematical economics – came about via Scarf's pioneering attempts to give numerical content to existence proofs.[3]

Thus, a restatement of problems in welfare economics, economic equilibrium, economic behavior, etc., in set-theoretic, model-theoretic and quasi-constructive terms "forced a re-examination of several of the primitive concepts" of economic analysis. Two of these "restatements" have led to fertile, progressive, research programs.[4] Then, why not try a "restatement" in terms of recursion-theoretic formalisms too? Perhaps there will be a fertile "re-examination of several of the primitive concepts" of economic analysis.

On the other hand, a different line of reasoning, starting from the impressive developments in computable general equilibrium theory, recursive economic dynamics, recursive computational equilibria, and computational economics, leads one to the following natural question:[5]

The idea of universal computation . . . One is led to ask: is there a computability property for the economy? This is clearly preliminary to any tentative computation. Given the difficulties we have been facing, one may well conjecture an impossibility theorem for economic systems: the economy is, simply, not computable. (Baum 1988: 252)

These questions can be asked, and answered, only after a recursion-theoretic formalization of economic analysis is attempted. Computable economics is, in part, about such an attempt.

If, now, I try to pull together these ideas in one methodological and epistemological credo, then the attempt to pursue computable economics can be realized as a definite and focused research program in one of two ways (or in an eclectic combination of the two): either

(a) seek or investigate the economic implications of recursion-theoretic restrictions to the standard primitive concepts of economic analysis; or

---

[3] But not going all the way with the constructivists in totally abandoning undecidable disjunctions.

[4] Even in the strict Lakatosian sense of the Methodology of Scientific Research Programs (MSRP).

[5] This refers, of course, to the *computability* of the formal model of the economy under discussion.

(b) go back to one of the nodes of the decision-tree that characterizes the development of the mathematization of economics (cf. Leijonhufvud 1991); e.g. to the nodes at which existence, uniqueness, and stability questions were rigorously posed and reconsidered for general economic equilibrium; then try to answer the questions recursion-theoretically, rather than set-theoretically or model-theoretically.

Let me take a concrete counterfactual issue in terms of (b). The device of ensuring that "the number of equations equals the number of unknowns" was known and considered to be insufficient to guarantee the existence of economically meaningful solutions to a problem of general economic equilibrium. The problem was then posed, and solved, with free-swinging, non-constructive, and non-algorithmic set-theoretic methods which guaranteed, ostensibly, the existence (and even uniqueness) of economically meaningful – i.e. non-negative – equilibrium solutions. But this resolution left two possible lacunae unresolved: the demonstrated solution could be any real number;[6] and the processes – whether virtual, like *tâtonnement*, or not – by which the demonstrated (unique) equilibrium was brought about were left unspecified. Developments in computable general equilibrium theory, following Scarf's quasi-constructive existence proofs, have partially resolved the second problem. Formulating the existence problem as a (combinatorial) decision problem, however, resolves both lacunae in one fell swoop. This latter approach is squarely recursion-theoretic; rational or integer constraints on data and solutions are explicitly introduced *ab inizio* and the solution brings with it an algorithm, a process, to achieve it. There will, however, be an open-endedness about the solution in that for most of the interesting economic decision problems – say, an increasing-returns-to-scale problem arising from indivisibilities – it will not be possible to decide whether or not a best algorithm exists.

To get back, however, to (a) and (b) and the path followed in this book, my own inclination is to go the latter way (i.e. (b)), although my limited knowledge and abilities force me to go the former way (i.e. (a)). As a result of these conflicting features, this work is mildly eclectic, dominated by the former method with a few infusions along

---

[6] To be perverse about this example, this means that a solution could, for example, be Euler's number, which, whether rational or not, is not known even at this point in time!

the latter path. Perhaps at some future date, when my knowledge and abilities mesh with my propensities, I may attempt a more coherent restatement based on trying to realize a research program based on (b).

Against the backdrop provided by the above ideas and conjectures, I will now try to summarise the story of some of the pioneers and precursors of computable economics.

2.3 PIONEERS AND PRECURSORS OF COMPUTABLE ECONOMICS

> The fact is that every writer creates his own precursors.
>
> Borges (1964: 201[7])

If we keep the Leibnizian injunction of "let us calculate" (when in doubt), it is possible to go back all the way to the founder of political economy to discover the precursor *par excellence*: William Petty. After all, he did set out to represent the concepts of political economics, as political arithmetic, entirely in terms of "number, weight and measure" – and long before Leibniz.[8] I shall, for the purposes of this book, restrain whim and concentrate on the pioneers and precursors of computable economics and their contributions, guided by the framework suggested in the previous section, in particular method (a). To make the story reasonably coherent, I will adopt a sub-schematization of method (a) as follows:

(i)   contributions that sought explicit recursion-theoretic characterizations of standard economic formalisms in specific areas, for example rationality, learning, games;

(ii) contributions that investigated the properties of economic entities and processes from the point of view of applied recur-

---

[7] "Kafka and his Precursors," *Labyrinths*, p. 201; emphasis added.

[8] Swift's inimitable satire must, surely, be mentioned as a noble precursor, too, of computable economics. Learned readers will recall that, in "A Voyage to Laputa," Gulliver was guided around the grand Academy of Lagado where, at the residence of the Projector in Speculative Learning, a professor described his ingenious "Project for improving Speculative Knowledge by Practical and Mechanical Operations." I have often wondered whether this particular aspect of Swift's satire was aimed at Leibniz and whether, also, Babbage was inspired by Swift in some of *his* projects for improving!

sion theory, for example the computational complexity of optimization operators or production processes with increasing returns to scale resulting from indivisibilities;

(iii) those contributions that utilized recursion-theoretic tools and concepts within the standard formalisms of economic theory, but, paradoxically, almost never with recursion-theoretic questions or solutions in mind;

(iv) finally, those contributions that raised important recursion-theoretic issues in economics but not necessarily within a systematic computable economic framework; Herbert Simon's lifelong research program comes to mind as the paradigmatic example of this case. Nothing can be more recursion-theoretic than procedural rationality or satisficing behavior; but neither of these was set in its paces in a computable economic setting.

Recursion-theoretic characterizations

The core areas in which explicit recursion-theoretic characterizations were sought for economic fundamentals have been games, rationality, learning, equilibria, and rational expectations. The pioneers and precursors, in approximate chronological order, are: Rabin (games), Lewis (games, rationality, equilibria), McAfee (games, rational expectations), Spear (learning), and Rustem and Velupillai (rationality). It is a striking and melancholy fact that between Rabin's classic work in 1957 and the contribution by Rustem and Velupillai in 1990, a period spanning over thirty years, the pioneers have been so few and – proverbially – far between. I have no useful explanation for this surprising fact except to conjecture that other, more exciting and pressing, concerns and developments in economics left little time for economists to embark on mastering and applying wholly new tools and concepts. After all, this period coincided with the great advances and consolidations in mathematical general equilibrium theory, a series of revolutions in macroeconomics, impressive developments in game theory, experimental economics, computable general equilibrium theory, and so on. Applying the economic principle to the classic problem of competition for the scarce resource of technically able economists pursuing interesting, useful, and frontier problems, it is perhaps not surprising that computable economics had to take a back seat, in particular because results in computable economics, under category (i) above, were predominantly and spectacularly negative – effectively undecidable and unplayable games, effectively unrealizable choice functions, uncomputable equilibria, effectively unlearnable REEs, and so on. Perhaps it was the fault of the pioneers that they emphasised the (universal) negative results rather than the positive aspects of the negative results.[9]

All these issues and results, and summaries and generalizations of the above pioneering works, literally span the basic contents of this book. Thus, the classic framework and results of Rabin form the subject matter of Chapter 7; aspects of Lewis's sustained and deep research program in computable economics are discussed in Chapters 3, 7, and 9; the starting-point for the subject matter of Chapter 6 on learning is the contributions of McAfee and Spear; a complete elaboration and generalization of Rustem and Velupillai on rationality is the main theme of Chapter 3. However, in contrast to the uniformly universal negative results reported in the original works, I try, wherever possible, to emphasize an interpretation that stresses the positive aspects of the negative results. Taken together, these works reiterate Debreu's message, but with "set-theoretical terms" replaced by "recursion-theoretical terms"; i.e., to paraphrase Debreu, "Especially relevant to my narrative is the fact that the restatement of . . . economics in *recursion-theoretic terms* forces a re-examination of several of the primitive concepts of economic theory" (1984: 269).

Above all, one is forced to re-examine the concepts of rationality, learning, the effective playability of games, and the diophantine complexity of simple (arithmetical) games. For example, a reconsideration of the notion of rationality leads to a natural definition in terms of procedures, which in turn forces – almost – the economic problem to be posed as a decision problem rather than an optimizing problem; such a series of re-evaluations brings back into the fold, quite naturally, satisficing behavior – but not simply as suboptimal behavior in a complex optimization problem (cf. Chapter 4).

Combinatorial and complexity considerations

Without the slightest doubt, the clear and distinguished pioneers and precursors under this definition are Herbert Simon (see below) and Scarf (1981a, b). The classics by Gomory and Baumol (1960) and

---

[9] As in formal recursion theory in general and in computational complexity theory and diophantine decision problems in particular (cf. Chs. 7 and 8 below).

Clower and Howitt (1978) also belong to this class of pioneering works, as does the whole tradition of combinatorial optimization coming down from Karl Menger's original statement of the famous *travelling salesman problem* (TSP). These contributions investigate the role and feasibility of decentralized pricing mechanisms, and their optimality, in the presence of computational complexities in the strict recursion-theoretic senses of the term. A model of computation – usually the Turing machine model although, of course, under the Church–Turing thesis any equivalent model could be used (cf. the appendix to this book) –underlies the theoretical analysis of the solution methods (algorithms). In general, the computational complexities arise because of the intrinsic combinatorial or diophantine nature of a standard integer programming problem, and these in turn are due to the existence of essential nonconvexities in economic entities and behavior.[10]

I shall, however, also include the whole of the literature on the so-called socialist calculation debate in this category. I believe it is feasible – indeed, quite easy – to give a computational complexity-theoretic characterization of the fundamental points made by von Mises, Robbins, and Hayek: they, as precursors in the sense Borges uses in "Kafka and his Precursors", were making the obvious point that certain processes were computationally intractable. In modern jargon, certain algorithms are computationally complex even though they can be shown to be *theoretically* feasible.

The work by Clower and Howitt is remarkable in that they found the need for combinatorial constraints and the theoretical technology of number theory for proofs[11] in an elementary domain of economic theory: the transactions theory of the demand for money. It is not too difficult to recast their problem and analyze it within

[10] As Gomory and Baumol noted, almost 40 years ago, "Among the economic problems which are related to integer programming are the travelling salesman problem and problems in which fixed (inescapable) costs are present. A surprisingly wide range of problems *including diophantine problems* and the four colour map problem can be given an integer programming formulation" (Gomory and Baumol 1960: 521; emphasis added). We may have come the proverbial "full circle" in this "inclusion relation." It is now the case that integer programming problems are given a diophantine formulation.

[11] As they note with characteristic candor, "These proofs necessarily involve the use of number theory – a branch of mathematics unfamiliar to most economists" (p. 452, fn.3). I suppose the task I am attempting in this book is to try to familiarize economists with another branch of mathematics with which they are unfamiliar and, hence, unable to harness for the purpose of mathematizing economics in effective ways.

the framework of a recursion-theoretic decision problem. Unfortunately, such an analysis within the framework of computable economics must be postponed for the sequel to this book. (See Velupillai 1999a for a complete study of Clower and Howitt within the framework of computable economics, and Velupillai 1998a for an initial attempt.)

The common economic implications in all these contributions, from Hayek to Simon, from Baumol–Gomory to Scarf, was a "restatement of the tractability of decentralised economic processes analyzed in computational complexity terms which forced a re-examination of the traditional interpretations of pricing, associated resource allocation mechanisms, competition and institutions." Indeed, in the series of classic works by Simon (Simon 1947 to Simon 1983 and beyond) and by Scarf (1989, 1994), the imaginative economic implication of viewing institutions as algorithms is one result of such computational complexity considerations; moreover, even the origin, evolution, and survival of firms and markets are given an algorithmic interpretation with a basis for an analysis of their computational complexity – hence economic efficiency – built in, so to speak.[12]

I will include two other classes of contributions under the present classification: my work with Rustem, going back to the late 1970s, on the efficiency analysis of the algorithms used in policy optimization, estimation, and learning exercises (Rustem and Velupillai 1985, 1990); and Kislaya Prasad's interesting and isolated work on applying algorithmic complexity theory to investigate simple decidability questions in standard "polynomial" games (Prasad 1991). To the best of my knowledge, Rustem and I initiated the application of Khachiyan's celebrated result on the tractability of linear programming to policy optimization and related problems. This work is adapted and applied in Chapter 8.

In a certain precise sense, Prasad's work is an explicit application of two fundamental applied recursion-theoretic results: algorithmic complexity theory, and diophantine decision problems. He uses the former approach to try to answer questions on the determinateness of the number of equilibria in a class of standard games, and the latter to investigate the decidability of finding equilibrium strategies in

---

[12] I would even include Hayek's classic works on information and knowledge husbanding in decentralized economic systems (e.g. Hayek 1945) in this class of pioneers and precursors.

a polynomially constrained cooperative game. I discuss these issues in Chapter 7.

Early utilization of recursion-theoretic tools and concepts

In a fundamental contribution in the 1960s Hilary Putnam utilised, with characteristic imagination and foresight, the notion of Turing machines to model rational behavior as defined in standard economic theory (Putnam 1967). So far as I am aware, this was the first explicit case of modeling rational economic agents as Turing machines, albeit the purposes were philosophical rather than economic.

Moreover, Putnam was also a pioneer and a noble precursor of the modern theory of induction (cf. Putnam 1963a, 1951). These remarkable and pioneering contributions by Putnam had their origins in the works of Reichenbach on probability and Carnap on inductive logic.[13]

There is, however, an uncharacteristic and surprising technical slip in Putnam's use of a finite automaton to encapsulate rational economic behavior.[14] Some marginal notes on this issue can be found in Chapters 3 and 4 below. On the other hand, as the precursor of the modern theory of induction, Putnam deserves a wholly separate and independent study. My inadequate comments on his important and pioneering work in this area can be found in Chapter 4 (but cf. Velupillai 1998a for a much more detailed study and appreciation of Putnam's contribution to a formalism for induction and inductive logic from a recursion-theoretic point of view).

Gerald Kramer tried to formalize the idea of bounded rationality with the device of a finite automaton in an early and unduly

---

[13] It is surely not a coincidence that an early impetus for Herbert Simon's lifelong research program were Carnap's lectures on the philosophy of science in the Chicago of the 1930s.

[14] The technical slip occurs, I believe, in postulating an equivalence between a *finite automaton* and a *rational agent* as defined in economic theory: "In short, our machines [i.e. finite automata] are *rational agents* in the sense in which that term is used in inductive logic and economic theory. If the rational preference functions of these machines resemble the rational preference functions of idealized human beings, and the computational skills of the machines are approximately equal to the computing skills of human beings, then the behaviour of these machines will closely resemble the behaviour of (idealized) human beings" (Putnam 1967: 409–10). There are problems with these claims, however, even if the rational agent is modelled as a Turing machine (cf. Ch. 3, below).

neglected study (Kramer 1968). Not long after that, Carl Futia used the framework of the algebraic theory of automata to investigate, formally, the complexity of (sequential) decision rules (Futia 1977). For pedantic reasons, I am forced to take a puritanical attitude to the definition of computable economics – even granting the latitude via categories (i), (ii), and (iii) above. I can, therefore, no more than mention these important and interesting contributions as examples of a vast genre of work and results that have connections, albeit tangential, with computable economics according to the above definitions. This is particularly so for the class of work in which finite automata and their (algebraic) complexity properties have been used in repeated games. Some of this literature has been surveyed in Jerker Holm's doctoral dissertation (Holm 1993) and I direct interested readers to that work and to the recent textbook by Osborne and Rubinstein (1994, particularly chapter 9) for an excellent introduction to the frontiers of the field. Once again, as in the case of Kramer and Futia, important and interesting though these contributions are, they are better studied from the point of view of the algebraic theory of automata (and perhaps to some extent also on the basis of graph theory).[15]

Finally, there is the crucial contribution by Binmore (1987, 1988) which, like those by Simon and Scarf is essentially, a wholly new research program. I am convinced that this will lead to the genesis of an entirely new sub-branch of economics which would be best called *algorithmic economics*, on the same footing as Simon's behavioral economics, Scarf's computable general equilibrium, and Vernon Smith's experimental economics. I suspect that what I have called computable economics will, eventually, turn out to have a large intersection with Binmore's algorithmic economics without, however, being a proper subset of it. At this time, the results and conceptual developments in algorithmic economics, singlehandedly created and nurtured by Binmore, seem to be confined to game-theoretic issues; but a close reading of what I consider to be the two classics of algorithmic economics (Binmore 1987, 1988), should convince any reader that the methodological and epistemological agendas have wider scope and deeper aims.

---

[15] This is, strictly speaking, not true for the work by Varian (1972), Gottinger (1987), and Kelly (1988). They belong to computable economics in the sense in which it is defined in this section, i.e. by definition (iii). Holm (1993) can be consulted for more detailed, albeit incomplete, description of these contributions.

There is, finally, Canning's work, in which, using the notion of the Turing machine, he investigates the constrained domain, in a certain precise game-theoretic sense, over which it is possible to be completely rational in the sense of economic theory (Canning 1992). There are some methodological similarities with Putnam's much earlier exercise (Putnam 1967). Neither of these contributions seems to have led to research programs in the sense in which I have referred to the works by Simon, Scarf, Smith, or Binmore. This is to be regretted, but I am sure their time will come.

Herbert Simon as a precursor

It is both impossible and, surely, unfair to try to summarize, under this heading, Herbert Simon's fascinating research program. But I must give it a try, and for my attempt to make any sense at all it is, I think, necessary to view economics within the broader canvas that is *cognitive science*.

When Herbert Simon made his first moves away from the Rational Man of Economics toward what he then termed the Thinking Man (of Cognitive Science), his justifications and definitions were as follows (all quotes are from Simon, 1979: ix–xiii and 3–5):

(a) "[When Allen Newell and I began discussing 'the prospect of simulating thinking in the summer of 1954' it was due to] my longstanding discontent with the economists' model of global rationality, which seemed to me to falsify the facts of human behavior and to provide a wholly wrong foundation for a theory of human decision making . . . "

(b) On looking, therefore, for a "foundation for a theory of human decisionmaking" that would not so blatantly "falsify the facts of human behavior," Simon's first steps were:

   (i) "to describe thinking processes as search processes" (p. 4), and, *pro tempore*, it was assumed that:

   (ii) "the search [is] a serial, one-thing-at-a-time exploration" (p. 4).

   This was not due to any dogmatic belief in the infeasibility or irrelevance of parallel architectures; it was simply a working hypothesis to get the research program going in its empirical and experimental paces.

(c) These broad, formal, and working hypotheses led to a more structured image of the Thinking Man (of cognitive science), one that would be reasonably consistent with "the facts of human behavior." This was the image that tried to encapsulate the boundedly rational behavior of decision-making when agents confront complex environments; the search – that "serial, one-thing-at-a-time" probing – was of the environment.

(d) But let me backtrack a little to get this point focused more clearly.

  (i) From the early 1950s Simon, with Newell, had empirically investigated evidence on human problem-solving and had "organised that evidence within an explicit framework of an information processing theory" (p. x).

  (ii) This led to "a general theory of human cognition, not limited to problem solving, [and] a methodology for expressing *theories of cognition as programs* and for using computers to simulate human thinking" (p. x; emphasis added).

Thus, the path towards Simon's behavioral economics began at the beginning, with the Rational Man of Economics; but, by studying human problem-solving in general, he moved in two parallel directions which facilitated a formal, experimental characterization of the Thinking Man: "inwards" to extract the cognitive architectures consistent with the evidence of problem-solving; "outwards" to define the domain of analysis in ways that would make experimental and behavioral sense. Thus, the Rational Man of Economics became the "Whole (or nearly whole) Thinking Man (of cognitive science) by way of the Problem-Solving Man (of normal science, *à la* Kuhn).

(e) The generalisation of human cognition – not limited to problem-solving – such that the restricted Problem-Solving Man became the (nearly whole) Thinking Man implied capabilities to "express cognitive skills in a wide range of task domains":

[L]earning and remembering, problem solving, inducing rules and attaining concepts, perceiving and recognizing stimuli, understanding natural language, and others. An information processing model of Thinking Man must contain components capable of humanly intelligent behavior in each of these domains; and, as these models are created, they must gradually be merged into a coherent whole. (p. x)

It is in this sense that an understanding and appreciation of Simon's research program necessitates a view of economics against a cognitive science background.[16] This path towards a broader base for economics, with Thinking Man replacing the traditional Rational Economic Man, stressed two empirical facts:

(I) "There exists a basic repertory of mechanisms and processes that Thinking Man uses in all the domain in which he exhibits intelligent behavior" (p. *x*);

(II) "The models we build initially for the several domains must all be assembled from this same basic repertory, and *common principles of architecture* must be followed throughout" (p. *x*; emphasis added).

It is at this point that I feel Simon's research program pointed the way toward computable economics in a precise sense. In a possible world, inhabited by Kafka's predecessors, the first precept could be interpreted as a tentative cognitive scientific statement of Church's thesis; i.e., the "basic repertory of mechanisms and processes" can be encapsulated by Turing machines and their formal equivalents under Church's thesis. The second precept could, on the basis of Rosenblatt's philosophy,[17] have had its basis in the neural network underpinnings of cognitive science. Together, they may have generalized the Thinking Man and led to the *Computably Rational Man* (cf. Chapter 3). But somehow Simon did not push his research program in that direction.

Instead, the direction Simon took codified his research program in terms of the familiar notions of bounded rationality and satisficing. The standard literature in formal economic theory has continued to interpret these notions as approximations to full rationality and its outcomes. My own interpretation of these fertile concepts is almost diametrically different. The reason I view them the way I do – reasons that are made formally explicit in Chapter 4 – is that I interpret Simon's precepts (I) and (II) above recursion-theoretically, i.e. within the context of decision problems in the strict recursion-theoretic sense.

---

[16] An interesting intellectual exercise would be to compare this evolution in Simon's research program and the almost parallel development in Polya's vision and interpretation of problem-solving by inductive, analogical, and heuristic methods. I have tried to interpret Leijonhufvud's methodology in the light of Polya's views on problem solving in Velupillai and Punzo (1996).

[17] Indeed, Simon's research program, the way I have outlined it, spans and characterizes the early definition of cognitive science.

I remain convinced that, had Simon made the explicit recursion-theoretic link at some point in the development of his research program, computable economics would have been codified much earlier.

2.4 CONCLUDING NOTES

> This is a story of how I changed my views from the belief that good knowledge must always be represented as a set of logical statements, within a suitable mathematical model of reality, to my present opinion that *knowledge is basically algorithmic*.
>
> Tseytin (1981: 390; emphasis added)

I have tried to tell a story of computable economics, its definition culled from "a road not taken" and the substantiation, *pro tempore*, of the definition, by means of a narrative of the way some of the pioneers and precursors of the subject tried to infuse recursion-theoretic considerations into economics. My formal starting-point was the fourfold division of logic and an implicit bewilderment that economic knowledge, activities, and entities had been, and are, modelled almost exclusively in set-theoretic and model-theoretic terms. What, I have asked myself over the years,[18] if "knowledge is basically algorithmic"? Are the tools and handmaidens of set theory and model theory, the standard framework of the predicate logic, and related familiar methods sufficient or even necessary to encapsulate algorithmic knowledge? If not, why not try other methods, more intrinsically algorithmic? Tseytin, that master analyst of learning systems and procedures, goes on (from the above quoted starting-point):

My logicist approach to applications was implicitly based on a presupposition that . . . the predicate logic is a universal representation of any regular reasoning, i.e., that any regular reasoning can be translated into the predicate logic by a suitable change of notation.

There were no direct objections to declarative representation of knowledge itself. Formerly I had to stick to it because it was the only form of knowledge supported by the logicist approach. Now I can view it as one special type of knowledge; and it cannot operate alone, without the aid of procedural

---

[18] Inspired by listening to my friend and mentor, Axel Leijonhufvud, deliver his Marshall Lectures at Cambridge University almost a quarter of a century ago, where I was first introduced to Herbert Simon's fascinating, algorithmic world.

knowledge. *No equation,* however general and elegant, *can be used without an algorithm for its solution.* . . . Thus the change to proceduralism was in three steps: lifting the restrictions imposed by logicism; extending the techniques of procedural knowledge; understanding the universal role of procedural knowledge. (Tseytin1991: 391–2; emphasis added)

Similarly, I conjecture – and hope – that the change to computable economics will proceed in a sequence of steps: first, lifting the restrictions imposed by formalism and Bourbakianism[19] which provide the mathematical underpinnings of economics; then extending the techniques of proceduralism, as Simon, Scarf, and Binmore have done, and continue to do; and finally, understanding the universal role of procedural knowledge, as Simon, almost more than any other single person, has been claiming for almost half-a-century.

My definition of computable economics, as given in Section 2.3 above, and the story of the pioneers and precursors were constructed with such steps in mind. Many have constructed individual, isolated steps, even whole segments of a path. The whole "road not taken" can be assembled from these individual steps and segmented pathways.

---

[19] As Binmore perceptively noted, "Not only are abstractions introduced that do not necessarily admit an operational referent: At the same time, operationally relevant factors are abstracted away together. This, in itself, is not necessarily invidious. However, *the Bourbaki ethos makes it inevitable that factors that are not taken account of formally are not taken account of at all*" (Binmore 1987: 183; emphasis added).

3
Computable Rationality

Turing's "Machines." These machines are *humans* who calculate.

Wittgenstein (1980: s. 1096)

3.1 INTRODUCTION

We see that reason is wholly instrumental. It cannot tell us
where to go; at best it can tell us how to get there.

Simon (1983: 7)

Can reason, in fact, tell us "how to get there"? The results in this
chapter point to a negative answer to this query. I begin starting from
fundamentals to try to substantiate the notion that rational economic agents can be viewed as Turing machines. By "starting from
fundamentals," I mean that I try to derive the mathematical equivalence between the choice behavior of rational economic agents and
the computational activities of a suitably encoded Turing machine
from the standard definitions and axioms of rational choice. This
might seem surprising in view of the fact that procedural elements
are, ostensibly, absent in rational choice, as conventionally defined.[1]
That this is not so will be demonstrated in the following section.
Another reason for the exercise in Section 3.2, apart from the above
and those stated in the general aims of Chapter 1, is that most discussions in which the rational agent is modelled as a Turing machine
– with a few notable exceptions in game theory – assume, *a priori*, an
equivalence. That this assumption is justified, under some mildly
restrictive assumptions, will be demonstrated.[2]

[1] One aspect of Herbert Simon's multifaceted research program for the Thinking
Man (cf. Ch. 2) is an attempt to rectify the procedural lacunae in the substantively
rational edifice of standard choice theory.
[2] The "negative" consequences of the equivalence assumption, some of which are
explored in this and the following three chapters, is quite another problem.

In Section 3.3, using the results obtained in Section 3.2, the undecidability of the *effective* generation of preferences and the impossibility of *effectively* identifying subclasses of rational choice functions will be stated and proved as theorems.

Another way to view the aims and contents of this chapter would be to read it in the light of Arrow's characteristically perceptive conjecture:

The next step in analysis . . . is a more consistent assumption of computability in the formulation of economic hypotheses. This is likely to have its own difficulties because, of course, *not everything is computable*, and there will be in this sense an inherently unpredictable element in rational behavior. (Arrow 1986: S398; emphasis added)

To wit, I shall explore the consequences of "a more consistent assumption of computability" in the formulation of some aspects of rational choice hypotheses. It will be useful to keep in mind, in order to grasp the intended meaning of some of the paradoxical and negative results, that Arrow links possibly unpredictable rational behavior with uncomputability rather than with probabilistic structures in the traditional sense.

The formalizations, formal results, and proofs harness elementary concepts from classical recursion theory: Gödel numbering, diagonalization, Rice's theorem, and the existence of *recursively enumerable but not recursive sets*. There recursion-theoretic concepts are set in their effective paces within the standard framework of the economic theory of rational choice.

3.2 THE RATIONAL ECONOMIC AGENT AS A TURING MACHINE

The present development . . . reveals the "Gödel Representation" to be merely a case of *resymbolization*, and suggests that with the growth of mathematics such resymbolization will have to be affected again and again.[3]

Post (1994: 377)

---

[3] The full paragraph of Post's seminal paper from which I have extracted this quote is particularly relevant for my essay: "Perhaps the chief difference in method between the present development and its more complete successors is its preoccupation with the outward forms of symbolic expressions, and possible operations thereon, rather than with logical concepts as clothed in, or reflected by, correspondingly

The equivalence I seek to demonstrate is that between the choice behavior of a rational economic agent and a suitably encoded Turing machine. I will try to build the choice behavior of the rational agent from first principles to extract, on the one hand, some of the implicit imperative contents of standard formalisms and to impute, on the other hand, procedural elements where ambiguity can be identified.

First of all, I take it that we study choice behavior with choice functions.[4] Formally, therefore, with

χ: a given universal set of alternatives;
Ω: a nonempty family of (finite) nonempty subsets of χ,

we have the following definition.

DEFINITION 3.1: THE CHOICE FUNCTION, $\mathscr{C}$.
(i) $\mathscr{C}: \Omega \to \Omega$.
(ii) $\mathscr{C}(\omega) \subseteq \omega, \forall \omega \in \Omega$.

Intuitively, this formalism encapsulates the elementary notion that choices are made from sets of alternatives, and that

A process (rule, mechanism, criterion) for making choices, individual or collective, is applicable to any finite, nonempty subset of some universal set χ of alternatives. (Schwartz 1986: 11)

In this interpretation, the process (or rule or mechanism) is called the *choice function*. We can immediately see that the intended interpretation gives an imperative content to the function concept underlying $\mathscr{C}$. This alone could enable one to leapfrog to a λ-calculus interpretation of choice functions and hence, by Church's thesis, to an assertion that rational economic agents are Turing machines.[5] I will,

particularlized symbolic expressions, and operations thereon. While this is perhaps responsible in part for the fragmentary nature of our development, it also allows greater freedom of method and technique. In particular, it reveals the 'Gödel Representation' to be merely a case of *resymbolization*, and suggests that with the growth of mathematics such resymbolization will have to be effected again and again" (Post 1944: 376–7; emphasis in the original).

   [4] In my formalisms of the basics I follow two of the classic texts in choice theory: Schwartz (1986) and Suzumura (1983).

   [5] In fact, in earlier work I felt able to use Schwartz's clear statements of an intended interpretation of the definition of the choice function – "C [the choice function] represents what I call (for want of a better label) a choice process – a rule, procedure, institutional mechanism . . . " (Schwartz 1986: 12) – by juxtaposing a reluctant constructivist's statement of a version of Church's thesis – "Every rule is reducible to a recursive rule" (Beeson 1985: 55) – and then going on to assuming the equivalence between rational economic agents and Turing machines.

however, pursue a more circuitous, but hopefully a logically better founded, path in the present attempt.

Ω is a collection of finite, nonempty subsets of the universal set χ, and therefore each ω is a finite, nonempty set. Thus, the choice function $\mathscr{C}$ picks out a finite, nonempty subset to every finite, nonempty subset of χ. Again I will rely on Schwartz's suggestive interpretative description, which gives behavioral content to the definitions in intuitive ways:

> $\mathscr{C}$ represents what I call (for want of a better label) a *choice process* – a rule, procedure, institutional mechanism, or criterion, or set of tastes, values, goals, or behavioral dispositions, that might govern the choices of some individual or group of individuals from finite subsets of χ. For $\omega \in \Omega$, $\mathscr{C}(\omega)$ comprises those members of ω that choosers governed by the given process might choose when ω is the feasible set. $\mathscr{C}(\omega)$ is the choice set from ω. (Schwartz 1986: 12)

Note also that the implication of (ii), indicated in the above quote, is that the choice function does not necessarily single out just one alternative; this means that a *nondeterministic* Turing machine should be the appropriate model for the rational economic agent (given that it can be shown to be equivalent to a Turing machine). The path from this very general definition of the choice function to a definition of rationality is not particularly complicated, from a formal point of view. The difficulty, if any, lies in unearthing various intended interpretations hidden behind some of the abstruse symbolisms. This is the main task in the rest of this section: to uncover the anatomy of the choice function, but via a dissection of the ideas and definitions behind (preference) orderings.

Arrow has demonstrated, in his classic piece on "Rational Choice Functions and Orderings" (Arrow 1959), that:

(a) "[b]oth demand function and orderings can be regarded as special classes of choice functions: (p. 122) and

(b) "an ordering can be interpreted as a series of statements about choices from sets containing two elements. Choices from larger sets . . . are defined in terms of binary choice" (p. 122).

With this background, it can be seen that the idea behind rational choice is as follows. It is the choice, by the choice function, of some class of maximal or optimal elements. These latter, in turn, are identified as a class of subsets of the Cartesian product over the set of alternatives. Hence, as pointed out by Arrow above, orderings are, in general, special cases of choice functions. In this sense, therefore, the given orderings – the traditional starting-point in economic analysis – via the choice function interpretation must have an imperative content. To unearth this I proceed as follows.

Using Arrow's result given in (b) above, I ask whether the rational economic agent can effectively generate, as a preference ordering, the relevant series of statements that are choices "from sets containing two elements." The formalism that enables me to ask, and answer, this question implies the equivalence I am seeking.

Taking, therefore, a few steps back from the standard, formal, starting-point of given orderings, I will ask the agents to generate their preference orderings.[6] This is, perhaps, to impose an unfair task; after all, the neoclassical closure is in terms of preferences (orderings), endowments, and technology. One is not supposed to ask how they came into being. There is, surely, no such thing as a totally endogenous field of inquiry: all science is in terms of judiciously chosen closures. Let me therefore pose my query in a different (sequence of) way(s).

1. What is the nature and size of the set of alternatives, χ?[7] For example, is χ countable? If not, how can we make sense of "orderings . . . as a series of statements"? Whether χ is countable or not seems to be the only important question requiring an answer under these headings.[8] Quite apart from, and prior to, the fabled numerical representation of preference orderings over sets of alternatives, there is

---

[6] Essentially, to generate them effectively. In my case, paraphrasing Nozick (cf. opening quote, Sec. 3.3, above), the "almost" equivalent query is: "In what other way, *if not effectively*, can we understand the process of generating orderings (equivalent to 'a series of statements about choices from sets containing two elements')?" It is clear that I am invoking Church's thesis.

[7] Duncan Luce's four-decade old observation seems to me to be still valid: "All of our procedures for data collection and analysis require the experiments to make explicit decisions about whether a certain action did or did not occur, and all of our choice theories – including this one – begin with *the assumptions that we have a mathematically well-defined set, the elements of which can be identified with the choice alternatives* . . . There are limited experimental results on these topics, but nothing like a coherent theory. . . . More than any other single thing, in my opinion, this Achilles' heel has limited the applicability of current theories of choice . . . " (Luce 1959: 3–4; emphasis added). It may, at this point, be useful to remind readers that Frank Ramsey, in his classic piece on Truth and Probability, considered only *finite* sets of alternatives, for the same reasons that motivated Alan Turing to constrain his machines to be equipped with a *finite* number of states.

[8] The interesting discussion between Chipman (1960, 1971) and Newman and Read (1961) is marginally relevant in this context. I will not, however, take it up in this book.

the question of describing the set of alternatives.[9] "An ordering . . . as a series of statements" requires each alternative to be described as a statement from a finite alphabet. The set of such statements from a finite alphabet can, at most, be countable. Finally, two-element sets from such a countable set are also countable and are effectively encodable, say by Gödel numberings. Before a demonstration of this encoding, another question should be asked.

2. What is the process by which economic agents are presented the alternatives, so as to exercise choice? There are various conceptual suggestions, in the form of thought experiments, in the standard literature, for example the Lucasian metaphor of the agent as a *signal processor*, or Patinkin's thought experiment of the agent as a *utility computer*, or the more recent New Classical suggestions of agents as *decision rules*. Patinkin conceptualized his utility computer as follows:

Indeed we can consider the individual – with his given indifference map and initial endowment – to be a "utility computer" into whom we "feed" a sequence of market prices and from whom we obtain a corresponding sequence of "solutions" in the form of specified optimum positions. In this way we can conceptually generate the individual's excess-demand [function]. (Patinkin 1965: 7)

Conjoining Arrow's results with Patinkin's assumptions in the above thought experiment gives the first hint for the equivalence that is being sought: the "given indifference map" (i.e. the given orderings) can, at most, be a countably infinite set of statements from a finite alphabet – indeed, *well formed formulas* (w.f.f.) – of a language. In a Turing machine formalism, this countably infinite list could be represented on the potentially infinite input tape, processed by a set of finite configurations of internal states and a finite set of transition rules. But, of course, for the processing to be implemented, the countably infinite set of statements encapsulating given orderings has to be represented *number-theoretically*. I turn, now, to these number theoretic representations.

3. Three sets have to be effectively encoded if the suggested equivalence is to be derived.

(i) the set χ of alternatives;
(ii) the series of statements about choices from sets containing two elements;

[9] As distinct from, and even prior to, the *framing* of alternatives: surely, a *formal language*.

(iii) the encoding of Ω in an economically meaningful way.

From the discussion in paragraphs 1 and 2, it is clear that there is a natural encoding of χ in terms of $\aleph$, the natural numbers. The encoding of the set in (ii) is, therefore, of the set $\aleph \times \aleph$. Following, for example, Rogers (1967: 63–4), the following number-theoretic encoding could be used: given any two alternatives $x, y \in \chi$ in a natural encoding in $\aleph$ (i.e., $x, y \in \aleph$), define:

$$\tau(x, y) = \tfrac{1}{2}(x^2 + 2xy + y^2 + 3x + y) \tag{3.1}$$

It is easy to show that (3.1) is a *recursive bijection* from $\aleph \times \aleph$ to $\aleph$.

Next, to effectively encode Ω, assume, as in Arrow (1959) and Suzumura (1983), that the economic agent's hypothetical "confrontation" is over the set of finite subsets of χ. Therefore, let $\omega \in \Omega$ be a finite set of alternatives denoted by

$$\{x\} = \{x_1, x_2, \ldots x_k\}, \tag{3.2}$$

where

$$x_1 < x_2 < \ldots < x_k \tag{3.3}$$

and denote by D_x the finite set that contains $\{x\}$. Then, each finite subset that is hypothetically presented to an economic agent is represented number-theoretically.

4. So far, the alternatives have simply been given a representation to be "registered" on the potentially infinite input tape of a Turing machine for effective processing. The elementary structures on the set of alternatives – $\tau(x, y)$, ω, and D_x – are, thus, effectively encoded. The equivalence I seek can be achieved if, in some recursion theoretic sense, I can also encapsulate a notion of rationality in an effective (or decidable) way. For this to be achieved, I need to investigate particular binary relations and the idea of maximal alternatives. Now, what is the meaning of binary relations over a set of alternatives facing an economic agent? To frame the question in a way that is relevant to my aims, note that a binary relation, say over χ, is a propositional function with truth values $\mathcal{T}$ (true) and $\mathcal{F}$ (false) that unambiguously decides[10] a membership relation for an ordered pair. Then the recursion-theoretic question would be: is this membership

---

[10] There is an implicit acceptance of the law of the excluded middle in the face of countable infinities at this point and, hence, would immediately disqualify standard choice theory from the constructivist's point of view.

relation effectively decidable? Define, therefore, the weak preference relation (e.g. Suzumura 1983: p. 7):

$$(x, y) \in \mathcal{R} \Leftrightarrow \text{according to the economic agent's view} \\ x \text{ is at least as good as } y \qquad (3.4)$$

or

$$(x, y) \in \mathcal{R} \Leftrightarrow \text{Proposition } (\mathcal{R}) \text{ has values } (\mathcal{T} \vee \mathcal{F}) \\ \Leftrightarrow \text{according to the economic agent's view} \\ x \text{ is at least as good as } y. \qquad (3.5)$$

What is the meaning of (3.5)? Since the effective encoding of all the building blocks has been demonstrated in paragraphs 2 and 3 above, this is a meaningful query for a Turing machine. Therefore the effective decidability of membership or truth values in (3.5) will depend on the recursive structure endowed to χ.[11] However, the economic agent's exercise of rationality also requires the definition of a maximal set of alternatives. Rational choice is the choosing of such a maximal set of alternatives by an economic agent. Define, then, the set of $\mathcal{R}$-maximal alternatives, $\mathcal{M}(\omega, \mathcal{R})$, as

$$\mathcal{M}(\omega, \mathcal{R}) = \{x \in \omega \mid \forall\, y \in \omega: (x, y) \in \mathcal{R}\}, \qquad (3.6)$$

where $\mathcal{R} \subset \aleph \times \aleph$ and $\omega \in \Omega$. Then, for example, a choice function $\mathcal{C}$ becomes a *rational choice function* (RCF) whenever, for all $\omega \in \Omega$, $\mathcal{C}(\omega)$ consists of the $\mathcal{R}$-maximal alternatives (3.6) of ω:

$$\exists\, \mathcal{R} \subset \aleph \times \aleph \text{ s.t. } \forall\, \omega \in \Omega: \mathcal{C}(\omega) = \mathcal{M}(\omega, \mathcal{R}). \qquad (3\text{-}7)$$

Clearly, $\mathcal{M}(\omega, \mathcal{R})$ is defined number-theoretically. A Turing machine can be programmed to test, for each given (pair of) encoded alternative(s), whether $\tau(x, y)$ has a certain decidable property (i.e. satisfies a membership relation or decides the truth value of a proposition) defining $\mathcal{M}(\omega, \mathcal{R})$.

5. Finally, we put together the elements discussed in paragraphs 1–4 to obtain the equivalence between the formal rational economic agent's choice process and the computing activities of a suitably initialized and configured Turing machine. As has been shown, every element going into the formal activity of choosing a subset from a given set of alternatives by a rational economic agent is effectively

---

[11] In other studies related to this one, more structure has been imposed directly on χ in order to characterize recursion-theoretic choice behavior. Alain Lewis (1985) is a brilliant and exhaustive study along such lines.

encodable. The only remaining unanswered question is the meaning to be given to choosing, or "picking out," a set of maximal alternatives.

The activity of choosing or "picking out" is one of comparing, for each $x \in \mathfrak{R}$, all $y \in \mathfrak{R}$ and identifying or verifying the membership relation $(x, y) \in \mathfrak{R}$ or deciding the truth value of the propositional function $\mathfrak{R}$. This too is an effectively encodable procedure, and hence can be processed by a Turing machine. Thus, every aspect of choice by a rational economic agent corresponds to an implementable procedure by a Turing machine. We have, therefore, the following proposition:

PROPOSITION 3.1. The process of rational choice by an economic agent is equivalent to the computing activity of a suitably programmed Turing machine.

Remark. If, as is sometimes standard, the rational agent is represented or identified with an appropriate RCF, then that RCF can be associated with a concomitant Turing machine.

In conclusion, it should be pointed out that I have eschewed the recent practice of endowing $\mathfrak{R}$, from the outset, with recursive structures, or of assuming, *ab inizio*, that rational agents are Turing machines. This was not for aesthetic, theoretical, or even empirical reasons. It was simply because I wanted to begin from standard fundamentals and to explore their effective content. It is clear that there are crucial – almost noneliminable – nonconstructive and noneffective implicit assumptions in the standard formalism. For example, from the constructivist's point of view, there is the implicit assumption of the law of the excluded middle in (3.5); and from the recursion theorist's point of view, there are the implicit noneffective assumptions in (3.5) and (3.7). Effectivizing them are crucial steps in deriving the equivalence Proposition 3.1.

3.3 THE NONEFFECTIVITY OF PREFERENCE GENERATION

> In what other way, if not simulation by a Turing Machine, can we understand the process of making free choices? By making them perhaps.
>
> Nozick (1981: 303)

Can economic agents act rationally, or choose optimally, without having access to their preference orderings, if these exist? Or without being able to rationalize their choice functions? It is one thing for the experimental–econometric investigator to endow agents with plausible utility functions[12] with which to interpret and organize data and the observed results of choice; it is quite another thing to assume that agents choose as they do because they have rationalized their choice function or have ordered preferences.[13] A plethora of dubious philosophical justifications have been harnessed to justify standard practice, from crude "as if" arguments to pseudo-scientific instrumentalist fundamentals. I do not know how to interpret the exact logical status of "as if" reasoning.[14] But ever since Machlup, Samuelson, and Friedman made their celebrated methodological statements, it has been hard to make a case for scientific realism in the formulation of economic hypotheses.[15] I will not even attempt to enter this particular minefield. Instead, assuming the Church–Turing thesis, I will simply ask whether there are effective procedures that rational economic agents, as Turing machines, can use to order their preferences (rationalize their choice functions[16]). If the answer is negative, I will assume that the following observation by Sen must be taken seriously in the formulation of testable hypotheses about rational behavior:

---

[12] But one must not forget Samuelson's original aim: "I have tried here to develop the theory of consumer's behaviour freed from any vestigial traces of the utility concept" (Samuelson 1938: 71).

[13] Or, to quote the master again, "the individual guinea-pig, by his market-behaviour, reveals his preference pattern – if there is such a consistent pattern" (Samuelson 1948: 243).

[14] As cogently argued by Musgrave (1981), "Are [as-if] . . . hypotheses convenient mathematical devices for predicting . . . ? Are they, in other words, mere instruments which do not really explain the facts which they predict? I do not think we are forced to such instrumentalist conclusions. For we can give our . . . hypotheses descriptive and explanatory force by [rephrasing] them. . . . I prefer the paraphrases. This is partly because I prefer scientific realism to instrumentalism. It is also because they eliminate 'as if': for the *logic* of 'as if' statements (what follows from them and what does not follow from them) is terribly unclear" (pp. 384–5). Musgrave means by this, for example, a rephrasing of "under a wide range of circumstances individual firms behave as if they were seeking rationally to maximize their expected returns" to "under a wide range of circumstances the conscious deliberation which underlie business behaviour have the overall effect of maximizing expected returns" (pp. 384–5, fn. 11).

[15] But see Ch. 9 for an "inductivist's" justification of a compromise between realism and instrumentalism, naively conceived.

[16] In an expectational context, the analogous problem would be whether there are effective procedures to rationalize expectations.

the fundamental assumption about the revelation of preference can be criti-
cized from many points of view, including the possibility that behavior may
not be based on systematic comparison of alternatives. (Sen 1973: 21)

If the rational economic agent can rationalize a choice function or
order preferences among alternatives, then this is equivalent to stating that

$$\text{Proposition } [\tau(x, y)] \text{ is } computable \qquad (3.8)$$

or that

$$\text{Proposition } [\mathcal{R}] \text{ is } decidable. \qquad (3.9)$$

The following theorem claims that neither of these assertions is true.

THEOREM 3.1. There is no effective procedure to generate preference
orderings.

Proof.[17] As pointed out above, formally a binary relation on $\aleph$ is a
proposition $\mathcal{R}$ such that, for any ordered pair (x, y), where $x, y \in \aleph$,
we can state unambiguously whether $\mathcal{R}$ is true or false. Thus, the
demonstration of the uncomputability of $\tau(x, y)$ will imply the truth
of the theorem.

The economic agent, in standard theory (cf. Sen 1973), is assumed
to systematically evaluate alternatives (pairwise – cf. the quotations
from Arrow 1959 above) in a rational choice situation such that the
observable results reveal consistent preferences. This "systematic
evaluation" means a sequence of computations of $\tau(x, y)$. Let agent
i, therefore, apply Turing machine *i*, TM_i, to evaluate the encoded
number $\tau(x, y)$ of the ordered pair (x, y); the agent faces, as in elementary consumer theory, the task of evaluating a countable infinity
of ordered pairs.[18] We can, of course, encode the two truth values
of $\mathcal{R}$ in appropriate numerals, say $\mathcal{T} = 1$ and $\mathcal{F} = 0$. Then, on input
$\tau(x, y)$, the TM_i should halt with values 1 or 0. (But will every possible Turing machine halt for any arbitrary input $\tau(l, m)$, $\forall l, m \in \chi$?[19])

[17] I will assume that each agent has access to any Turing machine and that, therefore, the collection of agents can also use them.

[18] Indeed I am assuming *much else*, since, in fact, the rational agent in elementary
consumer theory faces all the "points" in the nonnegative orthant – i.e. uncountable
infinities. I cannot see how this number of alternatives can be assumed and, at the
same time, agents be expected systematically to evaluate alternatives; or to be consistent with any of the standard thought experiments, without also assuming some form
of the *axiom of choice*.

[19] The proof can be concluded, in a simple way, with an appeal to the unsolvability of the halting problem at this point. Alternatively, we can endow $[\tau(x, y)]$ with an

Now, note that:

$$\exists TM_u: \aleph^2 \to \aleph, \text{ s.t. } \forall TM_i: \aleph \to \aleph;$$
$$\exists k, \text{ s.t. } \forall n: TM_i(n) = TM_u(k, n). \tag{3.10}$$

This kind of Turing machine, indexed by u, is the Universal Turing machine (UTM). Intuitively speaking, (3.10) asserts that a special purpose Turing machine can be constructed that can, in principle, simulate the actions of any arbitrary Turing machine for a given input. Consider the set

$$\{\Gamma = n: TM(n, n) \text{ is defined}\}. \tag{3.11}$$

This set is *recursively enumerable but not recursive* (which will be demonstrated). Hence $\Re$ is not (effectively) decidable. In other words, TM_n, say corresponding to the Turing machine used by rational agent n, when "fed" $n = \tau(p, q)$, may or may not output a truth value 1 or 0 for $\Re$. Thus, there is no effective procedure to decide whether a preference ordering can be generated by methodically – i.e. systematically – evaluating alternatives.

To complete the proof, it must also be shown that Γ is recursively enumerable but not recursive. This can be shown as follows.

It is clear that Γ is *recursively enumerable*. If, in addition, Γ were *recursive*, then the complement of Γ would be recursively enumerable, and therefore the (partial) characteristic function, say η, of this complementary set would also be computable. There would, thus, be a number m such that, $\forall x, \eta(x) = TM_u(m, x)$. Therefore, $x \notin \Gamma$ iff $\eta(x)$ is defined. However, we have defined Γ such that $m \in \Gamma$ iff $TM_u(m, m)$ is defined, and hence we have obtained the necessary contradiction.

The assumption that the countable infinity of Turing machines are (potentially) utilized – even if the number of rational agents is finite – is somewhat unsatisfactory. We shall, therefore, drop this assumption and, instead, ask whether we can effectively identify classes of choice functions, used by an arbitrary agent, that do generate his or her preference orderings. In other words, can we, given a class of choice functions, find a systematic procedure – i.e. an effective procedure – to decide whether this class does, in fact, pick out a set such

appropriate recursive structure and get direct undecidability results (as in Lewis 1985). I am, as mentioned earlier, following a more roundabout procedure which will also enable me to introduce the notion of a *Universal Turing machine*.

as 𝓜 of maximal alternatives? The next theorem asserts that the answer to this question is also in the negative.

THEOREM 3.2. Given a class of choice functions that do generate preference orderings (pick out the set of maximal alternatives) for any agent, there is no effective procedure to decide whether or not any arbitrary choice function is a member of the given class.

Proof. First of all, from the discussion in Section 3.2, we can safely assume that the class of choice functions can be effectively encoded and, therefore, *a fortiori*, those choice functions that are rationalizable are also effectively encodable. Moreover, dropping the assumption in footnote 17 used in proving Theorem 3.1, means that the class of choice functions is not necessarily countably infinite. In other words, we now have a subset of the class of Turing machines computing members from the class of all sequences $[\tau(x, y)]$ to evaluate truth values for (classes of) binary relations $\mathfrak{R}$. But by Rice's theorem no nontrivial property of this subset of Turing machines, i.e. the class of rationalizable choice functions, is effectively decidable. In particular, there is no effective procedure to decide whether or not any arbitrary given choice function is a member of the given rationalizable set.

This negative result, even more than Theorem 3.1, seems to be particularly depressing. But there are positive aspects to such negative results, some of which are sketched in the next, concluding, section to this chapter.

3.4 CONCLUDING NOTES

If we use a method which takes account only of recursive hypotheses, then if we live in a world in which human beings have the ability to calculate nonrecursive functions, and the true hypothesis involves a function of this kind, then we will never confirm the true hypothesis using a scheme of the kind just described.

Putnam (1951/1990: 10)

It is quite possible that economic agents are able to rationalize their preference functions using nonrecursive functions. Computable economics is, at least in part, about delineating the boundaries between the effective and noneffective processes. It must not, however, be forgotten that the notion of "effective" is predicated upon an acceptance of the Church–Turing thesis.

In an early and notable paper, Gerald Kramer sought to show the formal incompatibility of the assumptions underlying rational behavior and the "finite information-processing capabilities possessed by real decision-makers" (Kramer 1968: 39). In other words, if the latter idea is formally encapsulated in the device of a finite automaton, the question is whether the former behavior is possible, or whether a finite automaton can display rational behavior in the sense in which this is understood in formal economic theory (defined in Section 3.2 above). Kramer's negative result can be formally stated as follows:

PROPOSITION 3.2. For a countably infinite set of alternatives $\mathscr{X}$ and $\mathscr{J}$ the class of all finite subsets of $\mathscr{X}$, a rationalization of a choice function $\mathscr{C}$ by $\mathscr{R}$ cannot be realized by a finite automaton.

Remark. If we replace the finite automaton by a Turing machine, the equivalent result will be in terms of the effective undecidability of the rationalization of a choice function as in Theorem 3.1 above. Either Theorem 3.1 can be adapted to get a precise statement of Kramer's result, or, conversely, Kramer's methods can be modified appropriately to get the result with a Turing machine. In recent research – particularly in game-theoretic contexts but not exclusively so – attempts have been made to encapsulate the slippery notion of bounded rationality in the device of a finite automaton. Kramer's result lends partial support to such attempts in a very special sense. I will return to these themes in what follows.

I have underlined the importance of some of Putnam's seminal writings in Chapter 2. In his thoughts on "The Mental Life of Some Machines" (Putnam 1967), he tried to give recursion-theoretic content to an analytical category in economics in order to discuss issues in philosophy. In particular, Putnam wanted to debunk the idea that the "traditional mind–body problem" has something to do with the "supposedly special character of human subjective experience" (Putnam 1967: 408). By considering a community of *finite automatons*, each of which is endowed with a "rational preference function" in the sense of economic theory, Putnam assumes[20] that these

[20] More precisely, "In this paper, then, I am going to consider a hypothetical 'community' made up of 'agents', each of whom is in fact a Turing machine, or, more

machines can be considered "*rational agents* in the sense in which that term is used in inductive logic and economic theory" (p. 409). Thus, Putnam's assumption is that these machines – finite automata – can behave so as to maximize expected utility in the traditional sense in which this is held to be true in economic theory. But, by Kramer's result, his premiss is false. However, by simply modifying the premiss of finite automata to Turing machines, Putnam could preserve the substance of his analysis.

Perhaps the most general contribution to the genre spanned by Kramer (1968) and Putnam (1967) on the one hand and Rustem and Velupillai (1990) on the other is the brilliant piece by Alain Lewis (1985).[21] Lewis poses questions similar to those put by the above authors in the setting of quite general recursive structures *ab inizio*. I have explained my reasons for avoiding this path in Section 3.2 above. Lewis's main result (1985: 61, theorem 3.1) has a couple of precise implications, one of which I will reproduce here mainly because it ties up well with my Theorem 3.1 and Proposition 3.2.

Denote by:

$\mathcal{P}(\mathcal{X})$ the power set of the set of alternatives,

$\mathcal{M}(\mathcal{R})^n$ the image of a compact, convex subset $\mathcal{X} \subseteq \mathcal{R}^n$, and

$\mathcal{F}_R$ the collection of all recursive subsets of $\mathcal{R}(\mathcal{X})$.

DEFINITION 3.2. A choice function $\mathcal{C}: \mathcal{F}_R \rightarrow \mathcal{R}(\mathcal{X})$ is computationally viable if and only if there exists a Turing machine $\mathcal{M}$ such that $\mathcal{M}$ realizes $\mathcal{C}$ recursively.

Then we have the following proposition.

PROPOSITION 3.3. No *nontrivial* recursively representable demand correspondence on $\langle \mathcal{R}(\mathcal{X}), \mathcal{F}_R \rangle$ is computationally viable.

This result is a generalization of Proposition 3.3 and is an almost exact analogue of Theorem 3.1. The immediate consequences of these results, from a strictly economic-theoretic point of view, are expertly summarized by Lewis:

It is obvious that any choice function $\mathcal{C}$ that is not *at least computationally viable* is in a very strong sense *economically irrational*. Unless the computa-

precisely, a *finite automaton*. . . . In short, our machines are rational agents in the sense in which that term is used in inductive logic and economic theory" (Putnam 1967: 409; emphasis added).

[21] Campbell (1978) is, perhaps, of some marginal relevance in this discussion.

tion is trivial, i.e., involves no computation at all, and thus is both complete and accurate without the use of any Turing Machine, the choices prescribed by a *computationally non-viable* choice function can only be implemented by computational procedures that do one of two things: either (a) the computation does not halt and fails to converge, or (b) the computation halts at a non-optimal choice. (Lewis 1985: 45)

How are we to interpret, positively, these negative results? Perhaps one message is that we should be gentler in our demands on rational behavior – a message that Herbert Simon has been expounding tirelessly for almost half a century. But the negative results have a positive aspect in a more direct way. They are, in one sense, like counter-examples in mathematics,[22] and should be used the way George Polya used them – imaginatively, to push the outer boundaries of the subject. A demonstration that preferences cannot effectively be generated does not necessarily imply that preferences do not exist: it only means that computationally viable methods have no access to them. Whether there are other formal methods that can generate them, in analytically meaningful ways, is not a topic for discussion in this book – particularly because I work within the framework of the Church–Turing thesis. The negative results have to be accepted, and our frameworks adjusted to account for them, in the same way that social choice theorists and mathematical political scientists accepted, and adapted to, Arrow's celebrated Impossibility Theorem; and, as Suzumura pointed out, there are positive aspects to that result, too:

The implication of [Arrow's Impossibility Theorem] is very negative and sweeping indeed. But one should not fail to recognize that Arrow's theorem and related negative results may well serve as a signal that forces us to reexamine the conceptual framework of the analysis of rule design. Viewed in this way, the thrust of the apparently negative assertions may turn out to be quite positive after all. (Suzumura 1983: 62–3)

This observation applies, *pari passu*, to the negative results reported in Theorems 3.1 and 3.2, and in Propositions 3.2 and 3.3. It should lead us to "reexamine the conceptual framework of the analysis of rational behaviour." Again, it is not a particularly startling message to those who have followed Simon's suggestions for many decades. In later chapters I will suggest alternative ways to preserve the traditional conceptual framework, while remaining within a recursion-theoretic framework.

[22] This theme has been broached in more detail in Velupillai and Punzo (1996).

4
Adaptive Behavior

> What is ordinarily called adaptation is, when translated into mechanical terms, direct equilibration.
>
> Herbert Spencer (1866/1996: 234)

4.1 INTRODUCTION

> One can ask if solutions or trajectories exist for [an adaptive, evolutionary, economic] model and what is their dynamic and economic character. In particular we can ask if any such solutions would have the character of an intertemporal, general equilibrium and under what conditions the adaptive evolutionary economy would converge to one.
>
> Day (1993: 21)

If behavior in an economic context is always adaptive, then its "trajectory" must always represent transition dynamics to a steady state. If, moreover, behavior is assumed to be rational, then it must be characterized by the steady states of the dynamical system that corresponds to the above "trajectory." It is, therefore, legitimate to ask whether we can characterize rational behavior, as it is normally understood and defined in economic theory, in terms of the limit-sets of a dynamical system. Next, we may ask whether the limit-sets are computationally viable. Answers to these questions may suggest an observational fact: the persistence of adaptive behavior. These themes circumscribe the nature and scope of this chapter.

Fritz Machlup once described the word *structure*, as used in economics, as a weasel word[1] – "a word that makes a statement evasive or misleading."[2] Something similar can be suggested for the increas-

---

[1] In Machlup's characteristically pungent description, "Structure ... is ... a weasel-word used to avoid commitment to a definite and clear thought" (Machlup 1958: 280).

[2] Wordsworth *Concise English Dictionary*.

ing use being made of *adaptive, evolutionary, near-rational, boundedly rational*, and many similar evocative terms being harnessed by imaginative theoreticians to describe economic behavior that seems to be more realistic in descriptive and predictive senses. As Holland and Miller, themselves influential contributors to a fascinating research program on modelling economic environments as complex adaptive systems peopled by artificially adaptive agents (AAA), put it, "Usually, there is only one way to be fully rational, but there are many ways to be less rational" (Holland and Miller 1991: 367).

This suggests that the many ways in which we theorize about less than full rationality – as adaptive, boundedly rational, evolutionary etc., agents – are to be considered *approximations*, of one sort or the other, to the "one way to be fully rational." This is exemplified, for example, in the definition of ϵ-approximate rationality as boundedly rational.

But can we not go the other way? Can it not be the case that "full rationality" is the approximation to something more "realistic" in descriptive and predictive senses – indeed, even in a normative sense? More to the point, are there not more ways than one "to be fully rational"? I shall return to some of these issues later in this chapter and in other chapters, but for the moment it may be useful to remember that so-called theories of "full rationality" are good at being approximately correct only in descriptive and predictive senses. Why, then, should a "fully rational" model of rational behavior be a benchmark – if its predictive and descriptive powers are only approximately correct? Surely, it is the other way around in the natural and pure sciences. John Harsanyi, one of the great advocates of normative theories of human behavior and of the fully rational model, raised some of these key issues in the following way:

[H]uman beings often fall quite short of the perfect rationality postulated by normative theories of rational behaviour. . . . [One reason] is the *limited information-processing ability* of the human central nervous system, emphasized by Simon's theory of "limited rationality".

. . . [I]n actual fact these obvious limitations of human rationality do not generally present rational-behavior theories from yielding reasonably good approximate predictions about social behavior over a wide range of social situations. Of course, a good deal of further experimentation with various types of rational-behavior theories will be needed before we can ascertain how far these theories can really take us in explaining and predicting empirical social behaviour in each particular field. (Harsanyi 1977: 17)

Is there, then, more than "one way to be fully rational," as Harsanyi seems to be suggesting? This is my view, and I shall try to make my case for an alternative fully rational model in this and ensuing chapters. However, recall *pro tempore*, that I have identified a standard fully rational agent with a Turing machine (accepting the Church–Turing thesis).

In the next section I try to explore the recursion-theoretic characterization of a definition of adaptic behavior suggested recently by Lucas (1986). In Section 4.3 I continue my explorations on the connection between so-called fully rational and adaptive behavior, but this time in a more descriptively realistic way. Finally, in Section 4.4, I try to derive some hints, on the basis of the analytics in the preceding sections, on the path toward definitions of alternative ways to be fully rational.

4.2 DYNAMICAL RATIONAL BEHAVIOR

> One might question whether [processes that involve more or less mechanical following of a decision rule] involve much real choosing using the everyday sense of that term.
>
> Nelson and Winter (1982: 68)

Lucas discusses a dynamic characterization of rational behavior by suggesting that "all behavior is adaptive" (Lucas 1986: S408) in that "traditional demand functions are decision rules" (p. S410) and these, in turn are "steady states of some adaptive process" (p. S402) which are "arrived at after a process of deliberate experimentation and assessment of outcomes" (p. S410). The assessment of outcomes is by means of the traditional formalism of preferences. Thus, Lucas seems to be making explicit the *implicit dynamics* underlying formalisms of rational behavior. In fact, he states explicitly:

The behaviour implied by these decision rules is "rational" in the sense that economists use that term. But not only is it consistent with adaptive, trial-and-error behaviour; the experiment designed to discover this rationality assumes that, if it exists, it is the outcome of some (unspecified) adaptive process. (Lucas 1986: S4)

To explore the recursion-theoretic characterizations and implications, I shall work with the following two equivalences in addition to the one determined in Chapter 3 (here stated, for convenience, as (c)):

(a) Adaptive processes will be assumed to be dynamical systems (in the strict technical sense of the term).
(b) Dynamical systems capable of computational universality can be constructed from Turing machines.
(c) Rational behavior by an economic agent is equivalent to the computational behavior of a Turing machine.

With these equivalences, it will be possible to ask recursion-theoretic questions about the "steady states of . . . adaptive processes"; i.e. steady states of dynamical systems or the halting configuration of Turing machines which, by (c), depicts appropriate rational choice. Now, the equivalence in (c) has been demonstrated in Chapter 3; the equivalences in (b) will be shown in this section, while (a) will, as stated above, simply be assumed. The assumption of the equivalence in (a) is quite standard and is, indeed, implied in Lucas's suggestive descriptions.

To show a particularly simple construction of a dynamical system embedding the computational activities of a Turing machine (and, hence, rational behavior by an economic agent), I will describe, concisely, an ingenious recent construction by Moore (1995). However, before proceeding with a description of Moore's construction, let me point out that, ever since von Neumann (1966) constructed a 29-state cellular automaton (CA), there have been numerous successes in building simple dynamical systems capable of supporting computation universality – i.e., of simulating the behavior of a (Universal) Turing machine. More recently, for example, Berlekamp *et al.* (1982a, b) have shown how computation universality can be implemented on the initial configuration of the game "LIFE".

Now, Moore's starting-point was a construction suggested by Minsky in his seminal book (Minsky 1967: chs. 11, 14). Using what he called the *program machine equivalence* of the Turing machine – called a register machine in the more recent literature – Minsky showed, in theorems 14.1.1 and 14.2.1, how to construct a program machine with only 1 – or 2 – registers. For example, to simulate a register machine with three registers, say l, m and n, by a register machine with two registers, Minsky's result is:

For any Turing Machine $\mathcal{T}$ there exists a Program Machine $\mathcal{M}_E$ with just two registers that behaves the same as $\mathcal{T}$ . . . when started with zero in one register and $2^l 3^m 5^n$ in the other . . . (Minsky 1967: 257)

Moore, using analogous reasoning, combines the finite states (registers) of the Turing machine by putting

$$I = 2^l 3^m 5^n \tag{4.1}$$

and letting

$$x = nI + s, \tag{4.2}$$

where n is the number of (finite) states in the given register machine and the n states are labelled $s = 0, 1, \ldots, n - 1$.

Next, Moore embeds this in an analytic map of the reals. To check, then, whether or not the machine is in state s, define:

$$h_s(x) = \left(\frac{\sin \pi x}{n \sin \left[\frac{\pi(x - s)}{n} \right]} \right)^2. \tag{4.3}$$

It can be seen that $h_s(x) = 1$ on integer values if $x \bmod n = s$, and $h_s(x) = 0$, otherwise.

Next, to check whether the register k_s, for $k_s = 2, 3,$ or 5, is zero, put

$$g_s(1) = \left(\frac{\sin \pi I}{k_s \sin \left(\frac{\pi I}{k_s} \right)} \right)^2 \tag{4.4}$$

Then $k_s = 0 \Leftrightarrow g_s(I) = 1$ if $I \bmod k_s = 0$, and $k_s = 1 \Leftrightarrow g_s(I) = 0$ if $I \bmod k_s \neq 0$.

Next, as in a standard Turing machine, depending on the symbol read and the current state, there is a transition; i.e., depending on s and which of the registers is being accessed, I must be appropriately modified and the Turing machine must go to a new state, say t. Label them α_s, β_t, γ_s, and δ_t respectively. Then the transition can be affected by putting

$$f_s(x) = g_s \left[\left(\frac{x - s}{n} \right)(x - s)\gamma_s + \delta_t \right] + \left[1 - g_s \left(\frac{x - s}{n} \right) \right] [(x - s)\alpha_s + \beta_t], \tag{4.5}$$

if we define:

$$f(x) = \sum_{s=1}^{n-1} h_s(x) f_s(x). \tag{4.6}$$

This is the map that contains the Minsky program machine, which in turn simulates the original Turing machine, which is a representation of the rational economic agent's choice behavior. Furthermore, this map, as a dynamical system and a Turing machine, has embedded in it the undecidability of the halting problem. The undecidabilities of the limit-sets of its dynamics will not, for example, be due to sensitive dependence on initial conditions; i.e., even if initial conditions are precisely known, there will be undecidabilities of particular properties of the limit-sets of the dynamics of the maps.

At a more general level, once the Minsky construction is effected, the path from (4.1) to (4.6) can easily be replicated to tailor-make dynamical systems to specified prescriptions. Recall, further, that in a precise sense every Turing machine is also a Universal Turing machine; i.e., such a machine can be programmed to compute any theoretically feasible computation and mimic the action of any arbitrary Turing machine.

For ease of reference in the results to be stated as theorems and proved, I need two simple, synthetic, definitions.

DEFINITION 4.1. A dynamical system – discrete or continuous – is said to be *capable of computation universality* if, using its initial conditions, it can be programmed to simulate the action of any arbitrary Turing machine, in particular that of a Universal Turing machine.

DEFINITION 4.2. A dynamical system capable of computation universality will be called a *universal dynamical system*.

Remark. Clearly, it would have been sufficient, for my purposes, simply to use one of the cellular automatas – say, the relevant "LIFE" configuration – that have been shown to be capable of computation universality as the universal dynamical system. But the virtues of Moore's construction are that they are: (a) simple, (b) replicable, and (c) low-dimensional (indeed, one-dimensional).

I can now return to Lucas's suggested connection between adaptive behavior and rationality and state two precise results.

THEOREM 4.1. Only adaptive processes capable of computation universality are consistent with rationality "in the sense that economists use that term."

Proof. Recall, from earlier results, that the rational agent can be modelled as a Turing machine and that the rational behavior of the economic agent is equivalent to the appropriate computing behavior by a Turing machine (equivalence (c) above). By the construction above, equivalence (b) holds and (a) is an assumption. Then, by

Kramer's result on *finite* automata (Proposition 3.2) we know that such restricted Turing machines are inconsistent with rationality "in the sense that economists use that term." Thus, it follows that any dynamical system modelled by automata *not capable of computation universality* is similarly inconsistent, and hence only adaptive processes capable of computation universality are consistent with rationality "in the sense that economists use that term."

THEOREM 4.2. There is no effective procedure to decide whether given classes of decision rules are "steady states of (some) adaptive process."

Proof. Note, first of all, from the above discussions, assumptions, and results, that "steady states of adaptive processes" are "steady states of dynamical systems." Thus, given a class of decision rules, to ask whether they correspond to steady states of dynamical systems is equivalent to asking whether they belong to the basin of attractions of (some) such dynamical system. However, by the previous theorem, the dynamical system in question must be capable of computation universality, i.e. a universal dynamical system; for, if not, the steady states will violate some form of the rationality postulate.

Next, I claim that the basin of attraction of universal dynamical systems is recursively enumerable but not recursive. That it is recursively enumerable follows from the simple fact that trajectories belonging to it can be effectively listed by trying out initial conditions systematically.

On the other hand, suppose they are recursive. Then the halting problem would be solvable. For, given the basin of attraction and arbitrary initial points, this will mean that the dynamics will effectively answer questions of membership. Since this is a universal dynamical system, a query concerning whether or not a Universal Turing machine will halt, for arbitrary inputs, at a particular configuration can be answered. This contradicts the unsolvability of the halting problem. Hence, by Rice's theorem, there is no effective procedure to decide whether any given class of decision rules is in the steady state of (some) adaptive process.

These results, in a nutshell, state that there are no systematic procedures available *a priori* to study and characterize long-run properties of interesting dynamical systems. By "interesting dynamical systems" I mean those that can encapsulate fully rational behavior. Any economic dynamics that leads to limit-sets that are only limit-points (nodes, foci, saddle-points, even limit cycles) cannot represent fully rational behavior in a very precise sense. It is an aspect of this precise sense that I have attempted to capture in the above two theorems.

To put it another way, economic dynamics not capable of computation universality will be incompatible with the no-arbitrage hypothesis: there will be unexploited profitable opportunities in the limit. This is clearly one of the key reasons for the need to supplement simple dynamics with "*ad-hoc shockeries*"[3] in, for example, growth and cycle theories.

But, as always, these seemingly negative results have positive aspects. After all, these results only negate the feasibility of universally utilizable effective procedures to answer systematic questions about (dynamically) rational choice: they do not assert that *special-purpose procedures* do not exist, or cannot be found, to study the processes of rational choice.

For example, even although Lucas suggests that "all behaviour is adaptive" and that decision rules, such as demand functions, are "steady states of some adaptive process," he also seems to have had in mind a study of special-purpose dynamics:

In general terms, we view or model an individual as a collection of decision rules (rules that dictate the action to be taken in given situations) and a set of preferences used to evaluate the outcomes arising from particular situation–action combinations. These decision rules are continuously under review and revision, new decision rules are tried and tested against experience, and rules that produce desirable outcomes supplant those that do not. I use the term "adaptive" to refer to this trial-and-error process through which our modes of behavior are determined. (Lucas 1986: S401)

Against the backdrop provided by the formalism in this section, and the results obtained, how can we approach the systematic study of trial-and-error processes that are found to work over a range of situations from a recursion-theoretic viewpoint? Some answers to this are put forward in the next section.

---

[3] In the felicitous words of Richard Day (1992).

University of Ulster LIBRARY

4.3 A COMPUTABLE BASIS FOR THE STUDY OF TRIAL-AND-ERROR PROCESSES IN RATIONAL CHOICE

> [I]t is entirely permissible to regard the motion of an economy
> as a process of computing answers to the problems posed to it.
>
> Goodwin (1951: 1)

Richard Goodwin made the above interesting suggestion which, to the best of my knowledge, was the first explicit statement with a computable economic content. What Goodwin was suggesting, all those many years ago, was that any dynamical system encapsulating "the motion of an economy" could be interpreted as a suitable computing machine; if, in addition, "the motion of an economy" is driven by or represents rational choice processes, then the computing machine must be a Turing machine and the dynamical system a universal one. Goodwin's idea, and my remarks and results of the previous sections can be coupled to Ian Stewart's admirable summary of recent results in the interface between dynamical systems theory and computability:

> A huge range of questions . . . has been proved undecidable. . . . [U]ndecidability extends to many questions in dynamical systems theory. These include whether the dynamics is chaotic, whether a trajectory starting from a given initial point eventually passes through some specific region of phase space. . . . Indeed virtually any "interesting" question about dynamical systems is – in general – undecidable. (Stewart 1991: 664)

The results of the previous section could be considered as stepping stones toward an attempt to give positive content to these fertile ideas. In this section I take a few further descriptively conjectural steps in the same direction.

It is easy to see from the formalism and results in Chapter 3, that the propositional function the rational economic agent has to evaluate, or the function the Turing machine has to compute, includes – generically – the EXCLUSIVE OR; i.e., given propositions X and Y, the rational agent has to evaluate the truth value of X OR ELSE Y. This is true when, and only when, exactly one of the propositions is true.

Even more importantly, and independent of these immediately preceding remarks, every proposition (in the predicate calculus) can be expressed as a string of

$$\sim [(X \wedge \sim Y) \vee (Y \wedge \sim X)] \qquad (4.7)$$

(for given propositions X and Y).

This, i.e., (4.7), is the negation of the EXCLUSIVE OR:

$$X \; OR \; ELSE \; Y = (X \vee Y) \wedge (X \wedge Y)) \qquad (4.8)$$

$$= (X \wedge \sim Y) \vee (Y \wedge \sim X). \qquad (4.8a)$$

The negation of (4.8a) gives us (4.7), which, because of its property of being able to express every proposition (in the predicate calculus) as strings of itself, is called a *universal proposition*. In other words (4.7) is a universal proposition in the same sense in which we defined *universal dynamical systems*: it is capable of computation universality.

Recall, now, that the conventional reasons given for invoking boundedly rational behavior by economic agents are the physiological, physical, and other natural constraints on the information-processing capabilities of human beings. To quote Harsanyi again, [H]uman beings . . . fall . . . short of perfect rationality [owing to the] *limited information-processing ability of the human central nervous system . . .* " (1977: 17). In our case, the "human central nervous system" is required to process strings of the universal proposition. What is the architecture of the minimally complex unit of the "human central nervous system" that is capable of processing the universal proposition? Using standard McCulloch–Pitts neuronal units, we can explore some answers to this question.

McCulloch–Pitts neurons

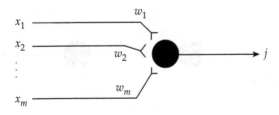

FIG. 4.1

(M–P) (see Figure 4.1) neurons are characterized by

(i) $m + 1$ numbers: inputs $\rightarrow x_1, x_2, \ldots, x_m$
                              output $\rightarrow y$.
(ii) threshold number: θ
(iii) "synaptic" weights: $w_1, w_2, w_3, \ldots w_m$, (where w_i is associated with x_i and y_j); the refractory period is taken as the unit of time.

ASSUMPTION 4.1. $y_j(n + 1) = 1$ iff $\Sigma\, w_{ij}x_i(n) \geq \theta$; i.e., the neuron fires an impulse along its axon at time $n + 1$ if the weighted sum of its inputs at time n exceeds the threshold of the neuron:

$w_{ij} > 0$: excitatory synapse;
$w_{ij} \leq 0$: inhibitory synapse.

Neural nets

A *neural net* is a collection of M–P neurons, each with the same refractory period, interconnected by splitting the output of any neuron ("axon to the dendrites") into a number of lines and connecting some or all of these to the inputs of other neurons.

PROPOSITION 4.1. Any neural net is a finite automaton.

Simple examples of neural nets to evaluate propositions

Three simple examples of how neural nets evaluate Boolean propositions prepares the groundwork for the main, universal, example of the text.

(a) Negation

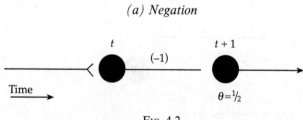

FIG. 4.2

The following remarks relate to Figure 4.2.

(i)   The left neuron emits a "spike" at time *t* if some proposition *A* is true.

(ii) If the transmission channel has weight w (-1), and the right neuron has the threshold $\theta = \frac{1}{2}$, then at time $t + 1$ the right neuron will not "spike"; i.e., $A \rightarrow \sim A$.

(iii) Conversely, when A is false, $\sim A \rightarrow A$.

(b) Conjunction

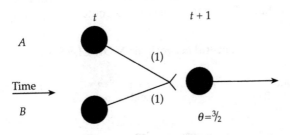

FIG. 4.3

The right neuron in Figure 4.3 will spike at $t + 1$ iff both neurons on the left spiked at time t, indicating that the propositions tested by these two neurons have both been true. Thus,

$$Aw_1 + Bw_2 = 1 \times 1 + 1 \times 1 = 2 > \theta = 3/2$$

when A and B are true. (Note the danger of diophantine formalisms.) If, on the other hand, A is true and B is false, then

$$1 \times 1 + 0 \times 1 = 1 < \theta = 3/2.$$

(c) The INCLUSIVE OR

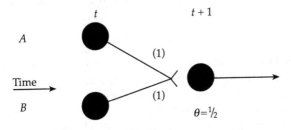

FIG. 4.4

If at least one of the left neurons in Figure 4.4 spike at time t, then the right neuron will spike at $t + 1$. Thus, if A is true (1), and B is false (0), we have

$$1 \times 1 + 0 \times 1 = 1 > \theta = 1/2.$$

Nothing more than a collection of these, and equally simple, elemental units is the basis for a neural network architecture to compute anything that a Turing machine can compute.

A neural network for X OR ELSE Y

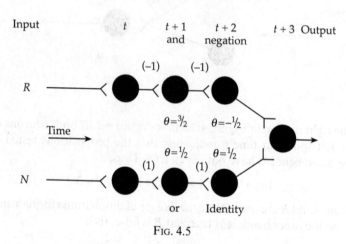

Fig. 4.5

Remark 1. The function of the "identity" operator in Figure 4.5 is to store $R \vee N$ while R is being evaluated – in this case negated.

Remark 2. No choice of weights and thresholds will allow the neuronal network to compute (evaluate) $R\ OR\ ELSE\ N$ in a single step.

(a) The geometry

The signal (input) can contain x, y, both or neither. Thus, the agent will have to identify four possible inputs and assign truth values to the output signals appropriately (see Table 4.1).

It is easy to see from Figure 4.6 that no "line" can be drawn such that $\langle (1, 0), (0, 1) \rangle$ is on one side and $\langle (0, 0), (1, 1) \rangle$ is on the "other"; i.e., the two sets of input signals are not (linearly) separable.

TABLE 4.1

Input[a]		Output[a]	
x	y		
0	0	→	0
1	0	→	1
0	1	→	1
1	1	→	0

[a] 0 = false
1 = true

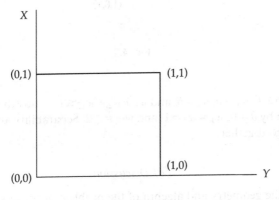

FIG. 4.6

However, if we allow second-order predicates, we can visualize a possible separation as in Figure 4.7. By introducing the second-order predicate XY, we are able to separate X and Y in three-dimensional space.

(b) The simple algebra

$$w_1 X + w_2 Y > \theta$$

where $\theta \geq 0$, $w_1 > \theta$, $w_2 > \theta$, and $w_1 + w_2 \leq \theta$, which is impossible. In the language of the above notations, *X OR ELSE Y* (the exclusive-or) cannot be evaluated (computed) by simple McCulloch–Pitts units. We have to nonlinearize the problem (a slight novelty in a procession that linearizes everything in sight) in the following way:

$$w_1 X + w_2 Y + w_{12} XY > \theta$$

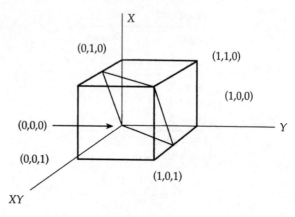

$$\text{Fig. 4.7}$$

where $\theta \geq \theta$, $w_1 > \theta$, $w_2 > \theta$, and $w_1 + w_2 + w_{12} \leq \theta$. A possible solution is given by $\theta = 0$, $w_1 = w_2 = 1$, and $w_{12} = -2$. Separability and nonlinearity go together.

(c) Discussion

From the geometry and algebra of the problem of processing a universal proposition, it is clear that some form of *nonlinearity* is essential. From the neural network architecture, we also note that *time-lags* are essential for processing a universal proposition; this is, of course, because no choice of weights or thresholds would allow the network to compute (evaluate) *X OR ELSE Y* in a single step.

We now have enough elements to give some concrete substance to the formal results of Chapter 3 and Section 4.2 above. First, note that all M–P units, and collections of M–P units, between those that have been initially identified as input and output groups of units are called *hidden units*. The adaptive, trial-and-error processes referred to in the previous section are, then, those procedures that assign sets of weights to the hidden units such that, for given input "signals," derived outputs can be reached.

Let me pose the problem in a slightly different way. The general problem facing the rational economic agent is to evaluate arbitrary propositions for truth values. Since a given proposition can be built up from strings of the universal proposition, the general problem will be to assign appropriate weights (w_{ij}) to hidden units. The key question, then, is:

> Given any arbitrary proposition, is there an effective procedure, determinable *a priori*, for assigning appropriate weights (to, say, construct the necessary "separating hyperplane") to evaluate it?

The various theorems of Chapter 3 and the previous section formalize and state the negative answer to this kind of question.

We can identify the reasons for the universal negative answers: the necessity of nonlinearity and time-lags.[4] Put another way, if we write the generalized algebraic expression for the input–output behavior of the neural network as

$$y = f(w, y), \qquad (4.9)$$

where f is nonlinear mapping, w is the vector of *integer* or *rational-number*-constrained connection weights, and y is the vector of input, output, and hidden variables, then finding an effective procedure for assigning weights to evaluate a given proposition is equivalent to finding an effective procedure to solve the diphantine equation (4.9). We know, from the celebrated negative solution to Hilbert's Tenth Problem (cf. Chapter 7), that there are no general effective procedures available *a priori* to solve a given, arbitrary, diophantine equation.

Furthermore, we can view (4.9) in a dynamic way, the solutions of (4.9) being the attractors for a dynamical system,

$$\frac{dy}{dt} = y - f(w, y). \qquad (4.10)$$

We know from the "geometry" of the evaluation problem for the EXCLUSIVE OR that the mapping f is both nonlinear and of dimension ≥ 3. The attractors of such a dynamical system, as solutions to (4.10), will in general be "strange," in the sense in which this is defined in formal dynamical system theory. Dynamical systems with strange attractors are minimally required if computation universality is to be feasible by them. Thus, we have the link between Goodwin's suggestion, Baum's query, and the results of Chapter 3 and the earlier sections of this chapter. In the final section of this

---

[4] As Richard Goodwin perceptively noted, "Combining the difficulties of difference equations with those of non-linear theory, we get an animal of a ferocious character and it is wise not to place too much confidence in our conclusions as to behaviour" (Goodwin 1950: 319).

chapter there is an attempt to tie up these disparate strands in a way that may suggest a micro–macro synthesis – albeit in a very speculative way.

We can now summarize and tie up the loose and disparate strange. The rational economic agent's problem of evaluating the truth value of given, arbitrary, propositions can be identified with:

(i) finding procedures to assign weights "appropriately" to hidden units in a neural network; or
(ii) finding algorithms to solve diophantine equations; or
(iii) finding effective methods to characterize strange attractors.

No known effective procedures exist to solve any of these problems in an *a priori* universal way; and in the case of (ii) it is known that no such effective procedures exist in general (negative solutions to Hilbert's Tenth Problem).

The best that can be done is to find a uniform procedure for special classes of propositions. Finding such uniform procedures, classifying classes of propositions, etc., are what count as "trial-and-error" procedures. This class of activities is what makes "all behavior adaptive" – except for the highly limited class of activities where propositions can be evaluated for their truth values without any hidden units. When a class of propositions has been classified and uniform procedures found to evaluate them, then there is a sense in which a "steady state" can be defined for them. Moreover, the modelling of "an individual as a collection of decision rules" can be interpreted in a similar fashion: collection of the uniform procedures that are used to evaluate classes of propositions.

4.4 CONCLUDING NOTES

Now if an organism is confronted with the problem of behaving approximately rationally, or adaptively, in a particular environment, the kinds of simplification that are suitable may depend not only on the characteristics – sensory, neural and other – of the organism, but equally upon the structure of the environment. Hence, we might hope to discover, by a careful examination of some of the fundamental structural characteristics of the environment, some further clues as to the nature of the approximating mechanisms used in decision making.

Simon (1956/1979: 21)

In the earlier parts of this chapter and in Chapter 3, we investigated some of the "characteristics of the organism" and the "structural characteristics of the environment" that cast doubt on the usefulness of working with the full paraphernalia of standard rational behavior. Now if the domain of the "structural characteristics of the environment" could also include the problems that confront a problem-solver, we might investigate the "nature of the approximating mechanisms" in use – implicitly and explicitly – in making them solvable. Approximating mechanisms have been devised for the rational agent, as an adaptive agent, as a boundedly rational agent, as a finite automaton; they have also been suggested for the "environment" – satisficing solutions, suitably chosen domains of definitions such as appropriate topological, measure-theoretic, and other spaces. I would like to suggest that there is an alternative way to approach this issue of "approximations" in a problem-solving context that leads to a more natural definition of boundedly rational behavior in which the agent becomes adaptive almost by necessity.

One way of specifying the standard economic problem (SEP) to be solved by "the Rational Man of Economics" is to formulate it as a mathematical programming problem (or an optimal control, game-theoretic, etc., problem). A simple (textbook)[5] formulation of an SEP is as follows (Papadimitriou and Steiglitz 1982: 343–6):

(SEP) Minimize $f(x)$
      subject to: $g_i(x) \geq 0$, $i = 1, \ldots, m$,
      and: $h_j(x) = 0$, $j = 1, \ldots, p$,

with standard assumptions on f, g, and h. Often the assumptions guarantee the *existence*[6] (for example) of a global optimum, as befits "a maximizer, who will settle for nothing less than *the* best."

Now consider the following variation of (SEP):

(SEP^a) An optimization problem is a pair $\{F, c\}$, where:
    F: any set (the domain of possible alternatives)
    c: $F \to \mathfrak{R}$ (e.g. criterion function)

---

[5] I follow the excellent notation and formulation in Papadimitriou and Steiglitz (1982), although, of course, I could have chosen any standard textbook in optimization, optimal control, or game theory for alternative – but formally equivalent – formulations and definitions.

[6] At the risk of belaboring a point beyond endurance, I cannot resist restating: guaranteeing the existence of an optimum is one thing; finding it is another thing; and finding it *tractably* is yet another thing.

PROBLEM. Find $f \in F$ such that $c(f) \le c(g)$, $\forall g \in F$.
Clearly, some meaningful structure, dictated by economic considerations, must be imposed on F, c, etc.

Next, consider yet another variant of (SEP) (and (SEP$^\alpha$):

(SEP†) (a) Given a combinatorial object (i.e. a number-theoretically specified object) f and a set of parameters S, decide whether $f \in F$ (where F is characterized by S). Assume that this decision procedure is executed by algorithm T_f (standing for the Turing machine indexed by f, which has been effectively encoded).

   (b) After the decision implemented by T_f, use another decision procedure (algorithm) to compute the value $c(f)$, where c is characterized by a set of parameters Q. Call this decision procedure T_c.

   (c) Note that S and Q are represented number-theoretically, for example Gödel-numbered.

Here is an example of (SEP†), the standard (integer) linear programming problem (SILP):

(SILP) Minimize $c\,'x$
       subject to $Ax = b$
       and $x \ge 0$(integer)
       (vectorial, of appropriate dimensions).

According to the (SEP†) interpretation, this means:

   (i) The parameters S, for the decision procedure T_f, are given by A, b.

   (ii) Given any integer (vector) x, T_f decides whether $Ax = b$ and $x \ge 0$ are simultaneously satisfied.

   (iii) "Then" T_c is implemented which has c for Q to evaluate $c\,'x$ for each x decided by T_f.

Note, however, that the "then" in (iii) above does not necessarily imply sequential actions by the Turing machines. More complex decision tasks, encapsulating richer varieties of (SEP†), will, of course, imply a set of Turing machines operating on a parallel architecture and sequentially (synchronously and asynchronously). Thus, in this vision every agent, and every problem in general, is a combinatorial object and a set of decision procedures; some of the decision procedures operate sequentially, with the output of a subset being inputs to other subsets; some operate (synchronously or asynchronously) in parallel. (SEP†) does not violate the setting in which "the Rational Man of Economics" is set in its paces. But it does give an entirely different perspective on the complexity and the dynamic nature of the decision problems executed by such a rational agent.

Now, for the way I have reformulated the rational choice problem in Chapter 3 and in Sections 4.2 and 4.3 of this chapter, it is (SEP†) that is relevant. The agent is, in general, interpreted as solving decision problems of which (SEP) will now be considered a special case. In such a case the "hidden units" are, or behave *as if* they are, dummy variables. All attention is focused on the input and output variables only, i.e. on the domain of *substantive rationality*. Whenever the "hidden units" drive a wedge between input and output variables, (SEP) (and (SEP$^\alpha$)) must be generalized to (SEP†) and we must focus on *procedural rationality*, i.e. on the rationality of the process of assigning weights to "hidden units."

In what sense, then, can we talk about the existence of the "one way to be fully rational"? Almost none whatever. There are many ways of being rational in the sense that classifying classes of problems, finding uniform, effective, procedures, etc., are more Linnean than anything else.[7] I think that induction and its formalisms provide discipling rules for this Linnean world of decision-making.

Let me, however, end this chapter with a tentative definition of boundedly rational agents and some equally tentative general notes.

DEFINITION 4.1. A boundedly rational agent solves decision problems in the sense of (SEP†).

Remark. This definition is completely consistent with the definition given by Osborne and Rubinstein in the context of repeated games (Osborne and Rubinstein 1994: 164).[8]

This definition makes it clear, I hope, that boundedly rational agents are *not approximately fully rational agents*. They are boundedly

---

[7] Or, in Rutherford's whimsical assertion, "science is largely 'stamp collecting' and . . . "

[8] In particular, sec. 8.4 and ch. IX of this excellent textbook: "we focus more closely on the structured equilibrium strategies rather than on the set of equilibrium payoffs, using the tool of a machine [which is intended as an abstraction of the process by which a player implements a strategy in a repeated game]. . . . A model that includes such 'procedural' aspects of decision-making is known as a model of 'bounded rationality'" (Osborne and Rubinstein 1994:163–4; emphasis added).

rational, according to these definitions, because the nature of the problems they face, and the way they view solutions to them, places bounds on the classes of problems they can solve. The substantively rational – or "fully rational" – agent of standard formalisms is a special case because such an agent is confronted with a special subset of the class of decision problems facing the boundedly rational agent.[9]

This brings me to one further, general, point. Much has been made, in recent years, of attempts to model emergent behavior on the basis of the interaction between collections of simple – even simplistic – agents. Connectionism, massive parallelism, cellular automatas, etc., are some of the "buzz" words in this vast literature, straddling fascinating interdisciplinary worlds. I believe this to be a fundamentally flawed vision.

The economic (or social or political) agent is anything but a simple or simplistic unit. I think it is imperative that we model the agent in its full complexity, i.e. as a Turing machine. It is the collective that is simplistic and may fail to have the capability of universal computation. How can the interactions of a collection of sophisticated agents – Turing machines – result in a system that cannot achieve what the individual units can achieve individually and separately? I think there are two reasons:

(a) First of all, the *system* does not try to solve decision problems: that is the individual agent's problem. The system simply acts as the ledger book, the classifier in the bucket-brigade algorithm, the noticeboard. It records the credits and debits. It is an accountant. In the extreme case it is Maxwell's Demon!

(b) Second, as the result of its being the accountant, it is not computation universality that is relevant for the system's behavior, but some conversation principle. Most of the natural sciences, in their phenomenological variations, have conservation principles; this is true even for many of the pure sciences (symmetry, modularity, and so on). The social sciences seem not to have succeeded in formulating useful conservation principles.

---

[9] In a curious collection of essays, with the attractive title *Artificial Intelligence and Economic Analysis* (Moss and Rae 1992), Huw Dixon states that: "A simple generalization of the orthodox approach is . . . sufficient to capture some elements of bounded rationality without the need explicitly to model reasoning" (p. 136). This is almost exactly the antithesis of my definition and is based on equating a boundedly rational solution with an approximately optimal solution in an otherwise orthodox setup. If all that bounded rationality meant was more constraints in the standard model, then, is the declarative a superset of the imperative (cf. concluding notes to Ch. 2)?

Thus, the question finally to be posed is: how can a collection of interesting Turing machines result in macro systems – institutions, laws, etc. – that have useful conservation principles? Computation universality is possessed by individual agents who behave rationally and implement the "no arbitrage" principle; conservation laws are possessed by aggregates. What, then, is the connection or relation between computation universality and conservation principles? An answer to this question should resolve the micro–macro divide.

A tentative step in the direction of obtaining interesting answers to this question requires recursion-theoretic formalisms at the macro level, too. For example, aggregate variables will have to be sequences that are recursively enumerable but not recursive. But, then, only dynamical systems capable of computation universality can generate such sequences. This means that *all* dynamical systems currently utilized to model growth and cycles in macroeconomics are inconsistent with the microeconomics of rational behavior. This is one reason why real business cycle theorists resort to *"ad-hoc shockeries"*; for no dynamical system that is asymptotically stable is capable of computation universality.

Most – if not all – of the assertions of the above paragraph can be stated and proved as theorems. I leave this as an exercise for a sequel to this work.

5

The Modern Theory of Induction

> The laws of nature are sufficiently simple that, following the
> *best available inductive methods*, man can in a reasonable period
> of time find them (or find a good approximation of them).
>
> Kemeny (1953: 402; emphasis added)

5.1 INTRODUCTION

> ... we may think of a system of inductive logic as a design for a
> "learning machine": that is to say, a design for a computing
> machine that can extrapolate certain kinds of empirical regu-
> larities from the data with which it is supplied.
>
> Putnam (1963/1975: 297)

In this admirable and characteristically well focused sentence,
Putnam has summarized, with customary finesse, the essential features of the modern theory of induction and its constituent elements:
inductive logic, learning machines, computing machines, and extrap-
olation of regularities. In other words, it can be asked whether there
is an inductive logical foundation for the construction of computing
machines to *learn* to extrapolate regularities. If an affirmative answer
can be found, the rational economic agent as a Turing machine could
be set in its paces to "learn to extrapolate regularities" on the basis of
"a system of inductive logic." This may help ground "economics as
an inductive science" (Clower 1996) and remove the deductive shack-
les to which economic analysis seems to have been chained ever since
Ricardo.

There have, however, been famous objections to such a "research
program," routinely referred to in Humean, Popperian and other
hand-waving modes. These have to be addressed, at least cursorily.

To suggest the way in which I believe the modern theory of induction comes to term with these objections, it may be useful to begin by noting Putnam's clear statement of the issues to be resolved:

Inductive logic is concerned with the relation of *confirmation*. Just as in deductive logic we consider certain correct inferences which lead from a set of sentences *P* (called the *premises* of the inference) to a conclusion *S*, so in inductive logic we deal with certain inferences which lead from a set of sentences *E* (called the evidence for the inductive inference) to a conclusion *S*. The premises of a good deductive inference are said to *imply* the conclusion *S*; the evidence, in the case of a warranted inductive inference, is said to confirm the conclusion *S*. The difference in terminology reflects some of the fundamental differences between the two subjects. The most important of these differences is that in a warranted inductive inference the sentences *E* may be true and the conclusion S may still be false. It is for this reason that we do not say that *E implies S* but choose the weaker terminology *E confirms S*. This difference has one immediately annoying consequence: it makes it somewhat difficult to state with any degree of precision what inductive logic is *about*.

Since deductive inferences are truth-preserving (this means: if the premises are true, the conclusion *must* be true) we can characterize deductive logic by saying that we seek mathematical rules for deriving conclusions from sets of premises which will preserve truth: which will lead from true premises only to true conclusions. But in inductive logic we seek what? Mathematical rules which will lead from true premises to conclusions which are probably true, relative to those premises. But "*probably*" in what sense? . . .

. . . If we seek rules which will lead to conclusions which are probably true on the evidence given in some *a priori* sense of "probably true", then what reason is there to think that there exists a defensible and scientifically interesting *a priori* notion of probability?

Let us by pass these difficulties for the moment by agreeing that, just as in deductive logic there are certain clear cases of valid reasoning, so in inductive logic there are certain clear cases of warranted inductive reasoning, and we can at least attempt to see if these have any mathematically interesting structural properties.(Putnam 1963: 294–5)

In the modern theory of induction, these difficult philosophical and methodological issues are dealt with in the following two analytical ways:

(1) The evidence for the inductive inference is characterized recursion-theoretically.
(2) The mathematical rules for confirming the recursion-theoretically characterized evidence is also formalized algorithmically.

Both of these analytical devices make it possible to circumvent, entirely, the need to rely on any *a priori* notion of probability. In the rest of this section I discuss the basis for these assertions in various *ad hoc* and intuitive ways. In the following section an outline of the mathematical formalism underlying the modern theory of induction is given (i.e. explicating (2) above). Finally, in Section 5.3, two explicit ways in which the "evidence for the inductive inferences" are characterized recursion-theoretically (i.e. following (1) above), and analyzed inductively, within the mathematical formalism of the modern theory of induction are stated and discussed.

Economic agents observe (the "evidence for the inductive infer- ence") sequences of, say, prices (and quantities), and adjust expendi- tures at the margins, to reach desirable situations. In some explicit and analytical sense, then, the observed sequences must contain information. An *induction process*, on the information contained in relevant sequences, will be the basis for decisions. If all the informa- tion relevant for the economic decision has been extracted by the induction process, then it is reasonable to surmise that the evidence has been "randomized." The classic "no-arbitrage" hypothesis underlying any statement on rational behavior, institutional asser- tions on efficient market hypotheses, etc., implies this kind of "ran- domization" of the evidence. If, however, the evidence retains "unexploited utility or profit generating possibilities" (Sargent 1993: 7), then, either agents are unable to exercise "full" rationality in some sense, or institutions exhibit some inefficiency, or else a combination of the two underlies the functioning of the economic system that gives rise to such evidence.

A broader interpretation consistent with the computable approach to economics would suggest an alternative combination of possible reasons for economic systems to generate unrandomized evidence. This broader interpretation implies that the reasons could be due to (a combination of):

(a) The intrinsic complexity of the observed sequence (i.e., the evi- dence);
(b) The inappropriateness of the mechanism (formalization) that is being used to model the agent or the institution;
(c) The suboptimality of the utilized induction process;

In traditional economic analysis, the theoretical technologies that have been harnessed to encapsulate these three subcomponents have not been derived in any consistent way. *Ad hoc* combinations of statistical and system-theoretic underpinnings for (a), Bourbakian and formalistic building blocks for (b), and a variety of alternative (*a priori*) probabilistic bases for (c) have caused the toolbox of economic analysis to resemble a veritable potpourri.

Imposing a rigid methodological discipline is not the main aim of the computable approach to economics. However, against the backdrop provided by (a)–(c) three interrelated questions could be asked:

(i)   What is the best way to model the inductive capabilities of a rational agent (or the best way to design or interpret the functioning of economic institutions from an inductive point of view)?

(ii) How is the complexity of the evidence to be modelled so that randomization can be studied without any *a priori* notion of probability being prejudicial to the formalism for (i) and the possible answer(s) to (iii) below?

(iii) Are there effective rules to decide when the no-arbitrage condition has been satisfied; i.e., are there effective rules to decide when the inductive process is to stop?

From a computable point of view, there are unambiguous and consistent answers to these three questions. The rational agent must be modelled as a Turing machine and the institutions of the economic system must be capable of *computation universality*; the complexity of the evidence is to be formalized in terms of a measure – effective – of the size and mode of its description or generation or, technically, in terms of its algorithmic complexity; as for an answer to (iii), in view of the remarkable theoretical result that the algorithmic complexity of randomized evidence is uncomputable, there can be no effective optimal stopping rule, valid in any general sense, for arbitrary inductive processes. These are all assertions that are consistent with the results, formalisms, and frameworks suggested and developed in earlier chapters.

Enough has been discussed about possible answers to (i) in previous chapters; some thoughts on answers to (iii) have also been discussed, in particular in Chapter 4. Answers to (ii), in conjunction with (a)–(c) above, delineate the basic material of this (and the next) chapter.

Ever since the microfoundation resurgence of the late 1960s, and the seminal work of Hayek, Stigler, and McCall, it has been fashionable, if not imperative, to refer to the "information revolution" in economics. This is perhaps most evident in the theory of finance, but surely not less so in conventional micro (and macro) economics and game theory. The economic cost of acquiring, utilizing, and transmitting information – indeed, of treating information as an economic good – has become very much part of the bread-and-butter training most graduate students receive in economics. In fact, it is just as important to state the nature of the assumptions underlying the place of information as it is to specify the exact role of endowments, preferences and technology in the traditional neoclassical closure. Phelps, and others following him – the New Classicals in particular – have augmented the neoclassical closure to include information almost on an equal footing with the other three constituent elements: endowments, preferences, and technology.

The suggestion to enlarge the *core* (to be very Lakatosian about it) is persuasive. However, I do not find the formalism that is used to encapsulate the intuitive notion of information equally persuasive, or even useful. It seems to be a case of repeating the same mistakes made in the formalization of preferences and technology, not to mention endowments, all over again. I have no adequate methodological explanation for this except to quote, on my side, Lucas's perceptive (and in my opinion correct) observation that:

To ask why the monetary theorists of the late 1940s did not make use of the contingent-claim view of equilibrium is, it seems to me, like asking why Hannibal did not use tanks against the Romans instead of elephants. There is no reason to view our ability to think as being any less limited by available technology than is our ability to act (if, indeed, this distinction can be defended). (Lucas, 1981: 286)

In other words, economists are often unaware of available theoretical technologies that can encapsulate the intuitive richnesses that, in turn, enhance "our ability to think." Thus, in standard theory it would be customary to interpret the evidence as a random variable drawn or generated in accordance with a probability density function which, in turn, is consistent with some *a priori* notion of probability. Haavelmo, for example, prefaced his seminal work on "The Probability Approach to Economics" with the following rationale for his "attempt to supply a theoretical foundation for the analysis of interrelations between economic variables":

it has been considered legitimate to use some of the *tools* developed in statistical theory without accepting the very *foundation* upon which statistical theory is built. For *no tool developed in the theory of statistics has any meaning* – except, perhaps for descriptive purposes – *without being referred to some stochastic scheme.*

  The reluctance among economists to accept probability models as a basis for economic research has, it seems, been founded upon a very narrow concept of probability and random variables. (Haavelmo 1994: *iii*)

Times have caught up even with the genius of Haavelmo.[1] There is a perfectly valid and mathematically rigorous way of founding (many of) the tools of statistics without any reference to a stochastic scheme; *a fortiori*, without reference to any kind of *a priori* notion of probability (narrow in concept or not). If this can be demonstrated in an analytically rigorous way, then there might be some basis for "the reluctance among economists to accept probability models as a basis for economic research." This will automatically imply that it will not be necessary to interpret evidence as a random variable drawn or generated in accordance with a probability density function.

  Even at the frontiers of business cycle research, such view are being questioned vigorously and imaginatively. Referring to the famous "measurement without theory" debate initiated by Koopmans against NBER methodology, Kydland and Prescott note:[2]

Koopmans's second criticism is that Burns and Mitchell's study lacks explicit assumptions about the probability distribution of the variables. That is, their study lack "assumptions expressing and specifying how random disturbances operate on the economy through the economic relationship

---

[1] This is the sense in which the above Lucasian observation on Hannibal's elephants must be interpreted. Moreover, recall the following observation by Keynes: "I have often pressed [Edgeworth] to give an opinion as to how far the modern theory of Statistics and Correlation can stand if the Frequency Theory fails as a logical doctrine. He would always reply to the effect that the collapse of the Frequency Theory would affect the *universality* of application of Statistical Theory, but that large masses of statistical data did, nevertheless, in his opinion, satisfy the conditions required for the validity of Statistical Theory, *whatever these might be*" (Keynes 1933: 281–2; second emphasis added). I am suggesting that the modern theory of induction resurrects the validity of the frequency theory *and* provides the alternative to the "stochastic scheme" that Haavelmo seeks.

[2] Kalman makes the same point even more pungently: "Although loud and opposing voices were raised, especially by Frisch, to the gradually prevailing dogma of imposing probability and then statistics on the treatment of noisy data – we may call this, roughly speaking, the Fisherian paradigm of sampling and estimation (Fisher: *'the World is a parametrized family of probability distributions'*) – somehow the addictiveness of the idea of probability resulted in weeding out the scientists from among econometricians" (Kalman 1994: 146; emphasis added).

between the variables".... Economists, he argues, should first hypothesize that the aggregate time series under consideration are generated by some probability model, which the economists must then estimate and test. Koopmans convinced the economic profession that to do otherwise is unscientific. On this point we strongly disagree with Koopmans: We think he did economics a grave disservice, because the reporting of facts – *without assuming the data are generated by some probability model* – is an important scientific activity. We see no reason for economics to be an exception. (Kydland and Prescott 1990: 3; emphasis added)

Kydland and Prescott (and indeed Kalman – cf. fn. 2) are trying to make a case for learning, inductively, from extractable patterns in reported data, data assumed to be generated from an *a priori* theoretical model. The patterns in the data contain and convey information. Filtering out noise from information is one way of analyzing data, the standard way; extracting patterns as information is another way. The modern theory of induction formalizes, on the basis of recursion theory, the latter mode.

The modern father of axiomatic probability theory, who happens also to be a parent of algorithmic complexity theory, pointed the way when he said:

it is not clear why information theory should be based so essentially on probability theory, as the majority of text-books would have it. It is my task to show that this dependence on previously created probability theory is not, in fact, inevitable. (Kolmogorov 1983: 31)

The traditional reason for basing information theory[3] "so essentially on probability theory" proceeds as follows. If the evidence, say X, is a random variable generated in accordance with a probability density function $p(x)$, then there is a clear sense in which the information content of $X = x$ is $\log(1/p(x))$.[4] Thus, ostensibly, the information content of the evidence depends, crucially, on the probability distribution, and hence on some *a priori* notion of probability. The circle is then completed by claiming that "probability models as a basis for economic research," information economics, stochastic macroeconomics, and the like are the natural vehicle for economic analysis.

But is this version "inevitable"? Or, as Kolmogorov challengingly notes, is it the case that "this dependence on previously created prob-

---

[3] Analogously, therefore, information economics "so essentially on probability theory," too!

[4] This is because $(\log(1/p(x)))$ is the number of bits required to describe x by a Shannon code.

ability theory is not, in fact, inevitable"? To begin at the beginning, is it absolutely necessary to interpret the evidence, say $X = x$, as a random variable, generated by an underlying probability density function, to encapsulate the unknown, the unknowable, and the fragility in the observed and the observer? What if we interpret the evidence $X = x$ recursion-theoretically? Surely, even at an intuitive level it is clear that the uncomputability, undecidability, and incompleteness inherent in complex entities, should be able to encapsulate the unknown, the unknowable, and the fragile in the evidence. In addition, this approach would have the advantage of characterizing the observer and the observed compatibly: the former, under the Church–Turing thesis, as a Turing machine; the latter, analogously, recursion-theoretically.[5] It is this possibility that Kolmogorov exploited, with characteristic finesse and originality, to free information theory from its probabilistic basis. Simply and directly stated, the basic idea is to formalize the difficulties inherent in describing the evidence recursion-theoretically, and to define randomness in terms of such a formalization, and then to build a basis for probability on such foundations: i.e., randomness on recursion-theoretic foundations and probability on randomness. This leads, directly and unambiguously, to a foundation for information theory in recursion theory.

Reverting to the mild formalism with which I began this discussion, the question is whether there is an analytical route to free ourselves from describing $X = x$ by some function of $\log(1/p(x))$. Kolmogorov's brilliant insight[6] was that a measure to describe the evidence can be defined on the basis of the *minimal length* of the algorithm that can generate the evidence, when implemented on a suitably defined universal computer. It will then be apparent that the evidence must, *ab inizio*, be endowed with some kind of recursion-theoretic structure. To this insight was coupled the conjecture, subsequently demonstrated, that such a description of the evidence does not depend, in any essential way, on the "suitably defined universal computer" utilized to implement the algorithm. It can thus be shown that such a measure – minimal over the resources needed to define

---

[5] E.g., characterizing the evidence $X = x$ as being recursively enumerable but not recursive, in general.

[6] Like all great and innovative ideas, there are parallel pioneers. In this case the obvious ones are Chaitin and Solomonoff; but Putnam, Löfgren, and Good should have some place in the list of parallel pioneers.

and implement the relevant algorithm – can characterize a universal code, valid for all (computable) probability density functions.[7]

Before proceeding with heavy formalisms in the next section, I would like to indulge in additional discursive comments on the intuitive basis for randomness in a recursion-theoretic framework. Terence Fine's excellent remark almost encapsulates the new view of randomness and contrasts it with the old:

Reflection on [the role of place-selection functions] . . . leads us from reliance on a pragmatic impossibility-of-a-gambling-scheme view of random sequences to an epistemic view that a random sequence is highly irregular or complex. (Fine 1973: 118)

It is this epistemic view that lies at the heart of the modern theory of induction and allows us to interpret learning as induction. Let me, therefore, ask: What is randomness? Indeed, is there such a thing as a "random number"? A master computer scientist suggested:

In a sense, there is no such thing as a random number; for example is 2 a random number? Rather, we speak of a *sequence of independent random numbers*. . . . (Knuth 1981: 2; emphasis added)

So, is randomness to be defined in terms of sequences? How, then, are the sequences generated? Leaving aside the deeper question of whether or not there are "random numbers," we can, perhaps, get some intuitive understanding of randomness[8] in general by looking at practical devices for generating random numbers. Shall we toss coins? Throw dice? Shuffle and deal out cards? Can a sequence of coin tosses generate "a sequence of independent random numbers"?[9]

Now, it is well known that it is fashionable, especially in economic theory, to dismiss any attempt at founding probability theory on frequency theoretic underpinnings. Knight, Keynes, Savage, and de Finetti rule! But it is only from the point of view of frequency theory that a serious attempt has been made to deal with the randomness of *finite* sequences. Rational agents, whether as Turing machines or not, have only a class, at most, of finite sequences to learn from. When

---

[7] In other words, it is possible, for example, to define a universal prior in the Bayesian context.

[8] One of the great results of the modern theory of induction is the fact that there are such things that can meaningfully be called "random numbers." Chaitin's Ω is one of them.

[9] Economists are not alone in their cavalier assumptions about independent and identically distributed (i.i.d.) "sequences."

learning stops, at a no-arbitrage state, the agent must be able to be sure that "the remains" are, indeed, random, and that they are, always, finite sequences. What, therefore, is the connection between *finite* and *infinite* sequences? How can we theorize about the randomness of finite sequences?

Assume we toss a fair coin twenty times and the outcomes are, for three trials:

$$1\ 0\ 0\ 0\ 1\ 0\ 1\ 1\ 1\ 0\ 1\ 1\ 1\ 1\ 0\ 1\ 0\ 0\ 0\ 0 \tag{5.1}$$

$$0\ 1\ 1\ 1\ 1\ 0\ 1\ 1\ 0\ 0\ 1\ 1\ 0\ 1\ 1\ 1\ 0\ 0\ 0\ 1 \tag{5.2}$$

and

$$0\ 0\ 0\ 0\ 0\ 0\ 0\ 0\ 0\ 0\ 0\ 0\ 0\ 0\ 0\ 0\ 0\ 0\ 0\ 0 \tag{5.3}$$

I suppose one feels that the third outcome is highly unlikely. Another way of looking at it would be to say that the first two seem to be patternless and the third full of structure. The third is the sort of sequence expected in economic series that are an outcome of "people . . . in recurrent situations" (Sargent 1993: 1); the first two are typical of outcomes that are a result of "people . . . confronted with new and ill-defined rules", people in "a daily struggle to determine the 'mechanism' that will eventually govern trade and production" (p. 1). But the people will have to determine the "mechanism" in real time; the mechanism is in operation in real time, too.

So we ask, about the first two sequences, "patternless" in what sense? The epistemic answer, as distinct from the pragmatic one, would be: *in the sense of not having a shorter description of itself than presenting it in its entirety.* This is rather like the difference between encapsulating a regularity by a formula and being unable to capture any regularity by a rule describing a time-series of outcomes of prices and quantities. In other words, we seek to identify randomness with some definition of patternlessness, of lack of structure; we say it is "difficult to describe," "hard to learn," etc. This is where algorithmic complexity theory meets randomness. Eventually we seek a definition of randomness for finite sequences in terms of the descriptional complexity (described by an algorithm) of a finite object embedded in a larger class of objects; this latter finesse means that we resort to the age-old strategy of embedding the finite problem in an infinite one. If we denote the infinite continuations of (5.1), (5.2), and (5.3) by the imagery of the familiar ellipses, we get

$$1\ 0\ 0\ 0\ 1\ 0\ 1\ 1\ 1\ 0\ 1\ 1\ 1\ 1\ 0\ 1\ 0\ 0\ 0\ 0\ \ldots \quad (5.1')$$

$$0\ 1\ 1\ 1\ 1\ 0\ 1\ 1\ 0\ 0\ 1\ 1\ 0\ 1\ 1\ 1\ 0\ 0\ 0\ 1\ \ldots \quad (5.2')$$

$$0\ 0\ 0\ 0\ 0\ 0\ 0\ 0\ 0\ 0\ 0\ 0\ 0\ 0\ 0\ 0\ 0\ 0\ 0\ 0\ \ldots \quad (5.3')$$

Next, after obtaining a definition of individual infinite sequences, we try to obtain a criterion for randomness for classes of finite sequences, keeping in mind the fact that the rational agent is trying to learn, above all, whether or not a (finite) sequence is patternless, in order to reach the no-arbitrage state.

It is here that the frequency theory of probability enters the induction problem with a vengeance! Leaving aside the colourful imagery of patterns and patternlessness, we turn to Richard von Mises and his valiant attempts to found a theory of probability on phenomenological grounds – like phenomenological thermodynamics and its laws. He did this in terms of two concepts: one, conceptual – the collective (randomness), the other mathematical – "stability of frequencies." There was a third to cement the above two: "place selection rules," to learn to randomize. It turns out that "place selection rules" are computable functions. Thus, an agent must be computably rich enough to have within "itself" enough "place selection rules" that can be activated when confronted with complex sequences from which to learn. Roughly speaking, the initial formalism took the following steps.

DEFINITION 5.1: FREQUENCY STABILITY. If

$$\lim_{n \to \infty}(v_n/v) = p,$$

where v_n is, for example, the number of zeros in the beginning segment of a binary sequence $a_0, a_1, a_2, \ldots, a_{n-1}$ of length n, then the binary sequence $a_0, a_1, a_2, \ldots$ has the property of frequency stability with limit p.

DEFINITION 5.2 (PRELIMINARY): RANDOM BINARY SEQUENCE. A binary sequence is random whenever any *suitably chosen* sub-sequence of it has the property of frequency stability.

These preliminary conceptual tools can be broken down into the following steps:

1. Given an (in)finite binary sequence, and
2. given a class of selection rules [to "suitably choose"], then

3. select a sub-sequence from the original sequence (using one of the selection rules given in step 2).

In other words, the trick is to link the definition of selection rules with the property of frequency stability. Thus,

A selection rule will extract a sub-sequence $a_{r0}, a_{r1}, a_{r2} \ldots$ from the original sequence $a_0, a_1, a_2 \ldots$ such that the extracted (sub)sequence has the frequency stability property.

The rational agent's learning task is exactly this (when modelled "artificially intelligently"), but with enough capacity to be the most powerful automaton: the Turing machine. *Learnable sequences* are those that such a machine can compute; unlearnable sequences trap the machine with the halting problem, undecidabilities, uncomputabilities and other menaces.

One last "doctrine-historical" observation before I conclude this section. Another pioneer, almost as influential as Haavelmo when measured in terms of his influence on the way economists model interrelations between economic variables, i.e. Rudolf Kalman, has in more recent times argued forcefully and cogently for the wholesale rejection of the Haavelmo–Cowles Foundation approach to quantitative analysis in economics. Put succinctly, and quite independently of the massively impressive developments in algorithmic complexity theory, Kalman has come to the conclusion that it was quite wrong to define randomness from the probability corner:

When we research and try to comprehend randomness in Nature we must try to avoid the temptation to automatically "explain" randomness in terms of (conventional = games-of-chance = Kolmogorov) probability.
It is our claim that

The majority of observed phenomena of randomness in Nature (always excluding games of chance) cannot be and should not be explained by (conventional) probability theory; there is little or no experimental evidence in favour of (conventional) probability but there is massive, accumulating evidence that explanations and even descriptions should be sought outside of the conventional framework. (Kalman 1994: 142; emphasis in the original)

Kalman's own definition of randomness is precisely the algorithmic one[10] – although he couches his discussion in different and idiosyncratic terminology and concepts.

---

[10] As he puts it with characteristic provocativeness, "Let us be bold and remove the question of independence, the method of generation and even probability from the

Are Kalman's observations sufficiently persuasive for abandoning the probability–randomness nexus? Is experimental falsification sufficient ground to abandon a methodology that seems to have "worked," with the help of judiciously chosen "ad-hockeries"? I doubt it. If scientific practice were so pure, nothing would ever get done. Dogmas, mythologies, and other alchemies are part of the small impurities that make the scientific enterprise robust, successful and relatively meaningful. One or two anomalies rarely sound the death knoll: *una rondine non fa primavera*! On the other hand, it is precisely the outlier, the odd swallow, that signals the onset of something new in the horizon.

5.2 THE MODERN THEORY OF INDUCTION

> If we could arrange *all* testable hypotheses in a single list, and then proceed to test hypotheses in the order in which they occur in our list, perhaps we could ensure that *if* there is a correct testable hypothesis, then sooner or later it will get tested (at least if there is an "immortal inquirer" or an immortal community of inquirers; *the problem of the finite case arises once more here*) . . .
>
> But . . . an empirical hypothesis is involved in saying that *all* testable hypotheses are in our list: Church's Thesis in itself an empirical hypothesis about the calculating powers of human beings, one which it needs induction to verify. If we use a method which takes account only of recursive hypotheses, then if we live in a world in which human beings have the ability to calculate nonrecursive functions, and the true hypothesis involved a function of this kind, then we will never confirm the true hypothesis using [a recursion-theoretic scheme].
>
> Putnam (1990: 9–10)

A colourful, possibly misleading, characterization of the modern theory of induction would be to say that it is about making precise, mathematically, the general notion of *Occam's razor*.[11]

way we look at randomness. Then the proper intrinsic definition of randomness becomes obvious. *Randomness is the opposite of regularity*" (Kalman 1994: 143).

[11] Apparently Occam's own most often stated version appears to be: "*Pluralitas non est ponenda sine necessitate*" (plurality is not to be posited without necessity); the form commonly attributed to Occam – "*Entia non sunt multiplicanda sine necessitate*" (entities must not be multiplied without necessity) – seems *not* to have been used by him (cf. Boehner, 1990: *xxi*).

In the previous section I suggested something like the following idea for learning as induction: given some set of information, say represented as binary sequences, can a learner find a (computable) rule to encapsulate this information set in such a way that the rule is "simple" in some well defined sense and can be used to predict "future" members of the sequence? In a nutshell, a scientific activity like learning is about finding rules to describe compactly the past evidence in such a way that predictions are implied in the compact rule.

The main idea in modern theory of induction is to formalize this activity in the following supposition. The given past (and contemporaneous) information set, the proposed hypothesis (rational expectations, for example), the mode of obtaining evidence and the evidence itself, the way this evidence is used to understand the hypothesis and, if necessary, to modify (RE to boundedly rational expectations (BRE)) the originally proposed hypothesis – *all of these should (and can) be encoded as the initial segment of a potentially infinite binary sequence.*

Now to some formalisms:

$B \{0,1\}$: the set of basic elements that constitute the infinite binary sequences;

$B \{0,1\}^*$: the set of all finite binary strings over B;

S: set of all one-way infinite binary sequences;

$\mu(x) = \Sigma \{P(xy): y \in B\}$ (measure μ over B).

Then, in terms of Bayes's formula,

$$\mu\left(Sa\middle|S\right) = \frac{\mu(Sa)}{\mu(S)}. \tag{5.4}$$

In this simple formalism, learning as induction implies *inferring the effective process* (e.g. the Turing machine) *that generates S* and, therefore, being able to forecast the next outcome a. This is how (and where) computability enters the picture. The question is then reduced to the search for an "absolute" prior or, in the language of the modern theory of induction, to the problem of the existence of a *universal prior*. The problem was solved by Solomonoff by imposing computability constraints on the allowable priors. This solution, which we will now describe, is the formalism for the modern theory of induction. The conceptual finesse is to use recursion-theoretic ideas to define the complexity of finite objects and then to identify simplicity with probably – i.e. more simple as more probable – and, via Bayes and Turing, formalize Occam *à la* Solomonoff, Kolmogorov, and Chaitin!

Denote by:

$l(x)$ the length of the (binary) string x;
T the Turing Machine.

We use the following encoding of strings:

   (i)   the empty string $\varepsilon \rightarrow 0$;
  (ii)   the string $\{0\} \rightarrow 1$;
 (iii)   the string $\{1\} \rightarrow 2$;
 (iv)   the string $\{0,0\} \rightarrow 3$;
  (v)   the string $\{0,1\} \rightarrow 4$;

and so on; i.e., the coding is

$$(\varepsilon,0), (0,1), (1,2), (00,3), (01,4), \ldots$$

DEFINITION 5.3. p is a description of the (finite) string x if, on input p to T, the output of T is x.

Remark. It is clear from the definitions that the description must be *effective*.

More generally, especially when Oracle computations are called forth, the Turing machine is allowed to use additional information y to generate x; this is denoted by

$$T(p,y) = x : T \text{ with input } p \text{ and } y \text{ terminates with output } x.$$

Intuitively, we would like to call a string *simple* if its description p, say in the form of a computer program, can be achieved easily. There is, of course, a circularity in this intuitive statement: "simple in terms of easy." But this will be clarified in a moment.

DEFINITION 5.4. $C_T(x|y) = \min\{l(p): p \in \{0,1\}^*, T(p,\uparrow y) = x\}$ and $C_T(x|y) = \infty$ if $\nexists p$ with such a minimum.

From standard results in algorithmic complexity theory, we know that the defined $C_T(x|y)$ is invariant with respect to the choice of T. In other words, there exists a universal Turing machine (UTM) such that, $\forall T, \exists c_T$ (constant) such that $\forall x, y \in B^*$:

$$C_u(x|y) \le C_T(x|y) + c_T. \tag{5.5}$$

DEFINITION 5.5: PREFIX CODE
(i) x is a *prefix* of y if there is a z such that $y = x\,z$ $(x, y, z \in B^*)$;
(ii) $A \subseteq B^*$ is prefix-free if $\forall x \in A$, x is not a prefix for any $y \in A$;
(iii) $F: B^* \to N$ is a *prefix code* if its domain is prefix-free.

DEFINITION 5.6: PREFIX MACHINE. A prefix machine is a multi-tape Turing machine such that the set of programs for which it halts is a prefix code. Thus, prefix machines can be effectively enumerated.

DEFINITION 5.7: PREFIX COMPLEXITY
$K_T(x|y) = \min\{l(p): p \in B^*, T(p, y) = x\}$ and, $\forall p$ for which there does not exist such a minimum: $K_T(x|y) = \infty$

$K_T(x|y)$: prefix complexity of $x \in B^*$ with respect to prefix machine T and binary string y.

In other words, $K_T(x|y)$ is the length of the shortest self-delimiting program that outputs x.[12]

Definition 5.8: INCOMPRESSIBILITY
$x \varepsilon B^*$ is *incompressible* (or random) whenever $K(x) \geq l(x)$.

Remark. $K(x)$ is uncomputable; it can be approximated by computable functions to arbitrary degrees of accuracy, but, paradoxically, the error of approximation cannot be determined at any point.

We need a few more notions before we can get to a definition of the universal prior, semicomputability, in particular. Semicomputability is related to computability, roughly speaking, as recursive enumerability is related to recursivity.

DEFINITION 5.9: SEMICOMPUTABLE FUNCTIONS. A function f is *semicomputable* from below if the set

$$\{(x,r): r \leq f(x), r \text{ is rational}\}$$

is recursively enumerable. (Analogously, f is *semicomputable from above* if $-f$ is semicomputable from below).

Remark. $C(x)$, $C(x|y)$, $K(x)$ and $K(x|y)$ are semicomputable from above, but are *not computable*.

DEFINITION 5.10: MEASURES AND UNIVERSAL MEASURES. If $\mu: N \to [0,1]$ and μ such that:

$$\Sigma_x \mu(x) \leq 1$$

---

[12] $C(x)$ and $K(x)$ are, respectively, unconditional algorithmic complexities (i.e. w.r.t the empty string ε). They differ by an additive factor of approximately $2 \log_2 k(x)$.

but satisfies the other Kolmogorov axioms for probability, it is called a *measure*. *Universal measures* are those semicomputable measures that dominate all measures in this class in the sense that, for the universal measure μ,

$$c\mu(x) \geq \mu'(x),$$

where c is a constant and μ' is an arbitrary semicomputable measure.

LEVIN'S THEOREM. There exists a universal measure in the class of measures that are semicomputable from below.

DEFINITION 5.11: UNIVERSAL PRIOR. From the countably infinite class of universal (semicomputable) measures, choose any arbitrary reference measure $\mu_0(x)$ and denote it by $m(x)$. This $m(x)$ is a *universal prior*.

DEFINITION 5.12: SOLOMONOFF–LEVIN DISTRIBUTION. For all p such that a reference UTM outputs x and

$$P_u(x) = \Sigma_p 2^{-l(p)}$$

denotes the Solomonoff (–Levin) distribution on the positive integers.[13]

Finally, we can state the main theorem of the modern theory of induction.

THEOREM OF THE MODERN THEORY OF INDUCTION. For all x, up to an additive constant c,

$$-\log_2 m(x) = -\log P_u(x) = K(x).$$

Remark. By linking the universal prior with the algorithmic complexity and the Solomonoff–Levin distribution, we link up the conceptual bases of induction in a rigorous way: *an outcome with the highest probability of occurring is also that which has the simplest description.* Because of the relations between $m(x)$ and $K(x)$ given by this theorem, it is also clear that $m(x)$ is uncomputable.

To close the loop with an estimate for μ in Bayes's theorem with which we started, we have one more definition.

---

[13] That this is a distribution can be shown by using *Kraft's inequality*. For any finite or infinite sequence $d_1, d_2, \ldots$, of natural numbers, there exists a prefix code with this sequence as length of its binary code words iff $\Sigma_n 2^{-l(p)} \leq 1$.

DEFINITION 5.13: *A Priori* PROBABILITY

$$M(x) = \Sigma\{m(xy): y \in B^*\}.$$

Thus, $M(x)$ is the prior probability of the output of the reference UTM that *starts with x*.

If we assume μ (in (5.4)) to be a recursive measure, then we can use M as an estimate of μ. This enables the highly technical results from the modern theory of induction to use the universal prior in Bayes's rule to yield Occam's razor: *if a sequence can be generated by many programs, choose the shortest one.*

Next, we use this framework and these results to show in what sense Gold's model of learning is a special case of the modern theory of induction.

5.3 GOLD'S LEARNING AND SOLOMONOFF'S INDUCTIVE INFERENCE

Accordingly, when we speak of a rule of induction, we mean a rule for making a series of approximations to the limit of the relative frequency. . . . This rule . . . formalizes the simplest of the classical modes of inductive inference – induction by "simple enumeration."

Putnam (1951/1990: 24)

The basic conceptual idea in Gold's model of learning is that of *identification in the limit*, and the method of implementing this is identification by enumeration. In a certain sense, it is classically Popperian in that the whole process is about conjectures and refutation until convergence.

In identification in the limit, learning a rule (rational expectations equilibrium (REE) for example) is an infinite process. In the terminology of the previous section, the method of learning (inference) that we use, say Ω, receives a longer and longer initial segment S. Corresponding to these sequentially larger initial segments, Ω generates a sequence of "conjectures" about R, say recursive functions f_1, $f_2, \ldots$ If, for some m and $\forall n > m$

$$f_m = f,$$

and if f_m is a correct description of R (e.g. if the algorithm for f_m generates R), then, according to Gold, Ω *identifies R in the limit*. But, surely, the ubiquitous halting problem precludes exact learning? In other words, can Ω, in general, know when to stop (perhaps if the $\{f_i\}$ are appropriately restricted, say, to the class of primitive recursive functions)?

Some observations by Gold should be kept in mind in the following paragraphs..

(α) Gold cautioned as follows:

I have been asked, "If information presentation is by means of text, Why not guess the unknown language to be the simplest one which accepts the text available?" This is *identification by enumeration*. It is instructive to see why it will not work for most interesting classes of languages: the universal language (if it is in class) will have some finite complexity. If the unknown language is more complex, then the guessing procedure being considered will always guess wrong, since the universal language is consistent with any finite text. . . . The problem with text is that, if you guess too large a language, the text will never tell you that you are wrong. (Gold 1967: 411; emphasis added)

(β) He was remarkably perceptive to note that:

Concerning inductive inference, philosophers often occupy themselves with the following type of question: Suppose we are given a body of information and a set of possible conclusions, from which we are to choose one. . . . The question is, of the conclusions which are consistent with the information, which is "correct"?

The difficulty with the inductive inference problem, when it is stated in this way, is that it asks: "What is the correct guess at a specific time with a fixed amount of information?" There is no basis for choosing between possible guesses at a specific time. However, it *is* interesting to study a *guessing strategy*. Now one can investigate the limiting behavior of the guesses as successively larger bodies of information are considered. This report is an example of such a study. Namely, *in interesting identification problems, a learner cannot help but make errors due to incomplete knowledge*. But, using an "identification in the limit" guessing rule, a learner can guarantee that he will be wrong only a finite number of times. (Gold 1967: 465–6; final emphasis added)

I shall now proceed to state the connection between identification by enumeration and Solomonoff's formalism for inductive inference (in essence, linking the observations in (α) and (β) in the form of a proposition).

Denote by
L: the class of languages, rules, etc., to be learned;
$\chi_L(x)$: the characteristic function of L;
R: the class of hypotheses (representing L) that are effectively enumerable.

ASSUMPTION 5.1. The effective enumeration of hypotheses $R_1, R_2, \ldots$ are codes for algorithms to compute the recursive functions $f_1, f_2, \ldots$

How are the data to be presented to the learner (a Turing machine)? Denote

$$\{s, f(s)\} \equiv (s_1, f(s_1)), (s_2, f(s_2)), \ldots$$

Then f has to be inferred, on the basis of R, from $\{s, f(s)\}$, which is an infinite sequence of examples.

DEFINITION 5.14: A POSITIVE EXAMPLE. When $f = \chi_L$, $\chi_L(s) = 1$ if and only if $s \in L$. Then s is said to be a positive example for L. (Conversely, s is a negative example for L whenever $s \notin L$.)

DEFINITION 5.15: CONSISTENCY. Given an initial segment of instances,

$$S = (s_1, a_1), (s_2, a_2) \ldots, (s_n, a_n) \tag{5.7}$$

a rule (i.e. recursive function) f is said to be consistent with s if

$$f(s_i) = a_i, \forall i = i, \ldots, n. \tag{5.8}$$

The task in Gold is to learn f. For the formalism, we proceed as follows.

Choose, for the prior probabilities of the effectively enumerated functions $\{f_i\}$ the universal prior given above, i.e.

$$m(f_k) \equiv m(k). \tag{5.9}$$

Using Bayes's rule,

$$P(f_k = f \,|\, f_k(s_i) = a_i, \forall i = i, \ldots, n)$$
$$= \frac{P(f_k(s_i) = a_i, \forall i = 1, \ldots, n \,\lfloor fk = f)m(k)}{\Sigma\{m(j): f_j(s_i) = a_i, \forall i = 1, \ldots, n\}} \tag{5.10}$$

In other words, the inferred probability of f_k being f after n instances is given by (5.10). As is usual in Bayesian exercises, the denominator is appropriately normalized. In fact, it denotes the combined prior probabilities of all rules consistent with S. From the previous results we know that

$$m(k) = c2^{-K(k)}, \qquad (5.11)$$

where c is a positive constant.

Now, for each k, all functions inconsistent with the current instance get zero for their probability values and remain zero for all future instances. As the instances increase without limit only those functions consistent with the presented S at that point have positive inferred probability. At this point we invoke (5.10) and use that f_k with the least algorithmic complexity of all those f that are consistent with S. Thus, we have Occam, Solomonoff, and Gold all dealt with in one fell swoop!

Put another way, since $m(k)$ is uncomputable, Gold's procedures are computable approximations to the evaluation of (5.8). But Gold's method of identification by enumeration is, in fact, an implementation of formula (5.10).

DEFINITION 5.16: IDENTIFICATION BY ENUMERATION. Given S and the current instance s, use as f the first rule that is consistent with S for generating $(s, f(s))$. If this can be effectively encoded, then the procedure is called *identification by enumeration*.

We can now state Proposition 5.1.

PROPOSITION 5.1. Identification by enumeration is a computable approximation to the inductive inference formula given by (5.8). An immediate consequence is a learnable class of functions.

PROPOSITION 5. 2. Functions in the class of primitive recursive functions (PRC) can be learned.

Proof. PRCs are effectively enumerable, say $\mathfrak{F}_1, \mathfrak{F}_2, \ldots$ Given any S, choose the least i such that $\mathfrak{F}_i$ is consistent with S.

PROPOSITION 5.3. The set of total recursive functions cannot, in general, be learned.

Proof. Suppose all total recursive functions can be learned. By diagonalizing over the set of consistent functions, we derive a contradiction. Define $f(\epsilon) = 0$. Using the effective encoding of instances, construct the sequence:

$$(\epsilon, f(\epsilon)), (1, f(1)), \ldots, (n, f(n)).$$

Diagonalize, for all n, $f(n + 1)$ such that it is $+1$ the prediction and equals, therefore, 0 or 1 if $f(n + 1)$ is 1 or 0. Thus, there exist recursive functions that can never be learned.

Remark. In the example to be discussed in the next chapter (from Spear 1989), Theorems 6.1 and 6.2 and Proposition 6.1 are direct applications of Propositions 5.2 and 5.3 above. And Spear's Proposition 3.4 is an indirect application of our Propositions 5.2 and 5.3. Furthermore, to prove Spear's Propositions 2.3 and 2.4, we simply invoke Rice's theorem; then, after using that theorem to prove the absence of effective procedures to determine the index set (Spear's Proposition 3.5) or membership in an index set (Spear's Proposition 4.1), Spear qualifies the scope of the respective propositions by referring to the Rice–Shapiro generalization of the Rice theorem.

5.4 CONCLUDING NOTES

the task of inductive logic is the construction of a "universal learning machine". Present day inductive logics are learning devices of very low power. But this is not reason for alarm. . . .

. . . In the future, the development of a powerful mathematical theory of inductive inference of "machines that learn", and of better mathematical models for human learning may grow out of this enterprise.

Putnam (1963/1985: 303–4)

I believe that the inductive tradition in economics should be given a new orientation on the basis of the recent developments in a recursion-theoretic approach to the principle of Occam's razor. In this chapter I have tried to give this belief some analytical and methodological focus; these should have been buttressed by a detailed doctrine-historical study of the inductive tradition in economics. Such a study would have to begin at the beginning – with the writings of Petty, the works of Hume, and Smith's essay on *The History of Astronomy* – and come via Malthus and Mill to Myrdal and Keynes all the way to Simon and Clower. That would be the mainstream; it is the others – the Ricardians, right up to and including the Formalists and the Bourbakian mathematical economists and the traditional econometricians – who were unorthodox.

But such a study would form the subject of a separate monograph. Neither space nor intellectual competence permits such an adventure within the framework of the present book. The message I wish to convey, however, is reasonably simple. The computable approach to economics enables the economic theorist to work within a consistent analytical framework in studying choice, learning from evidence, adapting to events, and exercising a broad concept of rationality, while going about the ordinary business of living as an economic person.

I have so far referred to, and assumed as a working hypothesis, the Church–Turing thesis. This "thesis" (referred to by Post as a "law") "legalises" the attempts that have been made to formally encapsulate the intuitive notion of effective calculability by Turing machines, Post machines, the λ-calculus, partial recursive functions, and so on. It remains a thesis, and has not been accorded the status of a theorem, because one cannot "prove," in any standard way, the equivalence between an intuitive concept and a formal definition. It is not inconceivable that some superior intelligence will, at some future date, be able to formally encapsulate Rado's "busy beaver" within the fold of the effectively calculable.

The exact analogy in the case with attempts to encapsulate the intuitive notion of randomness is the formal apparatus of the modern theory of induction. It is not that "Hume's problem" has been magically solved by the formalisms of the modern theory of induction: it is just that the modern theory of induction not only accepts the Church–Turing thesis, but also works within what may be called the "Kolmogorov–Chaitin–Solomonoff thesis." With these theses at hand, the modern inductivist can suspend doubts cast by "Hume's problem," at least provisionally. It is not unlike the deductivists' deft side-stepping of the difficulties posed by Gödel's results.

In Chapter 6 the ostensibly heavy machinery developed in this chapter will be applied to the economic example imaginatively developed by Spear (1989).

6
Learning in a Computable Setting

[T]here is reason to believe that human learning most kinds can be explained within the framework of [a] symbol processing system. . . .

Simon (1969: 119)

6.1 INTRODUCTION

All learning, including the process whereby the rules of induction are perfected, orders step by step an ensemble erstwhile chaotic.

McCulloch (1965: 274)

Much of the learning literature in orthodox frameworks, and with standard purposes, has been expertly summarized by Tom Sargent, my immediate predecessor as "Ryde Lecturer" (Sargent 1993). Sargent's work, in turn, has been brilliantly reviewed by De Vany (1996). In recent growth models, in traditional overlapping-generations (OLG) models, in the experimental economics literature, in game-theoretic settings, and in many other areas at the frontiers of economic theory, there is a learning component in the crucial senses.

As shown in the previous chapter, there is a more fundamental approach to learning than those applied in the above areas. This approach has been used by Spear in his pioneering article (Spear 1989), where the whole learning problem is imaginatively recast in a recursion-theoretic setting, and computability and decidability results are invoked to discuss the feasibility of learning *rational expectations equilibria* (REE).

In this chapter I simply describe Spear's model, interpret it as an application of Gold's learning paradigm, invoke the necessary results from Chapter 5 to prove the relevant propositions, and provide the background necessary to streamline the recursion-theoretic infelicities in the model. The aim is simply to show how to apply, in a standard economic setting, a recursion-theoretic learning paradigm. The need to extract the recursion-theoretic core of the economic setting[1] before applying the learning paradigm is emphasized.

Thus, in Section 6.2, the Spear model and its learning problems are interpreted and analyzed in the light of the results in Chapter 5. In Section 6.3, on the other hand, I attempt to analyze the nature of the computability constraints that have to be placed on the economic underpinnings of Spear's model (cf. fn. 1 above). The concluding section in this chapter is devoted to methodological and metamathematical observations that clarify some of the philosophically motivated economic infelicities in the background and interpretations provided by Spear.

6.2 USING GOLD IN LEARNING REE[2]

> And the stuff gathering in my ear
> . . .
> will have to be unlearned
> even though from there on everything
> is going to be learning
>
> Seamus Heaney, *Unwinding*

An abbreviated explanation of Gold's (1967) model of learning, from the point of view of the modern theory of induction, has been given in Chapter 5. The links with Bayesian learning, in a computable setting and as induction, were also discussed in that chapter. In this section I confine myself to the strict telegraphic task of transmitting the details of Spear's use of Gold's model for learning a rational expectations equilibrium under computability constraints. Spear's basic

---

[1] Akin to constructivizing a formalist mathematical framework. A clearer example will be found in the next chapter, where Rabin's perceptive exercise in stripping the noncomputable elements in the formalist Gale–Stewart game is described in detail.

[2] For the proofs in this chapter, as mentioned above in the introductory section, I refer the interested reader to p. 87 above.

analytical task is the modelling of the inductive learning of rational expectations equilibria. This is, therefore, a familiar exercise for those acquainted with investigating "fix-point" mappings that achieve equilibria in standard general equilibrium theory. Instead of inquiring into compactness and other topological conditions on the price simplex that are necessary (and sufficient) to prove the existence of an equilibrium "fix-point" mapping, Spear investigates the recursion-theoretic structure of price and forecast functions that could be "fix-point" mappings for a REE. In other words, instead of the topology of mappings, Spear looks at the computability of certain mappings.

Notations and assumptions

S: a *countable* set of state variables for the economy
P: a set of spot market prices for the economy
Φ: a set of total recursive functions on S that contains the set of (temporary) equilibrium (TE) price functions and the set of admissible forecast functions

$$\phi \in \Phi \text{ and } \Phi: S \to P; \quad \phi_0: \text{ forecast functions}$$
$$\phi_1: \text{ temporary equilibrium (TE)}$$
$$\text{price functions}$$

ASSUMPTION 6.1. The mapping from forecast functions to TE price functions, denoted by g, has a fixed point.

Remark. Using an effective enumeration of Φ, we can assume g to be a mapping from N to N. The fix-point assumption, therefore, asserts the existence of functions ϕ_1 and $\phi_{g[i]}$ such that $\phi_1 = \phi_{g[i]}$, where, ϕ_0 and ϕ_1 from $S \to P$ correspond to ϕ_1 and $\phi_{g[i]}$ from $N \to N$. This means, of course, that $p \to P$ is computable too.

CASE 6.1: TWO-STAGE LEARNING WITH FULL INFORMATION. I make the following assumptions:

(a) Agents hold fixed, common forecasts ϕ_i.
(b) Agents observe a *sequence* of temporary equilibrium pairs (p_t, s_t).

Learning problem: learn the function g. This is a two-stage problem in the following sense: given assumptions (a) and (b), agents attempt to learn the TE price function corresponding to the fixed, common forecast; if this is possible, at the next stage agents learn the function g by varying their forecasts to compute the TE price function correspondingly. Full information means that all prices and states, at every point in time, are observable.

The formalism. When the forecast is ϕ_i, agents observe s_t and prices are

$$p = \phi_{g[i]}(s_t). \tag{6.1}$$

PROPOSITION 6.1. If the TE price function is primitive-recursive, then it is computable; if not, it is not computable.

PROPOSITION 6.2. If the economy's mapping, g, is primitive-recursive, then agents can compute it.

Remark. The fix-point assumption means, in this recursion-theoretic setting, that there exists a computable function g that maps the space of forecast functions to the collection of functions actually used by the economy, such that there is a fix-point for this mapping. This is given by

$$p = \phi_{g[i]}(s). \tag{6.2}$$

Also, the REE is given by the forecasting rule ϕ_i such that

$$\phi_i(\ ) = \phi_{g[i]}(\ ). \tag{6.3}$$

Propositions 6.1 and 6.2 hold for this economy and for REE as given by (6.3).

DEFINITION 6.1. An economy is recursive if g, ϕ_i, and $\phi_{g[i]}$ are primitive-recursive.

Propositions 6.1 and 6.2 imply that, in a primitive-recursive economy, agents can learn the REE price functions.

CASE 6.2: TWO-STAGE LEARNING WITH PARTIAL INFORMATION. We now drop the assumption of full information; agents observe a signal $\eta_n(s)$ which denotes agent n's observation of a state-correlated signal. All other assumptions are identical to the full-information case; in particular, all agents hold, as before, a fixed common forecast ϕ_i. From the signal η_n, agent n has to learn the REE.

Denote

$$N(\overline{\eta_n}) = \{s \mid \eta_n(s) = \overline{\eta_n}\}. \tag{6.4}$$

From observations $\eta_n(s)$, agent n must learn the set of indices for which forecast functions are consistent with the economy's mapping $\phi_{g[i]}$. That is, agent n must learn the set of indices

$$\pi_n(i) = \{j | \text{range } \phi_j|_{N(\eta_n)} = \text{range } \phi_{g[i]}|_{N(\eta_n)}, \forall \overline{\eta_n}\}. \tag{6.5}$$

These formulas have the following explanations. For every state s, the economy has a mapping from S to P. A given signal $\eta(s)$ could have come from any one of many states $\langle s \rangle$; this set of states, for each signal observed by agent n, is given by $\pi_n(\cdot)$. For each such set of states $\pi_n(\cdot)$, by the fix-point assumption, there will be a collection of forecast functions for agents that are compatible with a collection of mappings by the "impersonal economy." If the agent can identify each collection $\{j\}$, then REE can be inferred via g.

PROPOSITION 6.3. The set $\pi_n(i)$ cannot be determined by an effective procedure.

Remark. The proof is obtained using a powerful result due to Rice (1953) (see the Appendix for statements of the theorem, variations of it, and a discussion) and belongs to a class of theorems in recursion theory that can be used with great force to obtain uncomputability and undecidability results. I have used it in Chapters 3 and 4 above; I shall also use it in the following chapters. It is important to note that the proposition's message is that there is no general method that will work effectively for all cases. This does not mean that special classes of effective methods cannot be found for particular sets of indices by various *ad hoc* procedures.

CASE 6.3: INCREMENTAL LEARNING. Let

$$[\phi_{g[i_o]}(s), \eta(s)] = \xi(s, i_o), \tag{6.6}$$

where, as before, $\eta(s)$ is the signal that agents receive for state s, and i_o is the index of a *common* initial forecast.

ASSUMPTION 6.2. Agents receive a common signal, and use a common updating scheme as functions of ξ. There exists a total recursive function f which maps i_t and ξ to i_{t+1} for given forecasts ϕi_t:

$$i_{t+1} = f(i_t, \xi[s_t, i_t]); \tag{6.7}$$

and if, for all s,

$$\phi_j = \phi_{f(j, \xi[s, j])}, \tag{6.8}$$

then we call the forecast ϕ_j consistent with the updating scheme, or a model consistent equilibrium. If a consistent forecast also satisfies the usual

$$\phi_j = \phi_{g[j]}, \tag{6.9}$$

then it is called a REE forecast.

The final assumption is as follows.

ASSUMPTION 6.3. There exist total recursive consistent equilibrium price functions.

PROPOSITION 6.4. There is no effective procedure for determining whether any given updating scheme yields a model-consistent REE forecast unless R_g is the trivial set, where

$$R_g = \{i | \phi f_{i[j, f]} = \phi_{g[j]}\}. \tag{6.10}$$

Remark. This is a "cheap" theorem, a mechanical application of Rice's theorem (or any variation of it). The interpretation of the set of indices R_g is analogous to the one for π, keeping in mind (6.8) and 6.9).

6.3 COMPUTABLE ANALYTIC UNDERPINNINGS FOR THE SPEAR MODEL

[C]omputable analysis differs profoundly from real analysis. This difference of computable analysis stems first from the restriction of the analysis to a subset of the real numbers – the computable numbers – and second from the restriction of the functions, sequences, etc., allowed over this subset to the algorithmically defined ones.

Aberth (1980: 3)

Spear states that he is working within "a stylized version of a simple overlapping generations model" (Spear 1989: 892). It is against the backdrop of such a model, and its equilibria, that Spear's assumptions on S and Φ are made. Thus, it is claimed that

For specificity, we will consider a stylized version of a simple overlapping generations model in which agents live for two periods, though the results developed here apply more generally, for any model in which the REE can be determined as the fixed points of a mapping taking forecasts into temporary equilibrium prices. (Spear 1989: 892–3).

The extent to which Spear's claim can be substantiated depends on the way a recursion-theoretic structure can be introduced into any "stylized version of a simple overlapping generations model"; and then it will be seen that the assumption on Φ entails that on S.

However, more importantly, the crucial question is whether, and in what sense, the REE learned within the recursion-theoretic framework of Gold's model corresponds to a traditional REE generated by a "stylized version of an OLG" model. If this question is not answered in a consistent and compatible manner, it is not clear whether the economic content of the inductively learned REE corresponds to that in the REE defined within a "stylized version of an OLG model." To answer this question meaningfully, I must investigate the recursion-theoretic content of the REE emanating from such a "stylized version of an OLG model."

For this purpose I can use any one of many standard OLG expositions; I choose to work with a particularly lucid one given in Azariadis (1993). A simple OLG model with standard assumptions (Azariadis 1993: 414–16) generates REE as solution(s) to the following type of functional dynamic equation:

$$\forall I_t,\ u'(e_1 - m_t) = E\left\{\frac{m_t + 1}{m_t} \frac{L_{t+1}}{L_t} v'\left(e_2 + {}_{mt+1}\frac{L_{t+1}}{L_t}\right)\Big| I_t \right\}, \quad (6.11)$$

where u and v are functional notations for the additive utility function; and L_t is the size of generation t (a discrete random variable with standard assumptions);

$$M_t \equiv \frac{M_t}{p_t L_t} \quad (6.12)$$

where M_t is the aggregate stock of currency, p_t is the realized price (of the one consumption good), e_t is the endowment at time t, and I_t is the information set, defined by

$$I_t = \{I_{t-1}, L_{t-1}, x_{t-1}, p_t, \theta_t\}. \quad (6.13)$$

It is clear immediately that, without a more precise recursion-theoretic structure on (6.11)–(6.13), Assumptions (6.1) and (6.2) are insufficient to ensure consistency between the REE defined by (6.9) and that generated by (6.11). Indeed, except for flukes, it is most likely that REE solutions to (6.11) are *nonrecursive reals*. How, then, can this nonrecursive real be learned by an observed sequence of state space and price realizations – even granting Assumptions 6.1 and 6.2?

The problem is to devise an *effective* mechanism to learn and identify a possible REE. The strategy to be adopted will be similar to that adopted by Rabin to effectivize a standard game. Rabin systematically stripped away the non-effective components in the Gale-Stewart game (to be discussed in the next chapter) and then posed recursion-theoretic questions. To make this possible here, (6.11)–(6.13) must be endowed with an appropriate recursion-theoretic basis. I now indicate the general nature of the minimum requirements.[3]

First and foremost, the derivative of the second-period component of the additive utility function, v:, must be a computable real function.[4]

Before proceeding to expand on this, a remark is necessary. A more elegant way would be to begin, from the outset, by defining choice over sets that have a suitable recursive structure. This strategy, however, leads to various undecidabilities that cannot easily be remedied and still maintain the framework of traditional choice theory (cf. Lewis 1985). An even more useful way would be to replicate Shepherdson's highly ingenious methods where only rational probabilities were used and still most of the traditional tools and concepts were preserved. By replacing the rational probabilities with the computable probabilities (cf. Gill 1977), one can proceed, with appropriate modifications, to use Shepherdson's framework to remain within standard choice theory. However, I now believe that my heuristic suggestions are simpler and more direct for the limited purposes I have in mind.[5]

To return to the question of v' and its status as a computable real function, it is important to remember that the computability of v does not entail, in general, the computability of v'. (See Myhill 1971 for this celebrated result, and Pour-El and Richards 1989 for a com-

---

[3] This is, of course, because there are many different ways of achieving the required recursive structures for (6.11)–(6.13), and my suggestion, though sufficient, may not be aesthetically the most pleasing.

[4] This is done exactly as in classical analysis. Thus, every classical real number x is associated with a classical total function f mapping N to Q such that $[x - f(x)] \to 0$ as $n \to \infty$, $\forall n \in N$. Replace the f with a total computable function and the above limit with: $x - f(n) \le 2^{-n}$, for each n, to get the computable reals. Real numbers for which there is no such total computable f are the *uncomputable reals*. In this interpretation, real numbers are functions from N to N. Therefore, a function of a real number will be a *functional*, say Ω, from real numbers to real numbers. Hence, a real valued function is computable if the corresponding functional, Ω, is recursive. This is the classic recursion-theoretic definition of a computable real function.

[5] See Shepherdson (1980), but also Bridges (1982), where only constructive methods are used to derive the standard framework of choice theory.

prehensive exposition of this and related results.) Roughly speaking, if the domain of v is chosen judiciously, and if $v \in C^2$ is computable, then v' is computable. But for this to be an acceptable assumption, the arguments of v' must, in turn, be computable reals, i.e. $e_2, m_{t+1}, L_{t+1}/L_t$. There will, of course, be no problem in ensuring this for e_2. However, L_t is another story; it is random variable, and hence we must give a recursion-theoretic interpretation to a kind of probabilistic computation.[6]

The random variables in the OLG model that resulted in (6.1) are characterized by finite means and stationary probability distributions. It is, therefore, easy to construct a probabilistic Turing machine endowed with an extra random-bit generator which generates, when necessary, the output that has the preassigned probability distribution. For the technical details of such a construction, I refer to Gill's classic work (1977).

Next, there is the question of the recursivity of the information set I_t. Given that a recursion-theoretic learning model requires this to be recursively presented to the learners,[7] it is only the element θ_t that remains to be recursively defined. But this is a pure exogenous variable and can be defined recursively in any arbitrary way.

Finally, I interpret the expectations operator in the customary way as an integration process. Then, noting that integration is a computable process completes my discussion of endowing (6.11)–(6.13) with enough recursion-theoretic structure to make the REE generated by (6.11) to be a recursive real.

In the next section the above assumptions are set in their paces in the form of a theorem. The method of proof I shall adopt is a minor variation of a standard technique in algorithmic complexity theory. (For an excellent exposition, see Li and Vitanyi 1997).

6.1 RESULTS AND INTERPRETATIONS

The recursive real(s) that are solutions to (6.11) as REEs can, surely, be learned by a wide variety of mechanisms. I am, however, concerned with an effective learning procedure (in the same standard

---

[6] By (6.2) this will, then, guarantee a recursive structure to m_{t+1} given an appropriate recursive assumption on prices.

[7] "Itself" essentially a Turing machine – if we should push the search for consistency to its limits.

sense of classical recursion recursion theory). The result, stated below as a theorem, utilizes a variation of Gold's model of recursive learning (Gold 1965, 1967) to identify and define a unique REE. I appeal to the auxiliary epistemological principle of Occam's razor (cf. Chapter 5) to justify some of the optimizations.

THEOREM 6.1. A unique solution to (6.11) can be identified as the REE and learned recursively.

Proof. The proof requires, first, that the REE generated as a solution to (6.11) is shown to be a recursive real. Second, it must be shown that there is an effective procedure, i.e. a recursive learning mechanism, to generate the recursive real that is the unique REE for (6.11). It will be shown that a version of the Gold model can be utilized to learn the REE given by (6.11). The learning procedure also identifies the unique solution that is to be the REE.

The first part of the proof is a trivial consequence of the assumptions. The second part is slightly more delicate in one sense but quite mechanical in other ways. Note, first of all, that the solutions generated by (6.11) are sequences of functions (cf. Azariadis 1993: 417). By the above assumptions, these functions are partial-recursive. The sequence can be given an effective enumeration, say by an appropriate Turing machine, for example $f_1, f_2, \ldots$. Observe, next, that we single out a particular function, say f, the REE, as the one to be inferred from the mapping of "the set of all possible histories" of the economy "into positive [recursive real] numbers that represent prices." That f which is "simplest" – in a sense to be defined – is, clearly the one to be identified economically as the one corresponding to a rational expectations equilibrium. In other words, to infer, inductively, the REE given by f, we observe a sequence of prices that are recursive reals, say $\Pi = p_1, p_2, \ldots, p_n$ containing elements of the form

$$p = \begin{cases} (x, y, 0) \text{ if } f(x) \neq y, \\ (x, y, 1) \text{ if } f(x) = y. \end{cases} \tag{6.14}$$

Now, we let $n \to \infty$. Denote by H_k the hypothesis that "$f = f_k$." Then

$$P(\Pi | H_k) = \begin{cases} 0 \\ 1 \end{cases},$$

depending on whether the upper or lower condition in (6.14) holds. Apply the Bayesian scheme,

$$P(H_k|D) = \frac{P(D|H_k)\,P(H_k)}{\Sigma\{P(H_j): f_j \text{ is consistent with } D\}}. \tag{6.15}$$

Now choose, for the prior, the Solomonoff *universal prior* (cf. Chapter 5), given by $P(H_k = \mathbf{m}(\cdot) = 2^{-K(\cdot)}$, where $K(\cdot)$ is the standard *prefix complexity* in algorithmic complexity theory. This prior is chosen for the intuitively obvious reason[8] that in this case $P(\cdot|D)$ will be maximized for the simplest hypothesis, which we identify with the REE. Then, as $n \to \infty$, this will hold for H_k where $K(k)$ is minimized and $f = f_k$.

Remark. The learning mechanism is called Gold's learning by *enumeration in the limit algorithm*.

Remark. The theorem, although effective in the technical recursion-theoretic sense at every stage of the argument as far as implementation is concerned, does embody an unfortunate epistemological consequence: there is no effective way for the agent to know when to stop applying the learning mechanism.

Remark. Nothing in my discussion guarantees any of the functions to be tractably computable. Indeed, once again, it is most likely that none of these assumptions guarantees *polynomial-time computability* of any of the constituent functions.

Discussion. Some justification will, surely, be warranted regarding the identification of the unique REE as that solution of (6.11) which is predicated upon the simplest hypothesis. Suppose, on the contrary, that some arbitrary prior other than the Solomonoff universal prior is chosen to implement the learning mechanism. In this case, $P(\ |D)$ will be maximized for some hypothesis that is not algorithmically the simplest, and hence costs of inferring, measured appropriately, *any* solution will be higher. By a standard application of the no-arbitrage hypothesis, all such solutions are dominated by the solution generated on the basis of the Solomonoff universal prior. Hence this latter solution is the natural candidate to be identified as the unique REE.

In an earlier paper (Rustem and Velupillai 1990) the question was raised of the effectivity of an agent generating his own preference function. Within the framework of classical recursion theory, the results were uniformly and disappointingly negative. This conclusion applies to a series of related pioneering contributions by Kramer,

---

[8] But also because it satisfies the obviously desirable scientific property of Occam's razor.

Lewis, and McAfee (1984). I have summarized and surveyed these contributions in some detail, in Chapter 2 above.

However, by replicating the procedures adopted in this section within the framework of recursive analysis, my conjecture is that it would be possible to construct effective mechanisms to generate preference orderings. The caveat is, of course, that tractability may be compromised. Moreover, there is also the unfortunate problem of recognizing when to stop whatever effective procedure is being used in the generation of preferences, rational choice functions, etc. This, I conjecture, is a direct consequence of the classic *halting problem* for Turing machines.

The fundamental methodological message of this chapter (and the previous one) is that learning problems in economics should be posed as induction problems. This gives us the chance to exploit the full scope of algorithmic complexity theory. I believe, therefore, that there are two immediate directions in which to pursue research along the lines adopted in this subsection – in addition to the suggestion in its opening paragraph.

First, and most immediate, would be to integrate estimation as part of learning in a model of induction. Here again, there is the made-to-order tools provided by Rissanen's "Minimum-Description-Length" principle.[9] The ad-hockery of nonrecursive learners using unrelated estimation techniques[10] can easily be eliminated in simple extensions of any standard model laterally, so to speak.

Second, I suggest that it is not only important to demonstrate the feasibility of computable inductive procedures, but is also necessary to investigate their tractability. An analysis of the computational and, when appropriate, diophantine complexity of learning procedures is at least as important.

---

[9] Or stochastic complexity.

[10] Even Sargent's admirable attempt to go part of the way by assuming that agents as finite automata implement the activities normally practiced by econometricians retains a great deal of the standard ad-hockery.

6.4 CONCLUDING NOTES

Why, when it was all over, did I hold on to them?
Seamus Heaney, *The Old Icons*

There are some technical and metamathematical slips in Spear's exposition of the learning model. For reasons of completeness and clarity, it may be useful to amend the slips, lest the fastidious computable economist be put off by them and throw the proverbial baby out with the bathwater. I have not attempted to organize this section thematically; instead, it is ordered sequentially, reflecting the order in which the themes appear in Spear's paper.

Spear, correctly and perceptively in my view, questions the refuge taken by economists in the quasi-logic of "as if."[11] He then goes on to make the following observation to buttress his defence of algorithmic modelling of rational agents.

Ultimately, the "as if" question is one of whether human mental activity is machine simulable or not. (Spear 1989: 891)

It is not quite clear in what sense machine simulability of human mental activity can settle "the 'as if' question," but this questionable statement is coupled to an incorrect metamathematical assertion:

Finite algorithms . . . are important because they determine the set of feasible computations that a human being can undertake. This is the content of the so-called Church–Turing thesis in formal logic. The Church–Turing thesis can be equivalently stated as the principle of noncomputability: if a function cannot be calculated by a Turing Machine, it cannot be calculated by a human being. (Spear 1989: 894)

However, Church's thesis – or the Church–Turing thesis – is about the formal equivalence of independently derived mathematical definitions of an intuitive notion: *effectively calculable*. One of the accurate – and, indeed, the "naming" – statement of the thesis, following the pioneer who gave it the name, is:

Every effectively calculable function (effectively decidable predicate) is general recursive. (Kleene 1952: 300)

---

[11] Cf. Musgrave's brilliant disposal of "as if" reasoning (fn. 14, Chapter 3, above) by pointing out its nebulous logical content (cf. Musgrave 1981).

A thesis is not a theorem; there is no such thing as a converse to a thesis, and taking a converse has no logical validity.

Next, continuing his scepticism on the "as if" theme, Spear states that:

> if one views the various constructs of economic theory as attempts to model realistically (rather than as if) the actual decision processes of agents, then the requirements that agents not be capable of deciding logically undecidable propositions is actually quite weak, since it leaves available the vast array of results in logic and mathematics which are, in fact, decidable. (Spear 1989: 891)

But, surely, Spear knows from his own deft use of the Rice and Rice–Shapiro theorems that there are no effective procedures to determine any nontrivial subset of "the vast array of results in logic and mathematics which are, in fact, decidable." This must mean that it is not possible to effectivize the decidable subset that is of particular relevance to economics. It is at least equally likely, in the unlikely event that they can be effectivized, that it is precisely the set of undecidable propositions that is of relevance to economic decision-makers.[12]

The next slip is a curious misunderstanding. Having assumed the state space to be countable (p. 895), Spear then goes on to claim that the "discreteness" associated with countability precludes continuity characterizations of such spaces. But there is a solid and well developed field of computable analysis – indeed, varieties of computable analysis – where quite rigorous definitions of continuity, compactness, etc., exist (cf. previous section for some references on this line of work). Moreover, whether "Continuity assumptions . . . are . . . only idealizations of the actual discrete computations performed in real economies peopled with real agents who always round off real numbers" (p. 895) or not is one thing; it is quite another thing to work on the space of the computable real numbers where the idealizations are not on the continuity assumptions. Above all, as pointed out in the previous section, the countability assumption is superflu-

---

[12] That great polymath, Stanislaw Ulam, pointed out with characteristic prescience that: "In the next fifty years there will be, if not axioms, at least agreement among mathematicians about assumptions of new freedoms and constructions, of thoughts. Given an undecidable proposition, there will be a preference as to whether one should assume it to be true or false. . . . " (Ulam, in Cooper 1988: 312). It is *as if* the analytical economist's pet domain, choice theory, will come into its own in the face of undecidable propositions.

ous in that it is entailed by the assumptions necessary to make the two REEs compatible. Perhaps Spear has forgotten the treacherous slips one can make when countable infinities are involved. I think the question about appropriate spaces should have been put another way – the way Hamming put it in a related discussion (but read "economics" for "probability"):

Thus without further examination it is not completely evident that the classical real number system will prove appropriate to the needs of probability. perhaps the real number system is (1) not rich enough – see nonstandard analysis; (2) just what we want – see standard mathematics; or (3) more than is needed – see constructive and computable analysis. (Hamming 1991: 190)

It is not only the cardinality of the domain that is the relevant item; it is also the nature of the *operations* and *operators*. Are we to allow the unrestricted use of the law of the excluded middle in a countably infinite space?[13] What is the status, logical or otherwise, of a theorem deduced in such nonconstructive ways, albeit in a countably infinite space? Or, if there is no possibility of effectivizing the Hahn–Banach theorem, are we justified in appealing to this – in the form of a separating hyperplane theorem – in our optimizing exercises? Or is Spear making a case for finiteness? In any case, the conflation of the countable and the discrete and then the negation of the feasibility of defining continuity seem both incorrect and somewhat misguided. Above all, the countability assumption is unnecessary – at least in its explicit form.

Finally, Spear seems to suggest that the assumption of the computability of nonequilibrium temporary equilibrium price functions "can be defended,"

by viewing these prices as computable approximations of the price functions associated with a given forecast. That such approximations exist (to any degree of precision) can be shown formally (though we do not undertake a proof here) by working with computable approximations to agents' excess demand functions) and applying the generalized Sturm algorithm . . . to compute the zeros of the approximation to the aggregate excess demand function. (Spear 1989: 895)

Spear's suggestion, therefore, is:

(a) Given an agent's excess demand function,

---

[13] For example, if there is no possibility to effectivize a fix-point theorem, are we justified in appealing to this – in the form of an existence theorem – in our equilibrium exercises?

(b) take a computable approximation to it, and
(c) apply the generalized Sturm algorithm to the computable
     approximation to the (individual) excess demand function,
     then
(d) the zeros computed by the generalized Sturm algorithm will be
     approximations to the zeros of the (individual) excess demand
     function.

Hence we are justified in working with the assumption of computable, nonequilibrium, TE price functions. Now, the first question
is: How does one take a computable approximation to an uncomputable function? Take, for example, the *busy beaver* function. This
is an explicit uncomputable function whose basic characteristic is
that it grows faster than any computable function in a certain precise
sense.[14] What would be the sense in which such an uncomputable
function becomes approximated by a computable function? Any definition of approximation involves, in general, two norms connected
by an inclusive inequality, e.g. something like

$$||\varphi - \psi^*|| \leq ||\phi - \psi||, \qquad (6.16)$$

where, say φ is some class of uncomputable functions, and ψ, ψ^* are
computable functions, say in a class ; and (6.14) should hold for all
$\psi \in \Omega$. But this is impossible to satisfy in general; the best that can
be done, via semicomputable functions,[15] is to assert an existential
statement for the approximation without any idea of the degree of
approximation. Moreover, even if it were possible to take a computable approximation to an uncomputable excess demand function,
there remains the thorny problem of the effective decidability of
computing zeros for special subsets of the computable functions. It is
easy to show, using variations of the theme broached by Richardson
(1968) and Caviness (1970) and the techniques developed to demonstrate the effective undecidability of Hilbert's Tenth problem (cf.
Chapter 7), that large classes of simple functions do not have effective procedures for the computation of their zeros. In this connection
it will be useful also to follow up on Spear's reference to Jacobsen's
classic text and to check, in turn, the demonstration of the Sturm theorem and further references to Seidenberg (1954); even further to van

---

[14] Like the way the Akermann function grows faster than any primitive recursive
function.
[15] Semicomputable functions were discussed in some detail above in Chapter 5.

der Waerden's remarkably lucid exposition of the Sturm algorithm (cf. van der Waerden 1970: 243 ff. and Seidenberg 1954: esp. 366, 374). A serious study of these classics will convince the reader that Spear's suggestions are infeasible.

Continuing on the approximation theme, Spear suggests that:

the question of whether one can uniformly approximate an economy with infinitely many state variables by one with finitely many is most interesting. One possibility for dealing with this issue when it occurs because of the inclusion of lagged endogenous variables would be to show a version of the shadowing lemma for compact, stochastic dynamic systems. This lemma states that for a nonstochastic, hyperbolic dynamic system, any approximation of a given trajectory is "uniformly shadowed by an exact trajectory. . . . " If such a result could be shown for stochastic dynamic systems, it would justify approximating price processes on finitely many ε-balls. (Spear 1989: 906)

Even if we grant success in this hope, it is unclear to me where finiteness enters the picture in the shadowing lemma – in an effective way. Indeed, I conjecture, adapting a version of the result that shows the failure of the Heine–Borel theorem in a recursive context (Bridges 1994: 69) that *this noneffectivity can be proved*.

Moreover, as noted by Spear himself, the available results on shadowing are for restricted classes of dynamical systems. These results, the early results of Anosov and Bowen, were for diffeomorphisms that are hyperbolic. Although I cannot see how and why price processes in RE models for generating REEs should be diffeomorphisms that are also hyperbolic, Spear may in fact be summarizing an acceptable assumption. In other words, once again, Spear may well be vindicated in that hyperbolic diffeomorphic price dynamics in an OLG setting is not an unacceptable economic assumption; and, because they are diffeomorphisms, they may satisfy the necessary computable analytic assumptions to make the model recursion-theoretically useful.

On the other hand, can it be shown that dynamical systems with the shadowing property are *computation-universal*? If not, it is hard to see how price processes can satisfy Assumption 6.2.

I believe that Spear's framework and results are of fundamental importance to economists interested in modelling learning. Spear has raised fundamental questions not just about the role of computability constraints in REE learning, but also about the nature and scope of induction in economics. In addition, he has broached the subject of finiteness assumptions in economics and the significance of approximation considerations in formal economic settings.

The weak links in his model and the metamathematical and technical slips are easy to rectify. The corrections strengthen his approach. In considering and suggesting extensions and emendations, we must above all bear in mind that Spear's fundamental message is that learning problems in economics should be posed as induction problems.

I hope that economists will take up the challenges posed by Spear in his imaginative suggestions to place learning squarely in the middle of the weird and wonderful world of induction. It is a refreshing antidote to the dominance of deductive theorizing in economics.

7

Effective Playability in Arithmetical Games

> On the first part of my inquiry I soon arrived at a demonstration that every game of skill is susceptible of being played by an automaton.
>
> Babbage (1864/1961: 153)

7.1 INTRODUCTION

> Given a diophantine equation with any number of unknown quantities and with rational integral numerical coefficients: *To devise a process according to which it can be determined by a finite number of operations whether the equation is solvable in rational integers.*
>
> Hilbert (1900/1902: 458)

I have, in earlier chapters referred to *decision problems*, suggesting that it is more general than the standard optimization formalism customarily utilized in economic theory. *Hilbert's Tenth problem*, the original statement of which is quoted above, is a paradigmatic example of a decision problem. Matiyasevich's lucid characterization of the essence of a decision problem might set the background against which to understand some of the discussions in this chapter:

The essence of a decision problem lies in the requirement to find a single method that can be used for obtaining the answer to any of the individual subproblems. Since Diophantus's time, number theorists have found solutions for many Diophantine equations and have established the unsolvability of many other equations. However, for many particular classes of equations, and even for certain individual equations, it was necessary to invent a specific method. In the Tenth problem, Hilbert asked for a *universal* method for deciding the solvability of Diophantine equations. (Matiyasevich 1994: 2)

In this chapter I attempt to discuss the question of *effective playability* and the computational and diophantine complexity of Rabin-type games[1] from various recursion-theoretic vantage points. The effective playability of an arithmetic game is rephrased as a decision problem for a diophantine relation.

There is a growing literature on applying recursion-theoretic concepts to traditional issues in game theory. I have, myself, been sceptical about the computable structure of many of these models. There are, of course, notable exceptions.[2] On the whole, my view on this literature is best summarized in the following important observation by Megiddo and Wigderson:

It has been said that the prisoner's dilemma may be "resolved" by "bounded rationality." One possibility of bounding rationality is to have players play the game through computing machines. . . . The only restriction is on the number of internal states of the machine . . . [However] it should be emphasized that *most of the results are nonconstructive and we do not believe that [this] approach . . . will lead to a practical resolution of the prisoner's dilemma.* (Megiddo and Wigderson 1986: 260; emphasis added)

As a matter of fact, it is easy to identify the nonconstructive nature of the results as emanating not only from the noneffective rules of the underlying games,[3] but also from the backward-induction proofs. It must be noted that it is customary to use nonconstructive methods in recursion theory too; but existential results come with effective processes to realize them. It is the (universal) undecidable results that are, in general, proved with free-swinging nonconstructive methods.[4]

I shall, instead, return to the Rabin tradition of seeking recursion-theoretic formalisms in game theory, and shall link it to some of the

---

[1] In other words, variations of the classic Gale–Stewart games which were perceptively stripped of their noneffective content by Rabin in his brilliant and pioneering contribution – now almost four decades ago. One of the aims of this chapter is to demonstrate that it is still a fertile framework in which to explore recursion-theoretic issues in games.

[2] Above all, Binmore (1987).

[3] As Rabin notes in his pioneering paper, "there should be no sense in worrying about the effective computability of a strategy when the rules of the game in which it should be applied are not effective" (Rabin 1957: 148, fn.3).

[4] As Davis *et al.* pointed out, "these [*reductio ad absurdum* and other noneffective methods] may well be the best available to us because universal methods for giving all the solutions do not exist" (Davis *et al.* 1976: 340).

classics as well. Indeed, a return to these classics makes it easier to link up with the frontiers in what I have earlier referred to as applied recursion theory, i.e. computational and diophantine complexity theories and an introduction to the use of new recursion-theoretic techniques to simplify proofs in arithmetical games.

This chapter is organized as follows. In the next section I discuss elementary examples and heuristic motivations for considering Rabin-type games as useful and fruitful frameworks in which to pose questions of *effective playability*. In Section 7.3, the formal structure of Rabin's effectivized Gale–Stewart game and an introductory discussion of Jones's variation of the Rabin game (Jones 1974) are presented. I outline the imaginative way Rabin stripped away the noneffective content in a Gale–Stewart game;[5] and, via Jones's modified version of the Rabin game, I introduce, in the proofs, the Busy Beaver game. Quite apart from the auxiliary benefit of literally seeing how an explicit noncomputable function is actually constructed from seemingly innocuous building blocks, this device prepares the analytical ground for the melancholy demonstration that very simple effectivized games, even when determined and playable, can contain intrinsic undecidabilities and intractable complexities.

The basic theme in Section 7.4 is to introduce the idea of arithmetical games and to show that they are a natural development of Rabin's effectivized Gale–Stewart game. Once we understand this, it is possible to exploit the elegant results that were byproducts of the long saga that led to the negative solution to Hilbert's Tenth problem: *the diophantine nature of recursively enumerable sets*. In other words, we reduce the analysis to questions of arithmetic (hence arithmetical games); the main question that Rabin posed, effective playability, is answered by looking at the effective solvability of diophantine equations by exploiting the above fundamental result.

The concluding section, is a brief introduction to the issue of diophantine and computational complexity in arithmetical games. The section also includes my suggestions for directions in which the themes of this chapter should, or could, be developed as part of a broad research strategy in computable economics.

---

[5] A formal and telegraphic description of a Gale–Stewart game is given in the appendix to this chapter.

7.2 EXAMPLES AND MOTIVATIONS

> The extensive form of a game is of considerable use in describ-
> ing the details of moves and the information conditions in an
> industry. A class of "games of economic survival" has been
> investigated . . .
>
> Shubik (1984: 60)

Consider a simple variant of the classic problem of "Long-run equilibrium in concentrated oligopoly" (Sylos-Labini 1962: 41 ff.),[6] as
imaginatively modified and illuminatingly discussed by Kreps (1990:
ch. 4, esp. 41 ff.), to illustrate the fertile uses of a game-theoretic
framework. A monopolistic manufacturer of one homogeneous
commodity, x, faces a classic downward-sloping demand curve and
a simple cost structure (in, say, dollar-denominated monetary units),
respectively, as follows:

(a) $x = 13 - p$,
(b) $c = x + 6.25$,

where p = price and c = cost.

Elementary analysis results in an optimum value of $x = 6$ at which
total profits are $28.75. Now consider a standard "von Stackelberg
story," where the monopolistic manufacturer is threatened by a
potential entrant. An extensive form for this story, in which the
potential entrant considers three levels of production, one for each of
three levels considered by the monopolistic manufacturer, is shown
in Figure 7.1. Conventional analysis would dictate, for example, that
we reformulate the extensive form as a strategic form and seek, say,
a Nash equilibrium. I wish, however, to highlight slightly different
aspects of this almost paradigmatic problem in elementary industrial
organizations theory. Observe, therefore, that:

---

[6] Recall, however, Shubik's important caveat: "Thus we shall not investigate
specific markets; nor shall we indulge in 'reaction functions' and quasidynamic
descriptions of the actions and reactions of duopolists or oligopolists in abstract
markets whose structural particulars are not described . . . several generations of graduate students have studied 'leader–follower' analyses . . . 'kinked-oligopoly-curve'
arguments, and a host of models that have in common a meager basis of extremely
casual empiricism, combined with a high degree of arbitrariness in modeling" (Shubik
1984: 60).

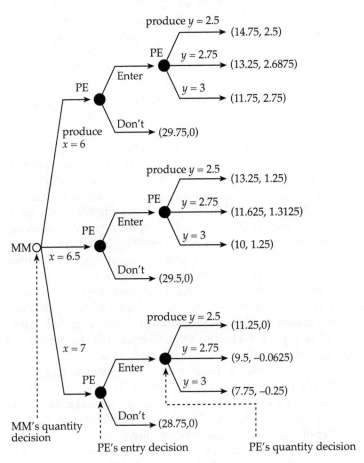

Fig. 7.1
MM: monopolistic manufacturer
PE: potential entrant
Source: Kreps (1990: 46)

(a) For each of three envisaged production decisions of the monopolistic manufacturer, the potential entrant considers four possible "reactions"; i.e. a total of $4^3 = 64$ possible reactions.

(b) The numerical values of the example – fortuitously or not – are "constrained" to be rational numbers. Kreps notes that: "In theory, the monopolist *can choose from an infinite set of actions*, as the quantity variable is perfectly divisible. If you find this bothersome, it will do to think that quantities must be in units no finer than hundredths" (Kreps 1990: 45; emphasis added).

I do find this bothersome! Hoggatt, in his pioneering study "An Experimental Business Game," also observed that: "The product is infinitely divisible, i.e., it can be produced in any fractional part of its unit of measure" (Hoggatt 1959: 192); he then added a footnote to this observation about potential (uncountably) infinite divisibility, to the effect that, "However, in the play of the game, numbers are rounded to two decimal places" (p. 193). I find these dichotomies analytically imprecise and intellectually disturbing. A constrained optimization problem in which the feasible domain is not[7] the whole of R cannot be guaranteed to yield "rounded" optimal solutions "near" a value yielded on the whole of R. In passing, it may be useful to remember that "the monopolist [in theory] can choose from an uncountably infinite set of actions." Somewhere, somehow, the axiom of choice is invoked and the whole experiment becomes noneffective in the strict recursion-theoretic sense.

(c) In this example, it is clear that the potential entrant can (easily!) compute an optimal response for each of the possible decisions by the monopolistic manufacturer. The only "curse of dimensionality" faced by the potential entrant is the number of computations, not their nature.[8]

(d) The extensive-form description highlights the sequential (or "dynamic") nature of the example (even if not the actual unfolding of events in the market).

(e) The way the problem has been presented indicates a termination point for the sequence of decisions and the outcome, which can be one of a finite number of cases. For example, the market could "evolve" into a duopolistic market, or remain one of two possible monopolistic markets. Thus, a standard

---

[7] By this I mean not integer, rational, or algebraically constrained number domains.

[8] Kreps notes that: "In general, we can compute the optimal response of the entrant to every choice of quantity output x by the monopolist. . . . [It] is *easy algebra as long as you know how to take the derivative of a quadratic* (Kreps 1990: 48; emphasis added).

"payoff" can be computed and associated with the finite number of alternative outcomes.

Stripped, therefore, of some of the paraphernalia, this problem can
be considered a determined, two-person, perfect-information, con-
stant-sum, finite-time game in extensive form. In its bare essentials, it
has the following structure. There are two players, I and II; player I,
choosing first, picks a number i; knowing I's choice, player II picks a
number j; depending on the value of $i + j$, the outcome is a continua-
tion of the status quo (player I "wins"), evolves into a duopolistic
market (a "draw"), etc.

Eschewing standard ad-hockeries in the analysis of oligopoly (cf.
fn. 1 above), Shubik has formulated a generalization of the above
kind of example as generic "games of economic survival" (cf. Shubik
1959: sec. 10.3). Apart from minor variations, all games of economic
survival have the essential structure exactly as described earlier in
this section.

A few additional technical characteristics could be pointed out.

(α) The sequential nature highlighted by the extensive form of the
example shows that the decision process has the classic form of
an *alternating game*; i.e., decisions or choices are prefixed
alternately by the existential and universal quantifiers until, at
the termination point, a polynomial is evaluated to determine
an outcome.

(β) The polynomials to be evaluated, in a general experimental
setting, are constrained to yield rational, non-negative values.

(γ) "Behind" the picking of integers (or rational numbers) i and j
by players I and II, there is a whole process of computation,
conjecture, evaluation, etc. Some of these sub-elements lurk-
ing "behind the scenes" may even have probabilistic elements.

Now, in the case of (α), technically this means that the problem can
be described in a prenex normal form (cf. Theorem 7.3 below). As for
(β), it is clear that, in general, a realistic experimental game of economic survival should be viewed as a diophantine decision problem
(cf. below). In other words, it is not sufficient "to know how to take
the derivative of a quadratic": it will also be necessary, for example,
"to know methods to extract roots."

As for (γ), it must first be noted that a probabilistic structure
is usually given to these games in view of – in my opinion – the

historical accident of the pioneers basing rational behavior on expected utility fundamentals. This is an inessential feature, but an expansion of this theme and a demonstration of its inessentiality will require space that is disproportional in length and nature to the main goals of this chapter. A few observations may, in any case, put the matter in some sort of perspective.

Expected utility maximization can be based on a definition for information that is wholly recursion-theoretic. This is implied by a recursion-theoretic basis for randomness (cf. Chapter 5 above) on which, in turn, probabilities are grounded.[9] Therefore, the "behind-the-scenes" processes[10] that are the bases for the players" choices of numbers[11] i and j, say, can be given complete recursion-theoretic underpinnings.

Furthermore, every decision-making unit, within any of the standard frameworks of economic theory – i.e. within the neoclassical closure – and the decision process itself, can be given a number-theoretic encoding.[12] The modifications and altered constraints on the domain of analysis will not be as drastic as is sometimes suggested.[13]

Let me next consider the example of a well known parlour game, "NIM", but in its form as the "Silver Dollar Game."[14] A row of squares, semi-infinite to the right, in the form of a tape is placed on a board. A finite number of coins, of which exactly one is a silver dollar, are placed on some of the squares, and a cash till at the left end of the semi-infinite tape. A legal move in the game consists of moving any one coin-heap from the square on which it is placed to any unoccupied square to its left without passing over any other coin heap. The cash till can hold any amount of coins, and the leftmost coin can be deposited in the cash till in one legal move. When a player making a move is forced to shift the silver dollar into the cash till, the game ends and the other player wins (gets the moneybag, for which a legal move is also defined).

---

[9] Indeed, the original definition and conceptual introductions of martingales goes back to such considerations (cf. Fine 1973: esp. ch. IV).

[10] In particular, expected utility maximization and the feasibility of choosing mixed strategies; but in general, almost all of standard theory.

[11] Only the computable numbers?

[12] E.g., Gödel numbering (cf. Ch. 3 above).

[13] In Spear (1989) or Lewis (1985). In the concluding sections of Ch. 6 – and related work in progress – I have developed a computable analytic framework within which standard results on REE can be retained in the face of "computability constraints."

[14] Brilliantly analyzed in Conway (1976) and Berlekamp *et al.* (1982).

A "Turing machine interpretation" of this game, heuristically, suggests the following intuitive ideas. Consider the semi-infinite tape as the conventional input tape for the computing activities of a Turing machine; however, the heaps of coins will be denoted by consecutive 1s with blank squares separating them. A program for the machine, in terms of its standard quadruple, can be written to encapsulate the rules of the game, with an appropriate interpretation for the terminal state given by the left-move end-state for the silver dollar.[15]

Although the game itself has a solution, in the sense of determining a winner, the point I wish to emphasize here is: *can we write an explicit sequence of instructions for the determinable winner to execute and reach the winning configurations?* The answer, in general, is negative.

Consider, now, a variation of the Silver Dollar Game. A win is determined for the player who makes a move that results in the number of heaps of coins[16] coinciding with the number of shifts made by an appropriately programmed Turing machine at that move. Then the above query, if answered in the affirmative, would provide an answer to a problem known to be effectively undecidable: *the unsolvability of the halting problem for Turing machines.* Many minor variations of the same theme – either in the rules or in the nature of the scope for the silver dollar in determining a win – with Turing machine dependence can be devised. It will then be possible to ask effective playability, decidability, and tractability questions more directly. For example, in any one of these variations of the Silver Dollar Game, the next question after the above query should perhaps be: *given an affirmative answer to the question on the existence of explicit sequence of instructions, how tractable is it?* In other words, how *fast* can a win be effectively prescribed?

Note, also, that the play can be cast in terms of an alternative sequence of existence and universal quantifiers. The player with the first move will be associated with the existential quantifier – choosing to move some one heap of coins to a feasible position on the left ($\exists$), taking into consideration all possible responses by the second player

---

[15] It is quite easy to convert this "finite" game into one of infinite heaps of coins using, as a model, the game of infinite NIM. With minor modifications, a variant of the game can be made into one without termination. This would mean that, in the Turing machine interpretation, we enter a "loop" or, perhaps, encounter a recursively enumerable set of coin heaps that are not recursive.

[16] Or their value as some function of the number or nature of the heaps.

($\forall$), and so on. The game is determined when one of the "win" conditions is satisfied; such conditions can be stated as Boolean expressions and then *arithmetized*, so that its satisfaction is equivalent to the decidability of a diophantine relation.

Finally, games of attrition (e.g. Isbell and Marlow 1956), games of timing, tactical air-war games (e.g. the Colonel Blotto game – cf., say, Karlin 1959: 82 ff.; Dresher 1961: chs. 9, 10), and "parlour" games of skill such as chess and variants of poker can all be studied in the generic form, intuitively suggested in the above discussion.[17] Moreover, even the famous Gambler's Ruin problem and the classic thought experiments underlying the genesis of calibration for logical and subjective probabilities by Ramsey, de Finetti, von Neumann–Morgenstern, and Savage can be reformulated as games in the senses discussed above.

In the next sections, in steps of increasing generality, a class of *arithmetical games*[18] will be defined, discussed, and analyzed. Such games encompass, as special cases, all of the above examples, when they are constrained computably in various ways. It is then possible to ask recursion-theoretic questions on the decidability, effective playability, and tractability of determined games.

It might be illuminating to conclude this section with Turing's remarkable, early, and general result; however, let me first proceed, as Turing (1954) did, with a series of increasingly general questions and possible answers. Think, first, of games in general. When asked to play the game, having been given an explanation of its rules, one may ask quite simply,

(a) Can this game be played?

Perhaps, as economists, we can take the concrete example of the classic parlour game with a clear economic content: Monopoly. With this game in mind, we know that the answer to (a) is "Yes"; but for

---

[17] Indeed, I have come to feel that the best starting-point for the analysis of all of these games is Conway's game-theoretic foundation for numbers – if, using Conway's own caveat, "We ignore some objections on the grounds of *ineffectivity*" (Conway 1976: 3; emphasis added).

[18] A more appropriate name may have been "recursive games." There are, however, two cogent reasons that mitigate against such a "naming." First of all, Everett (1954), more than 40 years ago, appropriated the word "*recursive*" for a special class of what has come to be called arithmetical games; second, the number-theoretic underpinnings of the methods devised to demonstrate the diophantine nature of recursively enumerable sets has made it natural to consider games studied in such contexts to be arithmetic in a foundational sense (as distinct from being analytic, algebraic, etc.).

games in general the admissible answers are "Yes," "No" or possibly, "Don't know." Indeed, "theoretically," a game of Monopoly, which has an elementary chance mechanism built into it, can go on "for ever." However, it does belong to Shubik's generic definition of a "game of economic survival" with, in principle, no termination point.

Next, one may ask, or be asked:

(b)   Is there a best way to play the game?

Again, the possible answers may, at first, be "Yes," "No" or "Don't know"; however, in the case of this question there is scope for further refinement of the query and the answer. I shall not elaborate further on this point but shall move to Turing's punch-lines:

When one has been asked a number of times whether a number of different [games] of similar nature can be [played] one is naturally led to ask oneself:

(c)   Is there a systematic procedure by which I can answer these questions, for [games] of this type?

If one were feeling rather more ambitious, one might even ask

(d)   Is there a systematic procedure by which one can tell whether a [game] is [playable]?

I hope to show that the answer to this last question is "No." (Turing 1954: 16)

Rabin's particular result, which I quoted at the beginning of Chapter 1, is a special case of Turing's more general result. With some of the intuitive background of this section as heuristic motivation, I begin with Rabin's framework and result and describe its progressive generalization in various directions. My conjecture is that, eventually, a general result similar to Turing's, applicable to arbitrary games when effectivized, can be demonstrated. These are tentative first steps in the direction of demonstration of such a conjecture.

7.3   RABIN'S COMPUTABLE GAME – AND EXTENSIONS

Mathematicians copied the example of philosophers; they derived logical principles from the language describing finite mathematics and without scruple also used them in their pure mathematical study of infinite systems.

Brouwer (1929/1998: 50)

Rabin's starting-point is the abstract Gale–Stewart game described in the appendix to this chapter. However, he focuses on the actual playability of a game in *real time*; hence the first modification would be to do away with the assumption of infinite plays.

Rabin's Assumption 1

(a) Each play terminates with a terminal position.
(b) There exists a 1–1 correspondence between terminal positions and plays.
(c) The set of terminal positions T of Γ (is defined by:

$$T = x - f(X - x_0).$$

(d) x is finite or countably infinite.

Remark. It is interesting to note Rabin's motivation for assumption (d):

In order to make communication between the players possible, they must have some fixed system of naming or denoting all the different positions of the game. Since any one notational system contains at most a countable number of different symbols we must impose the condition that the set x of positions of Γ is finite or countably infinite. (Rabin 1957: 150)

This important constraint is hardly ever considered in standard game theory – indeed, not even in ordinary economic analysis, where agents routinely face an uncountable infinity of alternatives over which they are able to assign preferences. I tried to point this out in the discussion of the "barriers to entry" example in the previous section. This basic building block is never, in general, relaxed when agents play, say, the prisoner's dilemma with finite automata, or when the algorithmic and computational complexity of Nash equilibria are investigated.

Rabin's Assumption 2 (Towards Effectiveness)

The following information must be *effectively ascertainable*:

(a) for all $x \in X$: who makes the next move;
(b) given: $x \to x'$, *effective verification* of $f(x') = x$, i.e. the effective verification of the validity of a move that is observed;
(c) for all $x \in X$, whether

(i) the play terminates at that x,
(ii) and if so, who won.

Rabin's Assumption 3

For X *countably infinite*,

(a) X_I and X_{II} are recursive sets;
(b) f is a computable function from $(X - (0))$ to X;
(c). T is recursive; and T_I and T_{II} for S_I and S_{II} are also recursive sets.

DEFINITION 7.1: ACTUAL GAMES. $P \equiv \{x_0, X, X_I, X_{II}, f, S, S_I, S_{II}, \Phi\}$ is called an actual game if:

(a) all plays $s \in S$ are finite;
(b) X is finite *or* countably infinite.

D*iscussion.* (i) If X is finite, the game is actually playable. This is because the effective instructions to play the game can be given in a finite list which enumerates the sets: X_I, X_{II}, T, T_I, T_{II} (recall that these are now recursive sets).

(ii) If X is countably infinite, too, the game is actually playable, this time because the finite list of effective instructions to compute the characteristic functions of X_I, X_{II}, T_I, T_{II}, and the computable function, f, can be given. Whenever the player faces one of the questions (a), (b), or (c) in Rabin's assumption 2, an answer can be given by computing the necessary recursive set or computable function and proceeding to play or terminate.

DEFINITION 7.2: (EFFECTIVELY) COMPUTABLE STRATEGY (RULE). σ is a(n) (effectively) computable strategy if it is defined by

$\sigma'(x) = \sigma(x), \forall x \in X_I$ and $\sigma(x) = 0, \forall x \in X - X_I$;

and is (effectively) computable. Similarly for τ.

DEFINITION 7.3: THE ACTUAL EFFECTIVE GAME. For $g(x)$, a computable function, $g: N \to N$, an actual effective game Γg is played as follows:

(i) Player I picks any integer I.
(ii) Player II, knowing I's choice, picks any integer j.

(iii) Player I, knowing i and j, picks an integer k.
(iv) Compute $g(k)$.
(v) If $g(k) = i + j$, then player I wins the play.
(vi) If $g(k) \neq i + j$, then player II wins the play;

Finally, we have Rabin's theorem.

RABIN'S THEOREM. If $g(x)$ enumerates a *simple set*[19] G, i.e. if the set of values of $g(x)$ is simple, then there is no (effectively) computable winning strategy in Γg.

Proof. Player II has the winning strategies because, given i, II could choose j so that $i + j \notin G$. This is possible because, by the definition of a simple set, G is infinite. Therefore, a winning strategy for II is any computable function $\tau(i)$, such that $\forall i, i + \tau(i) \notin G$. In fact, if I picks i and II picks $\tau(i)$, then no matter what k player I chooses in the third move, we have: $g(k) \in G$ and $g(k) \neq i + \tau(i) \notin G$. So player II always wins.

Next, assume that player II has the winning strategy $\tau(i)$ and that it is a computable function. Clearly, $h(i) = i + \tau(i)$ is also a computable function.[20] Now, the set of values taken by $h(i)$, call it H, is recursively enumerable. H is also infinite. Because $i + \tau(i) \in \bar{G}$, $H \subseteq \bar{G}$. But this means that $\bar{G}$ contains an infinite set which is recursively enumerable. This contradicts the assumption that G is simple. Hence $\tau(i)$ cannot be a computable function.

This whole section may appear arid and antiseptic. But is is never useless to know what the pioneer did – and *why* he did it. More importantly, it gave me the chance to describe a minor research program, on effectivizing standard concepts and tools. In the process I was able to introduce important definitions and two techniques customarily used in proving uncomputabilities: the diagonal argument, and existence of recursively enumerable nonrecursive sets.

Jones's version of Rabin's Gale–Stewart game differs, ostensibly, only in the way a win is determined; the play, in its basic first three steps, proceeds identically. Thus, the definition of the way the result is determined is:

---

[19] A *simple set* is a recursively enumerable set whose complement is infinite but which contains no infinite recursively enumerable subset. Simple sets were introduced by Emil Post in his pioneering paper of 1944, where what has come to be known as "Post's problem" was first formulated. It is not an exaggeration to state that the conceptual and epistemological innovations of this paper by Post heralded the transition from "Classical Recursion Theory" to "Generalized Recursion Theory."

[20] This is the diagonal method.

Player I wins if some (two-symbol) i-state TM halts in exactly $i + k$ shifts[21] when started on a blank input tape. If not, player II wins.

Now, in a perfectly intuitive sense, this game should be effectively playable. Why? Because, after I and II have elected i, j, and k, an impartial umpire should be able to list all possible (two-symbol) i-state TMs effectively. By a simple counting argument, it is easy to show that there are $(4i + 4)^{2i}$ such machines. Then, the umpire needs to go down the effective list of $(4i + 4)^{2i}$ (two-symbol), i-state TMs and operate each of them to see if any of them halts after exactly $(i + k)$ shifts. If any does, player I will be declared the winner; if not, player II is the winner. In this sense, this can be considered a variant of the Silver Dollar Game, discussed in the previous section, and hence a generalized form of NIM. Moreover, being a (modified) Gale–Stewart game, it is also provable that there is a winning strategy for player II. Even granting all this, it is still remarkable that:

THEOREM 7.1. In Jones's modified Rabin game, neither player has an *effective* winning strategy.

Some conceptual machinery must be introduced before the (simple) proof of the theorem can be given. Jones's original proof uses the formalism and results inherent in the "Busy Beaver Game." I will need to outline some of the basics of this game.

Tibor Rado's Busy Beaver game (cf. Rado 1962; Lin and Rado 1965) gives an explicit, intuitively clear, uncomputable function. Before defining it, consider, for example, a Rado-type description of a 3-state Turing machine (Figure 7.2). It functions as follows. The entry in the first row, first column signifies that the Turing machine scanning symbol 0, in state 1, writes 1 instead of 0, shifts right one square, and enters state 2. Now, denote by

$\Lambda(k)$: the set of all k-state Turing machines which eventually halt, after starting on a blank tape (*Note*: this number is finite since it is a subset of the number $(4k + 4)^{2k}$)

$\rho(m)$: the number of 1s finally written by a halting Turing machine m ($\in \Lambda(k)$), which is initialized on a blank tape (in Figure 7.2, $\rho(m) = 5$)

$s(m)$: the number of shifts made by Turing machine m ($\in \Lambda(k)$) before halting (having written $\rho(m)$)

$\Sigma(k)$: the kth Busy Beaver number, defined by

[21] A definition is given below.

| | (Scanned symbol) | |
	0	1
(Current state) 1	1R2	1R0
2	1L2	0R3
3	1L3	1L1

FIG. 7.2

$$\Sigma(k) = \max \{\rho(m) \; m \in \Lambda(k)\}$$

$S(k)$: the kth Busy Beaver shift number defined by:

$$S(k) = \max \{s(m) \mid m \in \Lambda(k)\}$$

DEFINITION 7.4: BUSY BEAVER GAME. Suppose we consider the set $\Lambda(k)$. Then the winner of a Busy Beaver game is that Turing machine, $m \in \Lambda(k)$, which generates $\Sigma(k)$.

DEFINITION 7.5: BUSY BEAVER PROBLEM. Find an effective procedure to determine $\Sigma(k)$.

THEOREM 7.2. For every computable function f, there exists an n, (depending on f) such that $\Sigma(k) > f(k)$, $\forall k > n$.

Proof. See Rado (1962) or, for a pedagogically masterful "constructive" proof, Boolos and Jeffrey (1989: 34–42).

An immediate corollary arises:

COROLLARY 7.1. The Busy Beaver shift number, $S(k)$, is uncomputable.

Proof. If $S(k)$ were computable, then $\Sigma(k)$ could be computed by a straightforward counting procedure. Simply run each Turing machine $m(\in \Lambda(k))$ through a maximum of $S(k)$ shifts; tick off the 1s on those Turing machines ($\in \Lambda(k)$) that halt and choose the one that scores the highest $\rho(m)$.

Remark. Just to get a feel for the orders of magnitude, note the following:

(a) There are $[4(2 + 1)]^4 = \Lambda(2)$, two-state machines, which is a manageable 20,730; $\Lambda(3)$, on the other hand, is $[4(3 + 1)]^6 = 16,777,216!!$

(b) As for the Busy Beaver number, $\Sigma(k)$, we have $\Sigma(1) = 1$; $\Sigma(2) = 4$; $\Sigma(3) = 0$; $\Sigma(4) = 13$; and then we reach monstrosities: $\Sigma(4) \geq 4,098, \ldots, \Sigma(7) \geq 22,961$, and $\Sigma(7) \geq 3 \cdot (7 \cdot 3^{92} - 1)/2$.

(c) The busy beaver shift number, as can be expected, is properly "Malthusian": $S(3) = 21$ (cf. Figure 7.2); $S(4) = 107$; $S(5) \geq 2,358,064$.

Note, above all, that these are two-symbol machines. For example, $S(2)$ for a three-symbol Turing machine is ≥ 38; and for a four-symbol Turing machine it is $\geq 7,195$. So far as I know, $S(k)$, for $k \geq 3$ and more than two symbols, has not ever been seriously calculated.

We can now prove Theorem 7.1.

Proof of Theorem 7.1. Assume that the Turing machine $m(\in \Lambda(k)$ is initialized in state 1 on a blank tape. Clearly, $\Sigma(k) \leq S(k)$. Now player II's strategy would be to try to find an l, as a computable function of k, say $f(k) = l$, so that the first player's third step is thwarted for *any choice* of k; i.e., l must be chosen so that $f(k) \geq S(k)$. Thus, there is a winning strategy, $S(k)$, for the second player. However, by Theorem 7.2 and corollary 7.1, $f(k) < \Sigma(k) = S(k)$. Hence there is no *computable* winning strategy for the second player.

Remark. The perceptive reader would have noticed that, both in Rabin's game and in Jones's variation of it, there are common elements, the most important of which are:

(a) The players *alternate* in their moves to choose.

(b) These alternations can be modelled by alternating existential and universal quantifiers.

(c) The existential quantifier moves first; if the total number of moves is odd, then an existential quantifier again fixes the choice of the last integer; if not – i.e., if the total number of moves is even – then the universal quantifier determines the value of the last chosen integer.

(d) One of the players tries to make an expression preceded by these alternating quantifiers *true*; the other to make it *false*.

Now, it can immediately be seen why Rabin-type games will be able to exploit the methods and results that were developed to solve Hilbert's Tenth problem (negatively) – especially when the expression to be satisfied, which comes after the alternating quantifiers, can be cast in conjunctive normal form. Recall that Rabin's G is a recursively enumerable set (which is not recursive). Then determining whether $i+j$ belongs to such a set is equivalent to determining whether there is an effective procedure to solve an associated diophantine equation. The negative answer to the latter can then be used to show that there is no computable winning strategy in the game. We will have occasion to return to these heuristic observations in more formal ways in the next and the concluding sections.

7.4 ARITHMETICAL GAMES

> The result that the proposition can be transformed into one about polynomials was very unexpected. . . . This is related to my early interest in number theory, stimulated by Furtwängler's lectures.
>
> Gödel (in Wang 1996: 84)

Gödel's celebrated result was that there were arithmetical problems that were effectively undecidable (or recursively unsolvable). Roughly speaking, what he showed was that there exist arithmetical equations, say linking two polynomials, preceded by some finite sequence of existential and universal quantifiers that are effectively undecidable. Now reflect on the way the moves are made in Rabin's effectivized Gale–Stewart game. The moves say: "there exists an integer i, for all possible choices of j, such that there is a $g(\cdot) = i + j \ldots$" – in other words, a form such as $\exists i \forall j \exists g(\cdot) \{ \ldots \}$. Inside the braces the win condition will be stated as a proposition to be satisfied. If we can extract an arithmetical form for the "win" condition, we can exploit the full force of the results coming down from Gödel and culminating in Matiyasevich's magisterial demonstration that Hilbert's Tenth problem is recursively unsolvable. It is here that we will exploit the fundamental result, i.e. the diophantine nature of recursively enumerable sets. When Rabin stipulated that g enumerates a simple set, he was, essentially, stating the "win" condition in the form of requiring a diophantine equation to be recursively solvable – an impossibility. This is the potted background to the work initiated by Jones, in a series of important papers, building on the suggestions made by Rabin. This whole line of thought has been almost totally ignored, as I mentioned in the introduction, by traditional game theorists who have attempted *ad hoc* effectivizing in special classes of games.

DEFINITION 7.6: ARITHMETICAL GAME OF LENGTH q. An arithmetical game of length q between two players, labelled I and II, is a game of perfect information and alternating choices of integers with, say, player I choosing the first and the final qth integers (i.e., q is odd); I wins if and only if $P(x_1, x_2, \ldots, x_q) = 0$, where $P(x_1, x_2, \ldots, x_q)$ is a polynomial with integer coefficients, $x_i, \forall i = 1, \ldots, q$ are the integers chosen, alternately, by I and II, and q is the length of game/total number of "moves," i.e. the total number of alternate choices made by I and II.

Remark. Note, in accordance with the previous remark, that the choices alternate. Indeed, I will be associated with the existential quantifier, and II with the universal quantifier. Essentially, what happens is as follows: I tried to find an x, $(\exists x_1)$ such that, for any choice of x_2 ($\forall x_2$) by II, I can find an x_3 ($\exists x_3$) such that . . . until, finally, an expression (in the case of arithmetical games, the expression is a polynomial) is to be satisfied by I (whilst II tries to make sure it is not satisfied). This, as I pointed out above, is exactly as in Rabin's effectivized Gale–Stewart game. From this, Theorem 3 follows immediately:

THEOREM 7.3: ARITHMETICAL GAMES ARE DETERMINED (Jones 1981: 64). In every arithmetical game either I or II has a winning strategy; either I can ensure that the polynomial is satisfied, or II can falsify it.

Proof. Note that the strategy of I or II is a series of alternating quantifiers beginning with the existential one for I and the universal one for II. For example, in a game of length q, with q an odd number, I's strategy[22] would look like:

$$\exists x, \forall x_2 \, \exists x_3 \ldots \forall x_{q-1} \, \exists x_q \, [P(x_1, \ldots, x_q) = 0].$$

Player II's strategy would, of course, be a negation of the above. Then, using the law of the excluded middle,[23] one or the other of the forms will be true; i.e., either I or II has a winning strategy.

It is, surely, intuitively obvious that one of the players has a winning strategy. Two obvious questions emerge from the result of the theorem, because to prove existence is one thing; but to actually implement it is quite another:

(a) Is the winning strategy easy to implement; i.e., is it tractable?

---

[22] Note that this is in prenex normal form.
[23] *Pace* the constructivists; but, of course, these are games of *finite* length.

(b) Even more fundamentally, is it computable?

I will postpone a discussion of the first question to the next section and concentrate on various approaches toward an answer to the second. For this I need two important results derived by Jones (1978, 1981). The first is theorem 2 in Jones (1978: 336).

THEOREM 7.4. The recursively enumerable sets $W_1, W_2, \ldots, W_n, \ldots$, can be represented in the *prenex normal form*:

$$x \in W_n \Leftrightarrow \exists ab \forall i \exists swpq \forall jv \exists eg$$
$$\{n + s + 1 - I\} \{[(s + w)^2 + 3w + s - 2I]^2 + [[(j - w)^2$$
$$+ (v - q)^2]$$
$$[(j - s)^2 + (v - p)^2 ((i - n)^2 + (v - q - x)^2)] [(j - 3I)^2$$
$$+ (v - p - q)^2]$$
$$[(j - 3i - 1)^2 + (v - pq)^2] - e - 1]^2 [[v + e + ejb - a]^2$$
$$+ [v + g - jb]^2]\} = 0$$

$$(7.1)$$

The second is lemma 2 in Jones (1981: 407):

THEOREM 7.5. For every recursively enumerable set W, there is a polynomial with integer coefficients given by $Q(n, x_1, x_2, x_3, x_4)$ such that, for all natural numbers n,

$$n \in W \Leftrightarrow \exists x_1, \forall x_2, \exists x_3, \forall x_4 [Q(n, x_1, x_2, x_3, x_4) \neq 0]. \quad (7.2)$$

These elegant results are direct, but ingenious, outcomes of methods and results, as mentioned above, developed for resolving Hilbert's Tenth problem.

An immediate application of Theorem 7.1 would be to consider a Rabin-type game of length $q = 6$. This is because we can put x_1 for I's first choice, x_2 for II's choice, and the winning condition would be exactly as in Rabin's game: I wins if $x_1 = x_2 \in G$. Then, analogously to Rabin's proof, II has a winning strategy, but has no computable winning strategy in a game of length $q = 6$ associated with a polynomial $Q(n, x_1, x_2, x_3, x_4)$ such that, for any choice of x_1 and x_2 by I and II, respectively, we have (putting $n = x_1 + x_2$ in Theorem 7.1).

$$x_1 + x_2 \in G \Leftrightarrow \exists x_3 \forall x_4 \exists x_5 \forall x_6 [Q(x_1 + x_2, x_3, x_4, x_5, x_6) \neq 0].$$

$$(7.3)$$

This is a recursively undecidable problem, and hence there is no computable winning strategy in the game. But, of course, this a general statement, i.e. without any demonstration of an explicit given polynomial Q. Jones however constructed such an example, which I report, again, in view of the neat way the first of the above two theorems is used in the proof. Jones (1981: 70–1) has shown that the arithmetical game associated with the following polynomial has no computable winning strategy for either player:

$$\{n + x_7 + 1 - x_6\} \; \{[(x_7 + x_9)^2 + 3x_9 + x_7 - 2x_6]^2$$
$$+ \, [[(x_{14} - x_9)^2 + (x_{16} - x_{13})^2][(x_{14} - x_7)^2 + (x_{16} - x_{11})^2 ((x_6 - n)^2$$
$$+ \, (x_{16} - x_{13} - x_1 - x_2)^2)] \, [x_{14} - 3x_6]^2 + (x_{16} - x_{11} - x_{13})^2]$$
$$[(x_{14} - 3x_6 - 1)^2 + (x_{16} - x_{11}x_{13})^2] - x_{17} - 1]^2 \; \{[x_{16} + x_{17}$$
$$+ \, x_{17}x_{14}x_5 - x_3]^2 + [x_{16} + x_{19} - x_{14}x_5]^2\}\}.$$

Since his proof of the above theorem gives the general method I am seeking, I will outline it.

Consider the above polynomial for a Rabin game, i.e. player I picking i, II picking j, etc. Then relabel, sequentially, the variables in Theorem 7.4 as follows: $i = x_1$; $j = x_2$; $a = x_3$; $b = x_5$; and so on. Replace them in (7.1) to get the above polynomial. This, then, is an arithmetic game of length 19; but x_4, x_8, x_{10}, x_{12}, x_{15}, and x_{18} are dummy variables; hence it is, in essence, an arithmetical game of length 13. Put, for the recursively enumerable set G in the Rabin game, W_n as in Theorem 7.4. Then, the nonexistence of a computable winning strategy for either player follows immediately from the diophantine nature of the above polynomial.

It will be clear that we have exploited results that are based on the diophantine nature of recursively enumerable sets. This means we can easily use these results in conventional (non-arithmetical) game theory by specifying various relevant functions as appropriate polynomials. The reason I have not done this in this essay is as follows. Recall that Rabin first effectivized the whole of the Gale–Stewart game. It is only after that task was accomplished that he investigated the existence of computable winning strategies. To repeat this procedure in more orthodox game theory would necessitate that we go back to basics: essentially, reducing rational players to Turing machines. At that point the games become those played by Turing machines approximately in the sense investigated by Ann Condon (1989). I refer the reader to this competent work as an excuse for not pursuing a similar exercise in this essay.

It must also be clear that the skepticism I indicated in the opening paragraphs of this chapter, regarding the conventional application, originates in reasons related to the remarks in the immediately preceding paragraph. But they are also due to the fact that I believe arithmetical games to be of more relevance to the kind of conflict and cooperative situations that economists ought to consider. A vision of an economy as a massively parallel distributed resource allocation system peopled by Turing machines in conflicting and cooperative situations generating emergent phenomena seems, to me at least, a far more interesting research strategy than pursuing the well-trodden path that appears to have exhausted itself. There are, of course, many who will disagree with this assessment; but there are also some who may agree.

7.5 CONCLUDING NOTES AND COMPLEXITY CONSIDERATIONS

> The traditional worst-case analysis – the dominant strain in complexity theory – corresponds to a scenario in which the instances of a problem to be solved are constructed by an infinitely intelligent adversary who knows the structure of the algorithm and chooses inputs that will embarrass it to the maximal extent.
>
> Karp (1987: 448)

Let me recall, from computational complexity theory, a few standard results.

(a) There is the well-known inclusion relation: $P \subseteq NP \subset PSPACE$.

(b) Quantified satisfiability ($QSAT$) is $PSPACE$-complete.

(c) Every Boolean expression is equivalent to one in conjunctive normal form.

(d) Finally there is the prenex normal form equivalent, with a Boolean expression instead of the polynomial, to Theorem 7.4, and now expressed as Theorem 7.1a.

THEOREM 7.1a (Jones 1978: 336, theorem 1). The RE sets, W_1, W_2, ..., may be represented in the form

$$x \in W_n \Leftrightarrow \exists ab \; \forall i_{i \leq n} \; \exists swpq \; \forall jv \; \exists eg \; \{(s+w)^2 + 3w + s = 2i \wedge [j = w \wedge v = q]\}$$

$$\vee [j = 3i \wedge v = p + q] \vee [j = s \wedge (v = p \vee (I = n \wedge v = q + x))]$$
$$\vee [j = 3i + 1 \wedge v = pq] \rightarrow a = v + e + ejb \wedge v + g = jb\rangle \}.$$

With this background, it is easy to see that all the arithmetical games that I have discussed in Section 7.4 have the *QSAT* form and are hence *PSPACE*-complete. In particular, Rabin's game is of this category. This goes to show that, even through the games are determined in principle, i.e. although the existence of a winning strategy for one of the players is provable, they are in fact – even in relatively simple cases – intractable. In other words, these arithmetical games would require at least exponential time to determine which player has a winning strategy. This is preliminary to determining whether the winning strategy is recursive!

One intuitively illuminating way to formalize the arithmetical games of Section 7.4 would be to have them played by alternating Turing machines. These machines, as the name suggests, allow the alternation of existential and universal quantifiers in the execution of a computational process.[24] Thus, Jones's modified Rabin game would be an ideal candidate for this reformulation. I leave this for a future exercise.

Denote, now, the polynomials in Theorems 7.4 and 7.5 generically as *D*. Then, recalling the fundamental result that recursively enumerable sets are diophantine, the facts stated in (a)–(d) at the beginning of this section, and the properties of alternating Turing machines (cf. esp. fn. 24), we can also ask for the *diophantine complexity* of *D* (or W_n or *G* in Rabin's game) in the following precise sense:

(i) What is the minimum possible degree with respect to the unknowns of the polynomial *D* in the diophantine representation of W_n given in Theorem(s) 7.4 (and 7.5)?

(ii) What is the minimum possible number of unknowns in *D*?

For example, in proving that the arithmetical game of length 6 (which was a variation of Rabin's game) had no computable winning strategies, we used a polynomial with 13 variables and the highest degree was 16. Call the degree condition the *order* of the set W_n and the condition on the minimum number of unknowns the *rank* of W_n

[24] Recall that in a standard nondeterministic computation one allows only existential quantifiers. Alternating Turing machines accept exactly the recursively enumerable sets. Hence they are ideal for verifying completeness properties of the arithmetical games of the previous section.

(cf. Matiyasevich 1994: ch. 8; Jones 1978: 338–9). Then we can define different diophantine complexity measures for W_n, based on combinations of the order and rank conditions for D.

This means that we can link up directly with computational complexity measures without going back to quantified Boolean expressions and then coming "down" through the complexity results for variations on the satisfiability problem. Note that in recent years there have been imaginative definitions of *nondeterministic diophantine machines* in terms of (parametric) diophantine equations like D. Then, its behavior, for given values of the parameter, is to "guess" the values of the (integer) variables that will ensure that $D = 0$. It has been shown that nondeterministic diophantine machines are as powerful as nondeterministic Turing machines. This means, of course, that we can also go, fruitfully, in the opposite direction: to give direct number-theoretic characterizations of standard computational complexity measures. But the obvious next step would be to define *alternating* diophantine machines, in analogy with the alternating Turing machines. These are issues at the frontiers of applied recursion theory. My aim was to start with a simple example and find a way to get to the frontiers in terms of just this one example: Rabin's effectivized Gale–Stewart game.

Clearly, the way to proceed would be first to take a series of traditionally defined, simple, two-person, perfect-information games and effectivize them. Next, take the definition of "solution" and reformulate it, say, in conjunctive normal form – if it is not possible to arithmetize it directly. After that, it would be the routine procedure described above: to verify that the game is determined, then to check that it is effectively playable, and finally to compute its relevant complexities and see whether it can be simplified, in terms of the complexity measures (computational or diophantine); eventually, also, to see what type of alternating machine can be simulated to play the effectivized game. The problem of "barriers to entry" in noncompetitive markets could then be put to experiment in the laboratory via simulation by alternating machines.

One other point should perhaps be made. Alternating Turing machines are, as mentioned above, generalizations of standard nondeterministic Turing machines. Now, the feature that distinguishes a nondeterministic Turing machine from its deterministic counterpart is that transitions are multivalued. This characteristic is, therefore, further generalized in alternating machines in that they can be viewed as simulating a certain type of parallelism in their computing activities. Thus, a state in an alternating Turing machine corresponding to, say, an evaluation at a universal quantifier will be "cooperating," i.e. taking into account all possible configurations in accordance with "for all." Similarly, when the state corresponds to an existential evaluation, it will be in a "conflict" situation; i.e., only one value will be evaluated, and all others ignored. Here I must refer again to the relevance of Condon (1989).

This interpretation can be developed to reduce some of the simpler "many-person," perfect-information, win–lose games to two-person games of the same sort. Perhaps we will then travel Convey's path in constructing surreal numbers in the opposite direction.

Appendix to Chapter 7: Gale–Stewart Games

The *binary game* is represented in extensive form (as a tree). Two players, I and II, choose, alternately, binary digits 0 or 1.

DEFINITION 7A.1: A PLAY. A play consists of a countable number of such moves; i.e., each play consists of a sequence $\Rightarrow s(0), s(1), \ldots,$ [$s(i) = 0$ or 1], and each such sequence determines a (real) number $\Rightarrow s = \sum_{n=1}^{\infty} [s(n)/2^n]$

DEFINITION 7A2: WIN–LOSE.
(a) Player I wins \$1 from player II if s belongs to a certain subset T of the unit interval;
(b) Player II wins \$1 from player I if s does not belong to T.

Main result

A set T can be chosen so that no matter what strategy player I chooses, there exists a strategy by which player II can win. (Contrariwise: for each strategy player II may elect to use, there exists a strategy by which player I can win.)

(NOTATIONAL) DEFINITIONS
(a) A game Γ is given by a set X of positions (vertices of a tree). Given a position $x \in X$, there must be a way of telling which are the next positions, x', obtainable from x on the next move, where: x' is the immediate successor of x, and x is the immediate predecessor of x'.
(b) $x_0 \in X$ in its initial position.

(c) There is an *immediate predecessor function f*, such that:
  (i) $f:\{X - x_0\} \to X$
  (ii) $\forall x \in X, \exists n \in \aleph \,(\geq 0)$, s.t $f^n(x) = x_0$
(d) A sequence $\{s(0), s(1), \dots\}$ is a *play* if:
  (i) $s(0) = x_0$;
  (ii) $\forall i \geq 0, s(i) = f[s(i + 1)]$
  S is the set of plays of Γ.
(e) X and S are partitioned into two mutually exclusive sets:
  (i) $X = X_I \cup X_{II}$, where: $X_I \,(X_{II})$ is the set of positions from which player I (II) has the right to move;
  (ii) $S = S_I \cup S_{II}$, where: $S_I \,(S_{II})$ are the sets of plays in which player I (II) wins a game.

(Win–Lose Game) Definitions. A win–lose game Γ is a collection of objects: $\Gamma = (x_0, X, X_I, X_{II}, f, S, S_I, S_{II}, \Phi)$, such that:

  (i) $x_0 \in X$;
  (ii) $X_I \cap X_{II} = \phi$; $X_I \cup X_{II} = X$;
  (iii) f is an immediate predecessor function;
  (iv) S satisfies (d)(i) and (ii) above;
  (v) $S_I \cap S_{II} = \phi$ and $S_I \cup S_{II} = S$;
  (vi) Φ is a real-valued function on S (payoff function).

A play of Γ, therefore is an element of S, and:

  (vii) a play is a win for player I if it belongs to S_I;
  (viii) a play is a win for player II if it belongs to S_{II}.

DEFINITION 7A.3: STRATEGY. Given a game P, the set of strategies (rules, procedures) for player I is denoted by Σ_I, the set of all functions σ with domain X_I such that:

$$\sigma(x) = f^1(x)$$

and similarly for player II (with Σ_{II} and τ replacing Σ_I and σ and X_{II} replacing X_I).

Thus, to every pair of strategies, σ and τ, there exists a unique play, s, of the game Γ; denote this as $s = \langle \sigma, \tau \rangle$. This play satisfies the following inductive definitions:
  (a) $s(o) = x_o$
  (b) if $s(n) \in X_I$ then $s(n + 1) = \sigma(s(n))$;
     if $s(n) \in X_{II}$ then $s(n + 1) = \tau(s(n))$.

DEFINITION 7A.4: A STRICTLY DETERMINED WINNING STRATEGY. A strategy (rule, procedure) σ is called a winning strategy for player I if $\tau \in \Sigma_{II}(\Gamma)$ implies $\langle \sigma, \tau \rangle \in S_I$, and similarly for player II with corresponding definitions. Thus,

A win-lose game is strictly determined if one of the players has winning strategies.

8

Notes on Computational Complexity

... I do think there are some very worthwhile and interesting
analogies between complexity issues in computer science and in
economics. ... They're in fact studying the limitations that have
arisen because of computational complexity. So there's a clear
link there with economics.

Karp (1987: 464)

8.1 INTRODUCTION

There is something very satisfactory in proving that a yes–no
problem cannot be solved in n, n^2 or 2^n steps, no matter what
algorithm is used.

Cook (1987: 417)

In most practical linear programming problems, with a constant
coefficient matrix A of dimension $m \times n$ say, the simplex algorithm
takes about $3m/2$ iterations to converge. But, theoretically, the algorithm can visit

$$2\binom{n}{m} = \frac{n!}{m!(n-m)!} > \left(\frac{n}{m}\right)^m$$

vertices. This number is at least 2^m, whenever $n \geq 2m$. Thus, the possibility of intractability, i.e. of computational complexity, is embedded in the algorithm. This intrinsic possibility was exploited by Klee
and Minty to show the existence of a class of (artificial) problems
with $m = n$ equality constraints in $2n$ non-negative variables where
the simplex algorithm required $2n - 1$ iterations, i.e. a visit to every
vertex of the problem!

Roughly speaking, the geometry of the reason for the intrinsic possibility of intractability is as follows:

(a) Since the simplex algorithm moves from vertex to vertex, first, find a polytope that has exponentially many vertices. Take, for example, a three-dimensional cube; it has 6 faces (i.e. 2×3 faces) and 8 vertices (i.e. 2^3 vertices), and thus a cube with $2d$ faces has 2^d vertices.

(b) Next, orient the cube such that the direction of decreasing cost is "upwards"; i.e., orient the sequence of exponentially many vertices (2^d), adjacent to one another, each higher than the "previously" (visited vertex).

(c) Then, for all $d > 4$, there exists a linear program with 2^d equations, 3^d variables, and integer coefficients with absolute value bounded by 4 such that the simplex may take $2^d - 1$ iterations to find the optimum.

Why, then, in practice, has simplex worked almost without exception? Is it luck, or could it have been human ingenuity and intuition in selecting judicious initial conditions? Or is it that the measure we have chosen to quantify intractability – the theory of computational complexity – is inadequate in nature and scope? Perhaps there is an element of truth in all of these possibilities.

Quite apart from this simple case, there is the recursion-theoretic status of the plethora of methods – ostensibly numerical, computational, and even tractable, if we are to believe textbooks – used in finding "solutions" to economic problems. I have in mind, apart from particular algorithms such as simplex, the recursion-theoretic status of general methods, widely used in economics: dynamic programming, the maximum principle, filtering, and variations thereof.[1] Do these methods come with tractable algorithms to compute their solutions? If not, what is the rationale behind the advocacy of the use of such methods by (even the) ideal economic decision-makers? Do such methods carry implicit solution techniques that have the status of the simplex algorithm, i.e., theoretically intractable but, practically well behaved and implementable?

---

[1] For example, in Ch. 6 part of the investigation was how to ensure, *a priori*, a computable REE which can then be learned by recursion-theoretic induction processes. This is, naturally, prior to any analysis or study of the tractability of the utilized induction process.

To even begin to answer these questions, it is above all necessary either to recast "the economic problem" recursion-theoretically, or to embed the methods in a model of computation (or, of course, both). Two ways to recast the economic problem recursion-theoretically were discussed in the previous two chapters. In this chapter, an intermediate strategy is adopted.

Thus, in Section 8.2, I begin by suggesting that the negative results of Chapter 3 can be circumvented by adopting, as a paradigmatic model of consumer behavior, Leijonhufvud's fertile construction of the *Marshallian Consumer* (MC). Then in Section 8.3 the Marshallian Consumer's sequential choice behavior is modelled algorithmically and shown to be tractable.

The concluding Section 8.4 summarizes the discussion and suggests broad directions in which the issues discussed in this chapter can be further developed. I want to suggest that the Marshallian Consumer is a far more plausible model of rational decision-making in economics than the Walrasian Consumer – the traditional rational agent in economic theory. The Marshallian Consumer is the one I had in mind as the paradigmatic case of the algorithmically rational agent in the formalisms of Chapter 3.

8.2 THE MARSHALLIAN CONSUMER'S TRACTABLE BEHAVIOR

> In Marshallian analysis, economic agents are conceived to be not so much rational as reasonable. Individuals fumble and grope rather than optimize.
>
> Clower (1984: 193–4)

It is now more than two decades since Axel Leijonhufvud suggested, in his remarkable Marshall Lectures at Cambridge,[2] that there was an alternative vision of procedurally consistent (descriptively more realistic) consumer behavior in Marshall (cf. also Clower 1984). I had the pleasure and privilege to be present at that lecture[3] and have tried, over the years, to extract the formal content in Leijonhufvud's

---

[2] Alas, the manuscript remains "unpublished" (Leijonhufvud 1974).
[3] Where, by the way, I was first introduced to the fascinating procedural world of Simon and the rich information and evolutionary economics of "old" UCLA.

reinterpretation of Marshall's *procedurally rational agent*. I have found it useful to characterize Leijonhufvud's Marshallian Consumer, and the underlying sequential choice behavior, in the following schematic way:

(i) Marshall's Consumer does not make an *ex ante* optimal choice of an entire basket of goods, all at once.

(ii) The conception is that of a consumer who starts out at some date with a sum of money (and credits and debits) which is to last for a (given) time period, and who has some fairly definite notion, based on past experience, of *what a shilling is worth to her*.

(iii) She then sets about making a series of consecutive purchases (choices) through time.

(iv) We are to imagine the Marshallian Consumer shopping and weighing, in a sequence of (binary) comparisons between money and commodities, and at each stage making the choice of buying or not buying.

(v) Thus, the entire basket is composed sequentially.

(vi) At each stage, the past period's "final utility of money" serves the Marshallian Consumer as a rough index of the opportunity cost of one good in terms of all other goods.

(vii) This spares the mental health and the computational burden of the Marshallian Consumer by eliminating the need to contemplate marginal rates of substitution in n dimensions.

(viii) The Marshallian Consumer proceeds, conceptually, from the (lattice of the) consumption–commodity space, by sequential choices, "out" towards the budget constraint.

(ix) When the constraints become binding, the basket has been *composed*.

(x) The chosen basket may not be "optimal"; this may lead to a recalibration of the various relevant measuring rods.

As encapsulated and summarized by Leijonhufvud:[4]

This mode of behavior-description frees us from the obligation to assume that the agent knows, or thinks he knows, or thinks he probably knows,

---

[4] As a matter of fact, Leijonhufvud went on to suggest that the Marshallian Consumer may reside more comfortably within the utility-tree framework of choice suggested by Strotz, Gorman, and others. This "extensive-form" depiction of the Marshallian Consumer's behavioral dynamics can be given an even more direct algorithmic interpretation. I leave this for a future exercise.

beforehand, all the conditions formally required in order to solve the relevant constrained optimization problem. This Marshallian Consumer is able to act even when ignorant – and not just "uncertain" about some of the prices he will face and some of the relevant characteristics of the goods available in the market. Besides not being lamed by incomplete information, he is able to muddle along with a "computational capacity" that is quite limited relative to the information actually on hand and relative to the complexity of the task of putting together an optimal basket in n-dimensions. (Leijonhufvud 1974: 48)

What, then, of my negative results of Chapters 3 and 4? The important point about the results of Chapters 3 and 4 (and of 7 too) is that they do not imply that specific procedures are not implementable in dynamic choice situations; nor do they mean that algorithms cannot be found in well specified special contexts.[5]

Now let us accept, at least *pro tempore*, the descriptive rationale for the behavioral realism of the Marshallian Consumer. How can the basic elements be formalized procedurally? In the first instance the following basic elements must be defined, explicitly or implicitly:

(a) the budget *constraint*;
(b) a *set*, perhaps existing only in the "mind" of the Marshallian Consumer, defining those amounts ("values") of the basket that are minimally acceptable or desirable;
(c) some feeling of the *priorities* over the elements of the basket (again, perhaps, existing only in the "mind" of the Marshallian Consumer) – exhibited, for example, in the precise sequence of purchases.

These are, obviously, minimal elements characterizing the Marshallian Consumer's behavioral profile.[6] Given the modern facilities for experimental home shopping, the plethora of software to analyze home and other accounts, etc., let me assume that the Marshallian Consumer tries to simulate the sequential behavior *before* embarking with the empty shopping basket and a reasonably full wallet. Taking all of the above into consideration, a plausible but approximate model could be the following.

Denote by

R the feasible region determined by the budget constraint;

---

[5] I cannot repeat too often that the negative results are so-called universal results; if we ask for too much, and give too little, the books will not balance.

[6] And indeed, that of the standard consumer.

Ω the set of admissible values for the commodity basket (existing, perhaps, only in the mind of the Marshallian Consumer);

x^d an initial conjecture on possible values for the (vector of) amounts for the basket of purchases ($x^d \in \Omega$).

To make a workable model I add the following more specific assumptions:

$$R \equiv \{x \in E^n | N^T x = b\}; \tag{8.1}$$

i.e., initially at least, the feasible region is taken to be a set of linear equality constraints, with N an ($n \times n$) matrix with linearly independent columns, and E^n the n-dimensional Euclidean vector space.

Next, I need a structured, specific, assumption to encapsulate the relative priorities over the (potential) elements of the desired basket of commodities:

$$q_c(x) = \frac{1}{2}\langle x - x^d, Q_c(x - x^d)\rangle, \tag{8.2}$$

where Q_c is the current $n \times n$ (positive definite) weighting matrix, and q_c the current quadratic criterion function; i.e., the relative priorities are formalized by a quadratic criterion function, but, as will be seen, there is no built-in assumption that this captures, *ab inizio*, the preference structure of the Marshallian Consumer. Indeed, quite the contrary. We can begin, at the initial stages of the conceptual experiment, by assuming equal priorities over all desired commodities.

Now, a possible conceptual choice procedure for the Marshallian Consumer is the following:

MC ALGORITHM

Step 0. Given x^d and R, assume (any) initial weighting matrix Q_c.

Step 1. Using Q_c, solve:

$$\text{optimize}\{q_c(x) | x \in R\} \tag{8.3}$$

such that (8.1), is satisfied, to obtain a set of initial values, x_c.

Step 2. Let the MC inspect x_c; if the MC finds it acceptable, then $x_c \in \Omega$ (in fact, $x_c \in \Omega \wedge R$), stop. If not, let the MC specify the changes required in x_c such that they also lie in Ω; i.e.,

$$x_p = x_c + \sigma \tag{8.4}$$

where σ is the vector of desired changes to x_c.

Step 3. Use the following formula to compute

$$Q_n = Q_c + \mu Q_c \sigma \sigma' Q_c \, / \, \langle \sigma, Q_c \sigma \rangle \tag{8.5}$$

for some choice of the scalar $\mu \geq 0$.

Step 4. Set $Q_c = Q_n$ and return to step 1.

Remark 1. The behavioral content of the processes in (8.4) and (8.5) can be depicted in the Figure 8.1. The economic meaning of this sequential updating is outlined below (cf. the explanatory paragraphs above and below (8.15)).

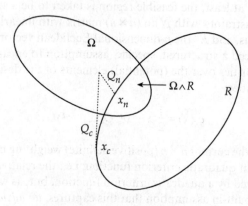

FIG. 8.1

Remark 2. The result of the MC Algorithm can be summarized as follows. Let the solution to (8.3) subject to (8.1) when Q_n in (8.5) is substituted for Q_c be denoted by x_n. Then (putting $H_c = Q_c^{-1}$)

$$x_n = x_c + \alpha P \delta, \quad P = I - H_c N (N^T H_c N)^{-1} N^T, \tag{8.6a}$$

$$\alpha = \mu \langle \delta, Q_c (x_c - x^d) \rangle / (\langle \delta, Q_c \delta \rangle + \mu \langle Q_c \delta, P H_c (Q_c \delta) \rangle)$$
$$= 1 / (n+1) \langle \delta, Q_c \delta \rangle^{1/2}, \quad \mu = 2/(n-1), \tag{8.6b}$$

and

$$\langle \delta, Q_c (x_c - x^d) \rangle = - (\langle \delta, Q_c \delta \rangle + \mu \langle Q_c \delta, P H_c (Q_c \delta) \rangle) / \mu (n+1) \langle \delta, Q_c \delta \rangle^{1/2}. \tag{8.6c}$$

Remark 3. A desirable local property of this algorithm is that, at every stage at which Q_c is updated and a new x_n is computed, the MC is more satisfied with this new solution compared with the "current" x_c.

I now come to the important technical question. Can it be shown that this innocuous-looking procedure converges *tractably*? The Marshallian Consumer makes choices in *real time*; hence, tractability is a crucial constraint.

8.3 KHACHIAN'S ELLIPSOID ALGORITHM AND THE COMPLEXITY OF POLICY DESIGN

Rather than revolutionizing the solving of linear programs, Khachiyan's publication has brought to the fore the gap between complexity theory and practice, and has caused a reconsideration of the value of "polynomiality" of algorithms.

Schrijver (198: 170)

In this section, the termination or tractable property of the MC Algorithm for the Marshallian Consumer's decision process is discussed in outline. In particular, I show that the MC's decision process terminates after a finite number of iterations if the model and the inequality constraints bounding the region Ω are assumed to be linear. The region Ω and the inequality constraints bounding it are still assumed to exist only in the mind of the Marshallian Consumer.

Convergence of the above algorithms in polynomial time is studied by establishing an equivalence with Khachian's (1979, 1980) ellipsoid algorithm for linear programming. The latter algorithm has been shown to terminate in polynomial time; i.e., the number of iterations required to arrive at a solution – or to establish the absence of one – is bounded by a polynomial in the original data of the problem (Khachian 1979, 1980; Kozlov *et al.* 1979).

In order to introduce the ellipsoid algorithm, consider first the problem of finding a feasible point satisfying the following system of inequalities:

$$\langle \mathbf{h}_i, \mathbf{x} \rangle \le g_i, \ i = 1, \dots p, \tag{8.7}$$

where $\mathbf{h}_i \in E^n$, $p \ge 2$, $n \ge 2$. Khachian's algorithm, summarized below, finds such a point, or establishes its nonexistence, in a finite number of iterations. Let L be the length of the binary encoding of the input data $\mathbf{h}_i$, $\mathbf{h}_i$, g_i, $i = 1, \dots, p$, i.e., the number of 0s and 1s needed to write these coefficients in binary form:

$$L = \sum_{i,j=1}^{n,p} \log_2(|h_{ij}| + 1) + \sum_{j=1}^{p} \log_2(|g_j| + 1) + \log_2 np + 2, \qquad (8.8)$$

where h_{ij} is the jth element of vector $\mathbf{h}_i$. Khachian's algorithm assumes that coefficients h_{ij}, g_j are integers. This can trivially be achieved, in general, by suitably scaling each inequality. The algorithm discussed below can also be used directly for nonintegers h_{ij}, g_j. In this case, the slight change in the properties of the algorithm are discussed in Goldfarb and Todd (1982).

KHACHIAN'S ALGORITHM
Step 1 (Initialization). Set $\mathbf{x}_o = 1$, $H_o = 2^{2L}I$, $k = 0$.
Step 2. If $\mathbf{x}_k$ satisfies

$$\langle \mathbf{h}_i \mathbf{x}_k \rangle < g_i + 2^{-L}, \ \forall i = 1, \ldots p, \qquad (8.9)$$

then terminate the algorithm with $\mathbf{x}_k$ as a feasible solution. If $k < 4(n+1)^2 L$, then go to step 3; otherwise, terminate the algorithm with the tractable, but negative, answer that no solution exists.
Step 3. Select any inequality for which

$$\langle \mathbf{h}_i \mathbf{x}_k \rangle \geq g_i + 2^{-L} \qquad (8.10)$$

and set

$$\mathbf{x}_{k+1} = \mathbf{x}_k - \frac{1}{(n+1)} \frac{H_k \mathbf{h}_i}{\langle \mathbf{h}_i, H_k \mathbf{h}_i \rangle^{1/2}}, \qquad (8.11)$$

and

$$H_{k+1} = \frac{n^2}{n^2 - 1} \left[H_k - \frac{2}{n+1} \frac{H_k \mathbf{h}_i \mathbf{h}_i^T H_k}{\mathbf{x}_p \mathbf{h}_i, H_k \mathbf{h}_i} \right]. \qquad (8.12)$$

Set $k = k + 1$ and go to step 2.

Some properties of the algorithm are discussed in Rustem and Velupillai (1985). The most important property, also referred to below, is that a feasible solution is returned or its absence is established in $4(n+1)^2 L$ iterations.

Consider now the problem of finding the solution to the system of inequalities (8.7) in the presence of linear equalities:

$$N^T \mathbf{x} = \mathbf{b}. \qquad (8.13)$$

In this case, given a starting point $\tilde{\mathbf{x}}_o$, the initial solution estimate is defined by $\mathbf{x}_o = \tilde{\mathbf{x}}_o - H_k N(N^T H_k N)^{-1}(N^T \tilde{\mathbf{x}}_o - b)$. It can be verified that $N^T \tilde{\mathbf{x}}_o = b$. In order that all $\mathbf{x}_k$ generated by the algorithms satisfy $N^T \mathbf{x}_k = b$, we have to replace (6a) by

$$\mathbf{x}_{k+1} = x_k - \frac{1}{n+1} \frac{P_k H_k \mathbf{h}_i}{\langle \mathbf{h}_i, H_k \mathbf{h}_i \rangle^{1/2}}, \tag{8.14}$$

where $P_k + I - H_k(N^T H_k N)^{-1} N^T$. It can also be verified that $P_k(\mathbf{x}_{k+1} - \mathbf{x}_k) = \mathbf{x}_{k+1} - \mathbf{x}_k$. All other steps of the algorithm remain unchanged. Thus, any feasible point generated by the algorithm also satisfies the linear equalities given by (8.13).

Let us now return to algorithm above and attempt to identify the reason why the Marshallian Consumer may wish to specify a given direction σ as a direction of "improvement." When the MC is asked in step 2 of the algorithm to specify σ or the preferred value $\mathbf{x}_p (= \mathbf{x}_c + \sigma)$, she is, in effect, required to specify the point, nearest to $\mathbf{x}_c$, that is in Ω. This "nearness" is measured with respect to the current weighting matrix Q_c. Thus, the MC is asked to specify $\mathbf{x}_p$, which is the solution of

$$\min\left\{ \frac{1}{2} \left\| \mathbf{x} - \mathbf{x}_c \right\|_{Q_c}^2 \middle| \langle \mathbf{h}, \mathbf{x} \rangle \le g \right\}, \tag{8.15}$$

where $\langle \mathbf{h}, \mathbf{x} \rangle \le g$ is one of the implicit constraints describing the region Ω and violated at $\mathbf{x}_c$. The MC may not know that such a constraint exists until he notices that $\mathbf{x}_c$ is violating it; i.e., $\langle \mathbf{h}, \mathbf{x} \rangle > g$. Clearly, the MC also does not know $\mathbf{h}$ and g, but can only specify $\mathbf{x}_p$. I argue below that this is sufficient to identify $\mathbf{h}$ to some degree, and thereby to quantify Ω, if $\mathbf{x}_p$ is interpreted as the solution of (8.15). This interpretation is shown to allow the use of Khachian's algorithm, discussed above, to solve for a feasible point of $\Omega \cap R$ in polynomial time by updating $H = Q^{-1}$ and using (8.11)–(8.12).

The solution of (8.15) can be obtained by writing the first-order necessary conditions of optimality.

$$\mathbf{x}_p - \mathbf{x}_c = -Q_c^{-1} \mathbf{h} \lambda, \quad \langle \mathbf{h}, \mathbf{x}_p \rangle \le g, \quad \lambda(\langle \mathbf{h}, \mathbf{x}_p \rangle - g) = 0, \quad \lambda \ge 0. \tag{8.16}$$

Thus, $\sigma = \mathbf{x}_p - \mathbf{x}_c = -Q_c^{-1} \mathbf{h} \lambda$ where the Lagrange multiplier (shadow price) λ is non-negative. It can be seen from (8.16) that

$$\begin{aligned} \lambda &= \langle \mathbf{h}, \mathbf{x}_p - \mathbf{x}_c \rangle / \langle \mathbf{h}, Q_c^{-1} \mathbf{h} \rangle \\ &= -\langle \mathbf{x}_p - \mathbf{x}_c, Q_c \mathbf{x}_p \mathbf{x}_c \rangle / \langle \mathbf{h}, \mathbf{x}_p - \mathbf{x}_c \rangle. \end{aligned}$$

Since $\lambda \ge 0$, these yield

$$\begin{aligned} \lambda &= \langle \mathbf{x}_p - \mathbf{x}_c, Q_c(\mathbf{x}_p - \mathbf{x}_c) \rangle^{1/2} / \langle \mathbf{h}, Q_c^{-1} \mathbf{h} \rangle^{1/2} \\ &\equiv \|\sigma\|_{Q_c} / \|\mathbf{h}\|_{Q_c^{-1}}. \end{aligned}$$

Thus, we have

$$\sigma / \|\sigma\|_{Q_c} = -Q_c^{-1}\mathbf{h} / \|\mathbf{h}\|_{Q_c^{-1}}. \tag{8.17}$$

It is shown in Rustem and Velupillai (1985) that the rank-one update (8.5) can be reformulated as (8.12) and that the algorithm can be made equivalent to Khachian's algorithm using (8.17).

8.4 CONCLUDING NOTES

> Perfection of a kind was what he was after,
> And the poetry he invented was easy to understand;
> . . .
>
> Auden, *Epitaph on a Tyrant*

The example in Section 8.2 has been chosen and discussed to show, partly at least, how and where the synergies are between traditional theory and computable economics: they complement each other in exactly the same way that classical, constructive, and computable analyses complement each other. In some sense I have tried to build up to this tentative conclusion by beginning with the negative implications of a recursion-theoretic vision of the standard framework.

On the more specific issue of computational complexity, are we, perhaps, asking for too much when we impose tractability requirements in economic choice situations? The example in Section 8.2 should give a negative answer to this question. On the other hand, it may be legitimate to ask whether computational complexity theory encapsulates the proper intuitive content of tractability.

In the earlier chapters I have worked, explicitly and implicitly, under the assumption of the Church–Turing thesis in computability theory and the Kolmogorov–Chaitin–Solomonoff thesis in algorithmic information theory. The former thesis is about the formal equivalence between the intuitive notion of effective calculability and the mathematical notion of (partial) recursive functions; the latter is about the formal equivalence between the intuitive notion of randomness and its mathematical encapsulation algorithmically. What, analogously, would be a thesis in computational complexity theory? What, in other words, is the intuitive notion we are trying to formalize mathematically?

The lack of an acceptable answer may be an indication of the existence of a variety of alternative measures of tractability: average-case complexity, computational complexity, information-based complexity, etc. I do not know whether there is any possibility of achieving consensus in the form of a thesis for tractability analogous to the Church–Turing and the Kolmogorov–Chaitin–Solomonoff theses. Until such time as there is a consensus on a thesis equating the intuitive and the formal, the sense of ad-hockery that pervades the field may have to continue. No one has stopped using the simplex algorithm simply because the Klee–Minty results demonstrate its intractability.

The best that can be done, in the interim, is to follow the Linnean precept suggested, with characteristic simplicity and blunt directness, by the great Rutherford: continue to study individual classes of examples and classify them as stamp collectors would. This will progressively "refine" and sensitize intuition, and the formal will emerge, eventually. But the album for the stamp-collecting exercise will have to be a *model of computation*, under the Church–Turing thesis.

Leijonhufvud's Marshallian Consumer is studied, in this chapter, with Rutherford's Linnean precepts in mind. If the generalized decision problem model for economics, suggested at the end of Chapter 4, is to be made inductively useful, then large classes of such special cases (like the MC) will have to be studied, categorized, and catalogued. The hope of achieving generalized solutions to whole classes of decision problems will then be facilitated by progressively more precise theses of the Church–Turing and Kolmogorov–Chaitin–Solomonoff variety: for complexity, for consumer choice, and so on. The humble step of analyzing special classes of decision problems has, for too long, been submerged in the blind adherence to the apparent power of the standard, but noneffective, choice-theoretic paradigm. To undo its stranglehold, it is necessary to have the decision problem framework as a backdrop to an analysis of special classes of procedural choice problems. It is in this spirit that I have tried to analyze and formalize Leijonhufvud's Marshallian Consumer.

9
Explorations in Computable Economics

> Are there general procedures for finding shortcuts? . . . If you
> look at a map there is a procedure for finding a shortcut, but if
> you look at mathematics, there is no such procedure . . . There
> is no way of making mathematical decisions; there are always
> theorems whose proofs may or may not turn up. Turing . . .
> loved making little machines, and so he invented a device called
> a Turing Machine, and the most important thing that we know
> is that all mechanisms which, *like science*, are of this kind are
> expressible as Turing machines.
>
> Bronowski (1978: 76–7; emphasis added)

9.1 INTRODUCTION

> [T]he house of analysis . . . is to a large degree built on sand. I
> believe that I can replace this shifting foundation with pillars of
> enduring strength. They will not, however, support everything
> which today is generally considered to be securely grounded. I
> give up the rest, since I see no other possibility.
>
> Weyl (1917/1994: 1)

I want to suggest three topics, circumscribed by the tools used and
the concepts suggested in this essay, that could point the way
towards some of the possible frontiers of computable economics.

One of the most fundamental results in economic theory is appropriately referred to as the second fundamental theorem of welfare
economics.[1] This is deep in economic content and wide in scope; and

---

[1] Have we, in economics, been influenced by the existence of such "fundamental
theorems" in analysis, algebra, and number theory in looking for, and naming, results
analogously? Are our two "fundamental theorems" as basic to economic analysis as

it is profound in the mathematical foundations that establish its analytical validity. It is, therefore, legitimate to ask whether its effective
content is as rich and, if not, why not.

Second, there is production theory. All the examples in earlier
chapters have been based on the framework of traditional-choice
theory, whether it be rationality, adaptive behavior, learning, or
games. Paul Romer, one of the pioneers of endogenous growth
theory, has suggested a formalism for production processes that
seems to exploit recursion-theoretic ideas. I want to explore some
directions in which Romer's characteristically fertile suggestions can
be taken in an elementary recursion-theoretic way.

Third, coupled to the question about the effective content of the
Second Fundamental Theorem of welfare economics, there should
be an analogous question about *tâtonnement*.

There are, surely, many other interesting problems at the frontiers
of economics that can be studied recursion-theoretically. Other
scholars, technically better equipped and deeper and abler in their
economic intuition and historical vision than myself, may be motivated to tackle them when the computable approach to economics
attains the proverbial status of Kuhnian "normal science" – as I hope
and expect it will. I shall discuss only selected aspects of the above
three problems, from a recursion-theoretic point of view.

The appendix to this chapter is an exercise in methodological
exploration. The only purely methodological chapter in this book is
the overly formal Chapter 5. The main theme of that chapter is the
link between induction and simplicity. In the appendix to this chapter, I extend that methodological framework to suggest a way of
resolving a perennial issue in business cycle theorizing: is there a "scientific" way of effectively deciding between alternative formalizations of mathematical theories of economic fluctuations? I pose this
question for business cycle theories simply because practitioners of
Real Business Cycle theories have been meticulously detailed and
precise about their methodological credo and precepts. But I relegate
the discussion to an appendix simply because it is a purely speculative exploration.

The next three sections discuss, somewhat discursively, the above
three issues – (efficient) decentralization, aspects of the modelling of

---

the analogous results in these other mathematical disciplines? I don't know that there
can be a clear answer to such a rhetorical, perhaps even counterfactual, question. If
pressed, my tentative answer would be in the negative.

production structures, and the effectivity of *tâtonnement* – recursion theoretically. In the final section, I summarize the discussion and try to extract simple, applicable, methodological precepts.

9.2 EFFECTIVE DECENTRALIZATION

Citizens:	How can we be rid of the plague?
Delphic oracle:	Construct a cubic altar of double the size of the existing one.
Arrow and Debreu:	Can we use the Hahn–Banach theorem?

pace Stan Wagon,
The Banach–Tarski Paradox (Wagon 1985: v)

Consider a simple, and numerically concrete, example (cf. Scarf 1989) of a straight forward linear optimization problem as a standard linear programming (LP) versus an integer programming problem:

$$\text{Max} \quad 2(x + 3y)$$
$$\text{s.t.} \quad 2x + 3y \geq 5, \quad x, y \geq 0 \text{ and integers}$$

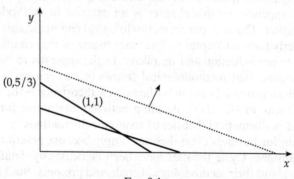

FIG. 9.1

The lessons and results seem to be as follows.

(i)   The solution to the LP version of the problem is $x = 0$; $y = 5/3$; and the optimal value of the dual variable (shadow price) is 1.

(ii) For the LP this means, according to the standard interpretation, that the second "industry" is activated and satisfies the zero profit criterion; the first industry is not activated since it makes a negative profit;

(iii) The optimal integer linear programming (ILP) solutions, on the other hand, are: $x = 1$; $y = 1$; and there does not exist an "optimal" value for the shadow prices such that the traditional zero profit condition holds simultaneously for the two activated industries.

(iv) In other words, in the standard LP case there is, for example, a clear economic interpretation of the (say, simplex) algorithm that substantiates the case for decentralized price and quantity decisions.

(v) In the ILP case, this classic "rule of free goods" and the "rule of profitability" fail; technically, this means that "unprofitable" industries may have to be activated at sectoral levels so that the overall (aggregate) economic system can be profitable.

(vi) Finally, there is no such thing as a uniform *procedure* – like simplex for LP – that can, in general, find the optimal solution (if it exists) to an arbitrary ILP.

The main implication of these lessons seem to be that we must ask a different kind of question when faced, say, with intrinsic indivisibilities: are there tractable methods to find feasible solutions? Surely, this is a move toward an economy peopled by boundedly rational agents satisficing their way through the intricacies of indivisible economic life tackling decision problems in their full generality? This was why I suggested, in Chapter 4, the latter as the paradigmatic choice framework and the boundedly rational agent as *the* general problem-solver, rather than proposing these two as special cases of the standard problem and orthodox rationality.

Leaving aside the indivisible – intrinsically nonconvex – case, let me now look at the standard mathematical justifications for decentralization via an appeal to the Second Fundamental Theorem of welfare economics. I cannot do better than to quote the maestro himself:

The second [fundamental theorem of welfare economics] provides a deeper economic insight and rests on a property of convex sets. It asserts that associated with a Pareto optimal state s of an economy, there is a price-vector p relative to which all the agents are in equilibrium . . . The treatment of the problem [of efficient decentralization] . . . given by means of convexity theory was rigorous, more general and simpler than the treatment by means of the differential calculus that had been traditional since Pareto. The supporting hyperplane theorem (more generally the Hahn–Banach theorem . . .) seemed to fit the economic problem perfectly. (Debreu 1984: 268–9)

Or did the economist transmogrify[2] "the economic problem" to "fit" the known theoretical technology? Every economist knows, or ought to know, that the Hahn–Banach theorem, as an extension theorem for liner functionals, can in fact be viewed as a generalization of the projection theorem[3] in appropriate spaces, i.e. the key analytical and conceptual device in generalizing optimization problems where, in particular, duality principles are exploited (as even in the simple numerical example above).

Now, the question I wish to pose is: what is the *effective content* of the Second Fundamental Theorem of welfare economics? I ask this question in the same sense, and in the same spirit, as I have asked analogous questions about rationality (Chapter 3), adaptive behavior (Chapter 4), learning REE (Chapter 6), and playability of (arithmetical) games (Chapter 7). Surely without an unambiguous answer to this question, it is not clear to what extent we have made a trade-off between rigor and numerical content.

There are at least two different ways to approach possible answers to this question, mirroring the two modes previously employed in this essay:[4] either we formulate the economic problem, *ab inizio*, recursion-theoretically and then appeal to a recursive version of the Hahn–Banach theorem (cf. Metakides *et al.* 1985: 87; or Metakides and Nerode, 1982: 128 ff.); or we take the standard formulation of the economic agent and her optimization problems and modify the framework to a computable analytic setting and, once again, rely on the recursive version of the Hahn–Banach theorem.[5]

I conjecture that the economic implications of the answers we get by choosing one or the other of the above two strategies will be funda-

---

[2] As in Auden's immortal lines:

> The students' flesh like his imagination
> *Makes fact fit theories* and has fashions too.

(letter to Lord Byron; emphasis added)

[3] Extensively used in my algorithm for the Marshallian Consumer's sequential behavioral activities, in the previous chapter.

[4] As in Chs. 3, 4, and 7, or as in the second part of Ch. 6.

[5] Again, this is in Ch. 6, where I investigated the computable content of REE from the point of view of computable analysis.

mentally different in precisely the sense suggested in the following way by Debreu (referring to his "topological" approach to economics):

Especially relevant to my narrative is the fact that the restatement of welfare economics in set-theoretical terms forced a re-examination of several of the primitive concepts of the theory of general economic equilibrium. (Debreu 1984: 269)

If we opt for the first solution, we will have algorithmically rational agents with their "rich" repertoire of incompletenesses, uncomputabilities, and undecidabilities operating in equally "exotic" recursively represented metric and other spaces; we may, I conjecture with even more conviction, have to be more modest than the maestro in our customary claims "for the success of the mathematization of economic theory":

one can describe the action of an economic agent by a vector in the commodity space R^l [when the commodities in the economy are l, finite, in number]. The fact that the commodity space has the structure of a real vector space is a basic reason for the success of the mathematization of economic theory. (Debreu 1984: 268)

On the other hand, if we choose to proceed along the second option, it is possible, I think, to continue "business as usual" – but at the price of some vagueness about the numerical content of our theorems and unclarity in the procedural status of decision-makers and their decision problems.

9.3 NOTES ON RECURSION-THEORETIC PRODUCTION THEORY

The same arrogance that made people at the turn of the century think that almost everything had already been invented sometimes leads us to think that there is nothing left to discover about the institutions that can encourage economic development. . . . Just as in a child's chemistry set, *there is far more scope for discovering new institutional arrangements than we can possibly understand.*

Romer (1992: 66, 89; emphasis added)

In a recent publication, Paul Romer broached new visions for an understanding of the growth process in widely differing economic systems (Romer 1993). He points out that the conventional modelling of growth processes are deficient in their incorporation of the role and genesis of *ideas*. To rectify this deficiency, he proposes an economic definition of ideas based, *inter alia*, on a distinction between their use and their production. These definitions have an evolutionary and algorithmic underpinning to them; moreover, the institutional setting in which ideas are used and produced is also given an evolutionary basis.

In this section I make an attempt to encapsulate some of these fertile and imaginative suggestions in a recursion-theoretic formalism. Thus, Romer's suggestions are first summarized with such a formalism as the backdrop for the interpretations; then, building on the skeletal model developed by Romer, an algorithmic interpretation of his formalism is suggested which makes the empirical implementation of the modified, computable model immediate. In particular, the framework becomes natural for a genetic (or any other evolutionary) programming implementation. This gives the algorithmic formulation an evolutionary flavor.

Romer's suggestions to formalize the use and production of ideas in growth models

The economic underpinning of Romer's definition of an idea is that it is *nonrival* and *excludable*.[6] "Nonrival" means that the use of an idea by one agent does not deprive other agents from using it. "Excludability" signifies the feasibility of an agent preventing other agents from using it.[7]

The functional characterization of an idea is based on the dichotomy between its use and its production. Romer explains this dichotomy in a characteristic economic setting: ideas are used for producing human capital; in turn, human capital is used to produce ideas.[8] This simple but illuminative description to evoke definitions suggests an economic setting in which ideas may usefully enhance the descriptive and explanatory power of (endogenous) growth models.[9]

---

[6] To put this definition in perspective, it can be contrasted with the characterization of a standard public good, which is nonrival but also nonexcludable.

[7] This is where cryptology, in particular public-key cryptology, enters the scheme of things.

[8] Human capital is, on the other hand, an excludable, rival good.

[9] I return to this theme later in this section.

For the formal definition of an idea, Romer resorts to the imaginative metaphor of toy chemistry sets.[10] Such sets typically consist of "a collection of N jars, each containing a different chemical element." Thus, in a set with N jars, there can be at least 2^{K-1} combinations of K elements ($K = 1, \ldots, N$). If we move from a child's chemistry set to a typical garment factory in the Free Trade Zone (FTZ) of a developing country, we might find that, say, sewing a shirt entails 52 distinct, sequenced activities. There are thus $52! = 10^{68}$ distinct orderings of the sequences in the preparation of a shirt. Now, as Romer perceptively notes,

For any realistic garment assembly operation, almost all the possible sequences for the steps would be wildly impractical,[11] but if even a very small fraction of sequences is useful, there will be many such sequences. It is therefore extremely unlikely that any actual sequence that humans have used for sewing a shirt is the best possible one. (Romer 1993: 69)

Thus,

The potential for continued economic growth comes from the vast search space that we can explore. The curse of dimensionality [i.e., 2^{K-1}, or $52! = 10^{68}$] is, for economic purposes, a remarkable blessing. To appreciate the potential for discovery, one need only consider the possibility that an extremely small fraction of the large number of possible mixtures may be valuable. (Romer 1993: 68–9)[12]

There are some problems with these imaginative and interesting observations, notwithstanding their casual and heuristic nature. First of all, there is the perennial question of the existence of a best sequence. Second, even if existence can be proved, in some mathematical sense – it is not clear that it can be discovered and implemented in an operational sense. Third, there will not be any feasible way of discovering, formally, even the "extremely small fraction" of sequences that may well be valuable. Finally, even in the unlikely

---

[10] Economists of my vintage will recall Trevor Swan's brilliant metaphor of Meccano sets "to put up a scarecrow . . . to keep off the index-number birds and Joan Robinson herself" (Swan 1956: 343). Is it a sign of the times that our metaphors have "evolved" from the *mechanical* to the *chemical?*

[11] I have, for example, personally seen the synchronized and immaculate sequencing of button-holes and buttons for shirts being prepared in exemplary fashion in Bangkok and compared it with the somewhat haphazard methods employed in Colombo.

[12] This, surely, is a basis for "learning by doing" emanating from Lundberg's famous "Horndal effect," made famous by Arrow (1962) and David (1975: ch. 3).

event that all of these issues can be resolved satisfactorily, there is the real question of the transition from the currently implemented sequence to a "more valuable region" of the feasible domain. Unless the currently utilized sequence is in the neighborhood of the "extremely small valuable fraction," it is unlikely that a transition will make economic sense in the context of a pure growth model with its given institutional background. The point at which development will have to be distinguished from pure growth may well be located in this transition manifold, to be somewhat pseudo-mathematical about it.

These problems need not be faced as squarely within the traditional production-theoretic framework with its handmaiden, the Book of Blueprints.[13] In the traditional framework, the well defined concepts of the efficient frontier and concomitant best-practice technologies and so on make most, if not all, of the above issues almost irrelevant. But, by the same token, they make it impossible to raise the interesting and important issues that Romer is trying to broach.

Romer emphasizes time-sequenced processes and, hence, must have something more than the Book of Blueprints metaphor for the repository or encapsulation of ideas. Not even "The Library of Babel"[14] can usefully encapsulate the vast vistas that Romer is trying

---

[13] Obviously, the book must have an "appendix" instructing the user on the necessity and mode of using the *axiom of choice*. Every indiscriminate reliance on indexing over a continuum of agents, technologies, etc., is an implicit appeal to the axiom of choice, or one of its noneffective and nonconstructive equivalents (cf. Velupillai 1999b).

[14] "The content of [the book] was . . . deciphered: some notions of combinative analysis, illustrated with examples of variation with unlimited repetition. These examples made it possible for a librarian of genius to discover the fundamental law of the Library. This thinker observed that all the books , no matter how diverse they might be, are made up of the same elements . . . He also alleged a fact which travellers have confirmed: *In the vast Library there are no two identical books.* From these two incontrovertible premises he deduced that the library is total and that its shelves register all the possible combinations of the twenty-odd orthographical symbols (a number which, though extremely vast, is not infinite): in other words, all that is given to express, in all languages. Everything: the minutely detailed history of the future . . . the interpolations of every book in all books" (Borges 1964: 54).
The operational content of the two propositions in this paper is philosophically interpretable in terms of this particular story by the inimitable Borges. The paradoxes and the treachery of the finite can, in my opinion, best be highlighted by *combinatorial* analysis within the discipline provided by recursion theory. Indeed, classic Gödelian incompleteness results can easily be invoked to cast formal doubt on the (effective) existence of "The Library of Babel." I have always been convinced that Borges must have such paradoxical conclusions in mind with this and many other related constructions.

to unfold. If it can, it will immediately be invalidated by a suitable application of one of the classic incompleteness theorems of Gödel. This, however, might be an unnecessarily nihilistic approach, and that is clearly not Romer's intention. I believe that he is trying to open some manageable vistas without trying to view all of the contents of Pandora's proverbial box. I believe it can be done, albeit with a good dose of ad-hockery. Such is the backdrop for my formal interpretation of the Romer suggestions and the basis for the two propositions I derive in this section.

To return to Romer's ideas on *ideas*, the casual empiricism of the above two quotes, underpinned by the metaphor of the child's toy chemistry set and its functions, suggests to him the analogy of ideas as mixtures, or as each of the potentially feasible 2^{K-1} mixtures (i.e., each of the $52! = 10^{68}$ ways of sequencing the sewing of a shirt):

Within the metaphor of the chemistry set, it is obvious what one means by an idea. Any mixture can be recorded as a bit string, an ordered sequence of 0s and 1s [of length N] . . . [A]n idea is the increment in information that comes from sorting some of the bit strings into two broad categories: useful ones and useless ones. . . .

When a useful mixture is discovered . . . the discovery makes possible the creation of economic value. It lets us combine raw materials of low intrinsic value into mixtures that are far more valuable. Once we have the idea, the process of mixing [the production function] will require its own (specialized capital and labor). For example, the bit string representing nylon requires a chemical processing plant and skilled workers. Important as these tangible inputs are, it is still the idea itself that permits the resulting increase in value. In this fundamental sense, *ideas make growth and development possible.* (Romer 1993: 68; emphasis added)

The final metaphoric invocation is to get hints on the way to encapsulate, formally, the role played by ideas, defined as evolving bit-strings, when "used to produce human capital." Here Romer relies on neurophysiological metaphors: ideas literally reconfigure the architecture of the neural network representation (cf. Chapter 4) of what Simon would term the Thinking (Wo)Man.[15] "Ideas . . . represented as pure pieces of information, as bit strings" (Romer 1993: 71) enhance the productivity of physical capital solely by a rearrangement of the possible permutations of the constituent

---

[15] I don't think there is the slighted hint or suggestion that Romer subscribes to any version of the serial, centralized AI propagandists when he makes these analogies and invokes such neurophysiological metaphors.

elements that go into its manufacture, be it a process, such as sewing a shirt, or a piece of equipment, say a computer. Similarly, they enhance the value of human capital by reconfiguring the physical architecture underlying, say, thought processes:

Now consider human capital. In my brain there are different physical connections between my neurons. . . . [T]he knowledge that reading a software manual [for a new computer and new wordprocessing software gives] rearranges connections in my brain and makes my human capital more valuable. . . . The increased value is created by new ideas. Whether it takes the form of a hardware design, software code, or an instruction manual, an idea is used to mix or arrange roughly the same physical ingredients in ways that are more valuable. And in each case, these ideas can be represented as pure pieces of information, as bit strings. (Romer 1993: 71)

Once again, therefore, ideas represented as bit-strings encapsulating "pure pieces of information"[16] function as inputs into a physical architecture representing human capital and transform its "wiring," so to speak, in such a way that it is able to process them more effectively. From standard results in automata and computability theory, going back to the classic works by McCulloch and Pitts (cf., again, Chapter 4), Kleene, and others, it is well known that neural network architectures can be given recursion-theoretic formalisms as automata of varying degrees of complexity. To be consistent with the standard postulates of rationality in economic theory, however, it is necessary to postulate an architecture that is formally equivalent to a Turing machine. Such an architecture allows rational decision processes to exhibit the kind of formal untamability of ideas.

Let me expand on the heuristics of this last comment a little more (to supplement the previous discursive comments). The inadequacy of the traditional Book of Blueprints vision of feasible technologies becomes patently evident if any such interpretation is attempted for ideas held by rational economic agents interpreted as Turing machines. The background to this statement is provided, for example, by the Busy Beaver (cf. Chapter 8). Even if the neurons in a brain are finite, not even the proponents of strong artificial intelligence (AI) would suggest that the world of ideas in any unit can be formally tamed or accessed – unless by magic or the kind of sleight of hand involved in invoking the axiom of choice. Somehow, somewhere, the

[16] The ideal way to proceed, at this point, would be to interpret and define information also recursion-theoretically, for which there is a well developed toolkit provided by algorithmic information theory (cf. Ch. 5 above).

open-endedness of ideas must assert itself in some kind of indeterminacy in models of growth and development. That is why the past can never hold all the secrets about the future. Trivial though this remark may sound, to encapsulate it formally in an interesting and operational way is not easy. And without such a formalism it will not be possible to delimit the range of validity of Romer's fertile ideas. Hence the attempt at a recursion-theoretic formalism – although this is only one of the reasons.[17]

This completes the background of intuitive building-blocks. We can now piece together a recursion-theoretic formalism. Before doing this, however, it is necessary to summarize Romer's production sub-model which is to be embedded in an (endogenous) growth framework. Romer considers output, Y, to be an additive function of a standard production function and a term representing the production of ideas, one for each of n sectors as follows:

$$Y = F(K, L, T) = \sum_{j=1}^{n} G_j(K_j, L_j, H_j; A_j).$$
(9.1)

In addition to the conventional notation, we have

H_j: human capital used in sector (or activity) j;

A_j: an "idea" characterizing sector (or activity) j;

The search for new ideas is formalized as a general dynamical system as follows:

$$A(t + 1) = S[H_A(t), (A_1(t), A_2(t), \ldots, A_N(t)), (H_1(t), H_2(t), \ldots H_n(t))].$$
(9.2)

This has the following interpretation: the genesis of new ideas is a function of:

$H_A(t)$ human capital used exclusively in the search of the "space" of ideas at time t;

$A_i(t)$ $(i = 1, \ldots, N(n \leq N))$, the collection of ideas available in a specified economic region at time t.

---

[17] In fact, and perhaps more importantly, the world of discovery is surely a subset of the world of inventions in the domain of ideas. Hence, also, my firm conviction that constructive mathematics, built on intuitionistic foundations, is a better framework in this particular area of economics. I view the recursion-theoretic messages of this essay as a halfway house between such an ideal and the current orthodoxy of Bourbakian formalism in standard economic theory.

The role of ideas in enhancing human capital and a learning-by-doing specification can together be captured in the following way to complete the output submodel:

$$H(t + 1) = \Omega\ (H(t),\ A(t)]. \tag{9.3}$$

Now, according to the intuitive definitions:

(a) $A_i(t)$, $(\forall i + 1, \ldots, N)$, are specified as bit strings.
(b) $H_j(t)$, $(\forall j + 1, \ldots, n)$, when considered as arguments of $G_j(\forall j = 1, \ldots, n)$, are neural networks; to be consistent with the rationality postulates of economic theory, these neural networks must be capable of computation universality.

Then, by the Church–Turing Thesis, we can represent each H_j, $j = 1, \ldots, n$, and H_a as programs (or algorithms) computationally equivalent to the corresponding Turing machine.

Next, by stacking the bit-strings A_i, $\forall i = 1, \ldots, N$, we can consider the prevailing collection of ideas as a program (or algorithm).[18] This means that the arguments of the function S in (9.2) are a collection of programs, and thus, search can be said to be conducted in the space of programs. At this point, a direct genetic programming interpretation of the (computable) search function S makes the dynamical system (9.2) naturally evolutionary. However, the bit-strings representing ideas can be retained as the data structures for the programs, partial recursive functions, and Turing machines in (9.1)–(9.3). Then search will be conducted in the space of programs and data structures.

A similar interpretation for (9.3) is quite straightforward. However, (9.1) is an entirely different matter. Standard definitions define the arguments of F and K_j and L_j as arguments in G_j on the domain of real numbers. Given the algorithmic definitions of H_j and A_j, it is clear that G_j must be a partial recursive function for the whole system (9.1)–(9.3) to make analytic sense. This means one of two possible resolutions:

- K_j and L_j $(\forall j = 1, \ldots, n)$ must be defined as computable reals; hence extended redefinitions of the domain of definition of H_j and A_j from the computable numbers to the computable reals; or

---

[18] Recall that "[A]n idea is the increment in information that comes from sorting . . ." In this connection see the illuminative discussion in Nelson and Winter (1982: ch. 4, §1) on "Skills as Programs," and Bronowski's Silliman Lectures (Bronowski 1978: ch. 3).

- K_j and L_j must be defined over the (countable set of) computable numbers.

Either way, on the one hand standard constrained optimization must be replaced by combinatorial optimization; and on the other hand one loses the applicability of separating hyperplane theorems – as discussed in the previous sub-section – and hence welfare and efficiency properties of equilibria cannot, in general, be derived. The next two formal propositions give recursion-theoretic content to this negative assertion .

PROPOSITION 9.1. Given the algorithmic interpretation of (9.2), there is no effective procedure to "locate" an arbitrary Pareto-improving configuration of ideas from the given configuration as an initial condition.

Remark. The proof of this proposition is based on a simple application of the Rice or Rice–Shapiro theorems.

PROPOSITION 9.2. Given an initial, empirically determined configuration of ideas represented algorithmically in (9.2), there is no effective procedure to determine whether S, implemented as a genetic program, will halt (whether at a Pareto-improved configuration or not).

Remark. This proposition can be proved by appealing to the halting problem for Turing machines or, alternatively, by exploiting the diophantine properties of recursively enumerable sets and then applying the results used in showing the unsolvability of Hilbert's Tenth Problem (cf. Chapter 7).

These two propositions cast doubts about the blessings of the "curse of dimensionality" to which Romer refers (cf. above and Romer 1993: 68–9). There are no effective procedures, discoverable *a priori* and systematically, to determine which "small fraction of the large number of possible mixtures may be valuable." This is why economic development, like the evolutionary paradigm itself, is so difficult to encapsulate in simplistic, formal, growth models – endogenous or not. Proposition 9.1, therefore, is a formal statement of the heuristic comments made earlier in this section as the background building-blocks for the model.

I suppose that the moral of the algorithmic formulation and the implication of the two propositions are that evolutionary models of growth *à la* Nelson and Winter have been, together with Molière's

M. Jourdain, speaking prose all along; and that Romer is absolutely right, on the basis of his intuitive definitions, to conclude that:

a *trained person* is still the central input in the process of trial and error, experimentation, guessing, hypothesis formation, and articulation that ultimately generates a valuable new idea that can be communicated to and used by others. (Romer 1993: 71; emphasis added)

To that extent, the model has to be formally open-ended; i.e. with some indeterminateness to be "closed" by the "trained person." However, the indeterminacy is not arbitrary: there must be, proverbially, *some method in the madness*. The above two propositions are an attempt to encapsulate formal indeterminateness in a structured way. Some kind of formal border between what can be known, learned, and "told" – i.e. formally described – and what cannot be so described defines the dividing line between the neat and determined world of formal growth models and the messy and evolutionary development process. The skeletal recursion-theoretic formalism, and the interpretation of Romer's ideas given above and the ensuing two propositions, make it possible to indicate the formal nature of this dividing line. In general, processes that are *recursively enumerable but not recursive* allow the kind of indeterminacy I am suggesting. The proofs of the above two propositions would locate the indeterminate range without actually determining it, to put it somewhat paradoxically. For, if not, there might be the unwarranted suspicion that I have tried to resurrect the logical positivistic dogma of the *Wiener Kreis*! Nothing can be further from my intentions. The existence of the dividing line and its formal indeterminacy is, more than anything else, what makes it necessary to resort to evolutionary selection criteria, and hence the applicability of genetic programming techniques.

But then, Simon, Nelson, Winter, Day, and others have been telling this to economists, within behavioral, institutional and evolutionary models of growth and development since at least the mid-1950s.

9.3 EFFECTIVE *TÂTONNEMENT*?

[P]erfectly respectable equations have a natural interpretation
as models of physically impossible devices.

Stewart (1991: 665)

The excess demand functions play a pivotal role in standard proofs of the existence of varieties of Walrasian equilibria. In view of the celebrated – almost startling – results of Sonnenschein–Debreu–Mantel (for convenience referred to as S–D–M) theorems, it is possible (and easy) to show that the dynamics of a *tâtonnement*, via the excess demand functions, is essentially arbitrary. In other words, the *tâtonnement* process can be represented as as:

$$\dot{p} = \varphi(p), \qquad (9.4)$$

where: $\varphi(p)$ is the vector of excess demand functions.

It is, then, a simple exercise to show that intuitively acceptable economic reasons underpinning the *tâtonnement* process in (9.4) induce a vector field on a relevant domain of the unit sphere. Then, in view of S–D–M theorems, the geometry of the resulting flow can be shown to be arbitrary. An interpretation of (9.4) as a differential, topological, or measurable dynamical object contains too little structure for it to be tamed even by the massive mathematical formalisms of such systems. The arbitrariness of the geometry (or the equivalent dynamics) of the flow is one of the reasons for the impossibility of extracting an economically meaningful procedure from conventional proofs of the existence of varieties of Walrasian equilibria.

The analogous result, when (9.4) is interpreted from a recursion-theoretic viewpoint, is that the characterization of its limit set is *effectively undecidable*. This means, simply, that the steady-state or equilibrium characterization of (9.4) is effectively undecidable. In other words, it is possible to encapsulate and delineate the meaning and scope of the notion "arbitrary' emanating in a dynamical systems context in the precise recursion theoretic notion of effective undecidability.[19]

At a more elementary economic level, there is the standard mapping:[20]

$$P_{t+1} = \frac{P_t + M(p_t)}{[P_t + M(p_t)]e}, \qquad (9.5)$$

where: $M(p_t)$ is based on the excess demand function $\varphi(p)$, and e is the appropriately dimensioned unit column vector. This mapping, interpreted as a (topological) mathematical object, is then shown to

---

[19] Of course under the assumption, once again, of the Church–Turing thesis.

[20] I follow the standard textbook notation, appropriately modified, in Arrow and Hahn (1971).

possess the fix-point property on the basis of various technical assumptions, not all of which are given readily intuitive economic interpretations. Next, the fix-point property is interpreted as an economic equilibrium "proof."

Nothing in this standard exercise, at almost any level of mathematical or economic sophistication, warrants the claim that one has: "been able to establish that for the economy here described there exists a set of 'signals' – market prices – that will lead agents to make decisions that are mutually compatible" (Arrow and Hahn, 1971: 29). It is "unwarranted' not only because of the standard criticism levelled against nonconstructive and noneffective existence proofs, but particularly because the fix-point itself is, in general, noneffective. In more vivid language, this means that the "signals' cannot be effectively encoded, in general, for economic agents to be "led to make decisions that are mutually compatible."

On the other hand we could adopt the alternative path of interpreting the mapping (9.5) as a recursion-theoretic object *ab inizio* and implement the economic procedure intrinsic to it, say on an appropriately encoded Turing machine (TM). This means that:[21]

    (a) the sequence of price vectors must, at least, be a recursively enumerable (RE) object;

    (b) the constituent functions, $M(p)$, and the underlying excess demand functions, $\varphi(p)$, must be at least partial recursive functions (PRC).

Both of these properties have natural and intuitive economic interpretations that are intrinsically procedural. Moreover, no hidden appeals to dubious set-theoretic axioms will have to be made at any stage of the analysis.

What would be the analogous recursion-theoretic question to be posed to the TM that has been encoded to implement the economic procedure inherent in (9.5)? "Analogous," that is, to the topological questions conventionally posed about the existence of a fix-point for (9.4), and "analogous" to the geometric questions posed to (9.4) viewed as a differential, topological, or measurable dynamical system? It will be the following:[22]

---

[21] There is an alternative strategy that can be pursued along computable analytic lines.

[22] Exactly analogous to the results in Ch. 4.

QUESTION 9.1. Given an arbitrary initial price "signal" as an input to the appropriately (and effectively) encoded TM, is there an effective procedure to determine whether it will "halt" at an economically meaningful final configuration?

In view of the diophantine nature of recursively enumerable sets, the general answer to this questions turns out to be negative. The negative result simply indicates that more structure has to be imposed on $M(p)$ and the implicit excess demand functions, $\varphi(p)$; but more interesting from an economic point of view is that there is a potential trade-off between *more* structure on $M(p)$ and $\varphi(p)$ as PRCs and *some* structure on the recursively enumerable sequence of price vectors. Either way, they translate into a restriction of power of the TM to, say, some particular finite automaton (FA). Then we can translate these structural assumptions to economic, behavioral, and institutional postulates implying constraints on rationality and market structures.

What, then, of the mathematical and economic statuses of the technique of proof utilized to prove Question 9.1 as the following proposition?

PROPOSITION 9.3. There is no effective procedure to determine whether (9.5) will eventually "halt" at an economically meaningful final configuration when initialized with effectively encoded price "signals."

Proof. By Rice's theorem and the "halting" problem for TMs, there is no such effective procedure.

Remark. Rice's theorem is exploited in interpreting the attempt to impose structure via an "economically meaningful final configuration."

This is nothing but a minor variant of the exercises in Chapter 4.

9.4 CONCLUDING NOTES

> It is so hard to dream posterity
> Or haunt a ruined century . . .
>
> Auden, *People and Places*

Two issues that are intimately related to the topics discussed in this chapter should have been at least mentioned in the main body of this chapter: the status of the socialist calculation debate in the light of algorithmic and computational complexity theories, and the recursion-theoretic sources of multiple equilibria in macrodynamic models of growth and cycles. But because this chapter has become disproportionately large, I must limit myself to cursory remarks on these two important issues.

Socialist economies may have collapsed with the paradigmatic and proverbial Wall, and the Iron Curtain too may have disintegrated,[23] but the "social planner" is alive and well in many representative agent models in macrodynamics. I have continued to be puzzled at the reliance on the feasibility of decentralization, on the basis of appeals to the Second Fundamental Theorem of welfare economics. It is as if the ghosts of Lange and Taylor have never been properly exorcised, in spite of the powerful empirical reasons put forward by von Mises, Hayek, and Robbins.

I conjecture that the tools of algorithmic and computational complexity theory can be used to indicate the computational infeasibility of the institutions of so-called socialist market economies based on Lange–Taylor type arguments. Moreover, until the effective content and status of the Hahn–Banach theorem is rigorously analyzed, I am equally convinced that reliance on the Second Fundamental Theorem of welfare economics to buttress the use of representative agent models is misguided.

In a paper, the origins of which were the Vilfredo Pareto Lecture, entitled "The Problem of Multiple Equilibria," Costas Azariadis states that:[24]

This essay regards multiple equilibria in dynamic economies as a departure from the Cauchy–Peano theorem and related results that ensure uniqueness of solutions to well-defined initial value problems. These violations are due to a shortage of initial conditions, indeterminate state spaces or else to set-valued laws of motion. (Azariadis, 1992: 2)

I conjecture, instead, that this lack of uniqueness should be interpreted as coming from the *lack of computability*. By this I mean a lack of sufficient recursivity in the underlying space in which the dynamics is embedded. Now, there are two ways in which this conjecture can be discussed:

---

[23] Although, of course, the bamboo curtain continues to flutter merrily onwards.

[24] I am not sure about the technical correctness of the above statement, i.e. that Cauchy–Peano guarantees existence; for uniqueness, one must add Lipshitz conditions or their equivalents. But let that pass.

(01)   by investigating the recursion-theoretic status of the set existence theorems that guarantee Cauchy–Peano; or

(001)   Or by constructing an uncomputable solution to a computable dynamical system, say an ordinary differential equation (ODE).

The more fertile way would be to proceed via (001). The reason is as follows. Take the standard, elementary exposition of the initial value problem to an ODE. I follow the lucid exposition in Coddington (1961: ch. 5). Find solutions to the equation

$$y' = f(x, y), \tag{9.6}$$

where f is any continuous real-valued function defined on some rectangle

$$R: |x - x_0| \le a, |y - y_0| \le b, (a, b > 0) \tag{9.7}$$

in the real (x, y)-plane. The idea is to show that on some interval I containing x_0 there exists a solution φ of (9.6) such that

$$\phi(x_0) = y_0; \tag{9.8}$$

in other words, there exists a real-valued, differentiable function ϕ satisfying (9.8) such that

$$(x, \phi(x)) \in R, \text{ and } \phi'(x) = f(x, \phi(x)), \forall x \in I. \tag{9.9}$$

ϕ is then called a solution to the initial value problem (IVP)

$$y' = f(x, y), y(c_0) = y_0 \text{ (on } I). \tag{9.10}$$

When we use the method of successive approximation to demonstrate the existence of solutions on an IVP, we begin by showing its equivalence to the following integral equation:

$$y' = y_0 + \int_{x_0}^{x} f(t, y) dt \text{ (on } I). \tag{9.11}$$

Again, by a solution to (9.11) on I I mean that there exists a ϕ, continuous and real-valued on I, such that

$$(x, \phi(x)) \in R, \forall x \in I \text{ and } \forall x \in I \Rightarrow \phi(x) = y_0 + \int_{x_0}^{x} f(t, \phi)(t)) dt. \tag{9.12}$$

Now, in solving (9.11), we consider, as a first approximation to a solution,

$$\phi_0(x) = y_0. \tag{9.13}$$

Obviously, (9.13) satisfies the initial condition given in (9.10). Compute

$$\phi_1(x) = y_0 + \int_{x_0}^x f(t, \phi_0(t))\mathrm{d}t = y_0 + \int_{x_0}^x f(t, y_0)\mathrm{d}t. \qquad (9.14)$$

If the space on which the flow takes place allows "contraction," we can expect ϕ_1 to be a closer approximation to the final solution than ϕ_0. If we continue this process, we get (again):

$$\phi_0(x) = y_0 \qquad (9.13)$$

and

$$\phi_{n+1}(x) = y_0 + \int_{x_0}^x f(t, \phi_n(t))\mathrm{d}t, \, n = 1, 2, \ldots \qquad (9.15)$$

Again, on a suitable space on which the flow takes place, we might take limits such that

$$\lim_{n \to \infty} \phi_n(x) = \phi(x) \qquad (9.16)$$

and ((9.12) again):

$$\phi(x) = y_0 + \int_{x_0}^x f(t, \phi(t))\mathrm{d}t. \qquad (9.12)$$

The functions $\phi_0, \phi_1, \phi_2, \ldots$ defined by (9.15) are the successive approximations to the IVP or to a solution to (9.11). At this point, Coddington gives a suggestive picture to describe or explain the method of successive approximations. Here I follow him quite literally:

One way to picture the successive approximations is to think of *a machine S* (for solving)[25] which converts functions ϕ into new functions $S(\phi)$ defined by

$$S(\phi)x = y_0 + \int_{x_0}^x f(t, \phi(t))\mathrm{d}t.$$

A solution to the initial value problem [(9.10)] would then be a function ϕ which moves through the machine untouched, that is, a function satisfying $S(\phi) = \phi$. Starting with $\phi_0(x) = y_0$, we see that S converts ϕ_0 into ϕ_1, and then ϕ_1 into ϕ_2. In general, $S(\phi_k) = \phi_{k+1}$, and ultimately we end up with a ϕ such that $S(\phi) = \phi$. (Coddington 1961: 201–2; emphasis added)

Now we want to grant the IVP all that is granted by the conventional mathematician both pure and applied (hence including economists). Then we want to ask whether the S-machine can get "jammed," enter a loop, or even break down when, finally, ϕ is its

[25] Could the S-machine be a Turing machine? The answer is: in general *no*; or not necessarily. If it is not a Turing machine, what can it be? A non-algorithmic machine!

input. The answer is in the affirmative, and can be summarized in the following celebrated theorem from computable analysis.

THEOREM 9.1. There exists an ordinary differential equation with initial condition

$$\phi'(t) = F(t, \phi(t)), \phi(0) = 0$$

such that $F(x, y)$ is computable on the rectangle $\{0 \le x \le 1, -1 \le y \le 1\}$, but *no solution* of the differential equation is computable on any interval $[0, \sigma]$, $\sigma > 0$.

Now rewrite (9.6) as an integral equation, as is done in Coddington's S-machine proof:

$$\phi(s) = \int_0^x F(u, \phi(u)) \mathrm{d}u \qquad (9.17)$$

Now integration is a computable process in the sense that $\int_0^x h(u)\mathrm{d}u$ is computable if h is computable.[26] So, if the theorem is correct there is an integral in (9.17) that generates a computable transformation – but has no computable fix-point (recall S-machine ϕ).

Another "aside." In 1974 Georg Kreisel posed the following problem:

We consider theories, by which we mean such things as classical or quantum mechanics, and ask *if every sequence of natural numbers or every real number which is well defined* (observable) **according to the theory** *must be recursive or*, more generally, *recursive in the data*. . . . Equivalently, we may ask whether any such sequence of numbers, etc., can also be generated by an ideal *computing* or *Turing Machine* if the data are used as input. The question is certainly not empty because most objects considered in a (physical) theory are not computers in the sense defined by Turing. . . . (Kreisel 1974: 11)

Thus, if the sequence is not recursive, then the nature of the theoretical knowledge required must be nonalgorithmic; for example, we will have to theorize about equilibria in formalistic, platonic, senses.

In our context of differential equations, Marian Pour-El and Ian Richards put it this way:

Our results are related to [the above] remarks of Kreisel. In [Kreisel, 1974 he] concerns himself with the following question: Can one *predict theoretically*, on the basis of some current physical theory, e.g. classical mechanics or quantum mechanics, the existence of a physical constant which is not a recursive real? Since physical theories are often expressed in terms of

---

[26] I have referred to this result in Ch. 6.

differential equations, it is natural to ask the following question: Are the solutions of $\phi' = F(x, \phi)$, $\phi(0) = 0$, computable when F is? (Pour-El and Richards 1979: 62)

If they are not, the most immediate implication will be the generation of multiple equilibria. In this sense, then, the genesis of multiple equilibria can fruitfully be investigated recursion-theoretically and will be a fertile source of a disciplining research program. It is, of course, only a conjecture. What it means is that the economic system, even if "fed" inputs in the form of initial conditions that are computable, can generate evidence, i.e. output or observables, that are nonrecursive (e.g. Coddington's S-machine generating a nonrecursive output).

Appendix: Simplest Fluctuation Theories

> Description must be non-linear, prediction must be linear
>
> Alan Turing (in Hodges 1983: 495)

In a famously polemical piece, Lucas and Sargent appear to have stated their methodological credo clearly:

Further, as Frisch and Slutsky emphasized, linear stochastic difference equations are a very flexible device for studying business cycles. It is an open question whether for explaining the central features of the business cycle there will be a big reward to fitting nonlinear models. (Lucas and Sargent 1979/1981: 314)

(It has never been clear to me[27] that "Frisch . . . emphasized linear stochastic difference equations [as] a very flexible device for studying business cycles," but let that pass.) In contrast to the New Classical credo, there is what may be called a new (or neo) Keynesian credo where the cycle theorist is advised to[28] "look more closely at the sort of mechanisms that may be responsible for significant nonlinearities in the economic system if they wish to have a proper foundation

---

[27] I have made my case as explicitly as possible in Velupillai (1992).

[28] A justification for the pursuit of nonlinear endogenous theories of economic fluctuations is provided by one of the leading theorists of modern dynamical system theory: "only *nonlinear* differential equations have interesting dynamics" (Hirsch 1984: 23). If, therefore, the stylized facts of economic fluctuations are interesting, the only way to model them mathematically must be in terms of *nonlinear differential equations* – at least, that is what Hirsch seems to be saying. But, surely, nonlinear difference equations and classes of partial differential equations are also candidates for possessing *interesting dynamics*?

upon which to build a sound business cycle theory" (Grandmont 1985: 1042).

Is there an effective procedure to decide this perennial dispute, one way or the other – or is it an undecidable question? So far as I can see, the controversy does not involve issues of fundamental economic principle. The question seems to be simply (!) the relative explanatory power of two alternative (theoretical) visions of the macrodynamic economic system. But, in fact, the issue is far from simple in (at least) one important respect: how are we to interpret "explanatory power"? Hard-core instrumentalists would reason in terms of *predictive* power; at the other end, realists may argue for *descriptive* relevance; in between, there is the amorphous world of ad-hockeries. I do not wish to enter this particular philosophical debate. However, I do wish to claim that recursion-theoretic tools can be used to advantage in going at least part of the way in resolving the controversy.

Before suggesting how this can be done, let me give a concrete example of the general idea I have in mind. Connoisseurs and students of the history of business cycle theory will be familiar with the devices of the full-employment *ceiling* and the investment *floor*, introduced by Hicks, to bound his piecewise linear model from exploding or collapsing away into oblivion. Richard Goodwin, by embedding the piecewise linear (deterministic) dynamics in a nonlinear (differential) dynamic model, was able to show that one of the economic constraints was sufficient – i.e. either the ceiling or the floor – to generate persistent (endogenous) economic fluctuations. Goodwin's stated purpose was to look for the simplest hypothesis with equal explanatory power. His trade-off was that between a second-order linear difference equation with two "nonlinear" constraints as against a second-order nonlinear differential equation with one "nonlinearity," in a precise sense. Which is the simpler theoretical system? Can we find a theoretical measure to quantify the simplicity in terms of these concepts, given that the two systems have equal explanatory power?[29]

A suggestive example may be useful in focusing attention on some aspect of the issue. Consider the famous Lorenz equations:

$$\dot{x}_1 = a(x_2 - x_1), \tag{9A.1}$$

$$\dot{x}_2 = -x_1 x_3 + \beta x_1 - x_2, \tag{9A.2}$$

[29] Granting this, *pro tempore*.

$$\dot{x}_3 = x_1 x_2 - \gamma x_3. \tag{9A.3}$$

Equations (9A.2) and (9A.3) contain the nonlinear terms $(-x_1 x_3)$ and $(x_1 x_2)$ respectively; but the system as a whole is homogeneous. Otto Rössler consciously sought a simpler system in terms of the number of nonlinearities; i.e., he sought to reduce the number of nonlinearities in the system as a whole[30] to the minimum of one. He "succeeded" in constructing, artificially, the following system:

$$\dot{x}_1 = x_2 - x_3, \tag{9A.4}$$

$$\dot{x}_2 = x_1 + \sigma x_2, \tag{9A.5}$$

$$\dot{x}_3 = \epsilon + x_1 x_3 - \eta x_3. \tag{9A.6}$$

It is evident that the trade-off in the Rössler system was for the elimination of *one nonlinearity* at the cost of introducing *an inhomogeneity* in the dynamics of the third variable,[31] which, now, is the simpler system. An immediate supplementary question would be whether it is

(a) simpler in terms of the theory utilized to summarize the evidence;
(b) simpler in terms of the data used;
(c) simpler in terms of the resources needed to use the data, in conjunction with the theory, to understand relevant regularities in the data;
(d) or, perhaps, a combination of some or all of these factors.

At this level of generalization, a first, tentative approach might be to use Rissanen's *Minimum Description Length* (MDL) principle. According to this principle, the scientific enterprise consists in:[32]

(i) starting with a space of theories or set of hypotheses characterized by the evidence;

[30] There is, of course, a simple combinatorial formula to compute the number of different ways three elements can be combined pairwise and represented in a maximum of 18 different ways on the right-hand side of (9.A1)–(9.A3) or (9.A4)–(9.A6).

[31] Recall, say, from elementary considerations in the case of linear differential or difference equations, that it is "easier" to solve the homogeneous equation than an inhomogeneous one.

[32] The backdrop for this definition is the implicit idea that, say, describing an inhomogeneous equation requires more bits of information than the corresponding homogeneous one, describing nonlinear interactions more than linear ones, and so on.

(ii) selecting, on the basis of some *a priori* criteria, a subclass or subset of theories or hypotheses;

(iii) encoding each of the chosen theories or hypotheses number-theoretically (say, Gödel numbering) and representing them in binary code;

(iv) choosing, finally, that theory and hypothesis which minimizes the sum of:

 (α) The length of the number theoretically represented theories or hypotheses.

 (β) The length of the data, represented similarly, and encoded utilizing the theories or hypotheses in (α).

However, we face, once again, the problem of "relevant regularities" and "characterized by the evidence." One may legitimately ask:

- Is the scientific enterprise restricted to finding mechanisms – theories, hypotheses – that can reproduce the evidence?
- Or, is it, perhaps, the more fundamental one of detecting the underlying mechanisms that gives rise to the evidence?

This is where the philosophical distinction between the instrumentalists and the realists becomes significant. To stay clear of this veritable minefield, I would like to suggest that the scientific enterprise must encompass both aspects. There will be, in any realized scientific exercise, a trade-off between the two aspects.[33]

Let me return to the problem of "relevant regularities" in the evidence for the subject being studied and the choice of the evidence for the theories or hypotheses. In the case of business cycle studies, there is, increasingly, a consensus about the nature of the evidence and the structure of the regularities in the evidence that characterize the subject. A brief aside on this issue, in business cycle studies, may put the problem in perspective. A succinct description of the scientific enterprise guiding Real Business Cycle studies is the following:

(1) Identify business cycle facts *a priori*.

(2) Construct and compute quantitative measures of business cycle facts from the actual evidence.

(3) Simulate the theoretical (stochastically perturbed) model economy and construct and compute similar quantitative measures for the model economy as in (b);

---

[33] This, I conjecture, is one of the reasons for Feyerabend to be able to detect seeming ad-hockeries in scientific practice.

(4) Compare the results from (2) and (3) and check the extent to which (stochastic) shocks "explain" deviations from trend.

(5) Repeat the whole procedure with progressively relaxed assumptions in (3).

What are *business cycle facts*? They are analogous to the familiar *stylized facts* of growth immortalized by Kaldor. In referring to a collection of the stylized facts of growth, two of the pioneers of Real Business Cycle theory, Kydland and Prescott, pointed out that:

These facts are neither estimates nor measures of anything; they are obtained *without first hypothesizing that the time series are generated by a probability model belonging to some class.* . . .

From [these facts] . . . Solow [developed] a parsimonious theory that rationalizes these facts – namely, his neo-classical growth model. . . .

The growth facts are not the only interesting features of these aggregate time series. Also of interest are the more volatile changes that occur in these and other aggregates – that is, the cyclical behavior of the time series. These observations are interesting because they apparently conflict with basic competitive theory, in which outcomes reflect people's ability and willingness to substitute between consumption and leisure at a given point in time and between consumption at different points in time. (Kydland and Prescott 1990:. 4; emphasis added)

Having identified the business cycle facts, the guiding principles for steps (2) and (3) can be gleaned from the following observation by Cooley and Prescott:

Lucas, following on the work of Burns and Mitchell, argued that the business cycle should be thought of as apparent deviations from a trend in which variables move together. An examination of the time path of output for any modern industrialized economy quickly reveals that output tends to fluctuate about a long-term growth path. These fluctuations about trend are what we most often think of as the business cycle. The fluctuations are typically irregularly spaced and of varying amplitude and duration. Nevertheless, the one very regular feature of these fluctuations is the way variables move together. It is these comovements of variables that Burns and Mitchell worked so hard to document and that Robert Lucas emphasized as the defining features of the business cycle. These are the features of fluctuations that we would like an artificial economy – a business cycle model – to replicate. (Cooley and Prescott 1995: 26)

In other words, we can detect, in the evidence from which we constructed business cycle facts, a set of (observable) *regularities* "in the comovements among different aggregative time series" (Lucas 1981:

217). At that point, like, say, Kaldor's or Solow's attempts to ratio-nalize growth facts, via the extracted regularities, in terms of a parsi-monious theory, we try to rationalize business cycle facts (step 1) and their constructed regularities (step 2) with a *parsimonious* business cycle theory (step 3). The next set of guiding principles, for step (3), would be, for Real Business Cycle theory, the following exercise:

(γ) Specify the economic environment in terms of the neoclassical closure.

(σ) Specify the economic environment's evolution through time.

In the case of (γ), we get the discipline and organizing principles from microeconomic theory; in the case of (σ) we get them from the growth theories that are based on (γ) but with the external con-straints imposed by the need to encapsulate elements from step (1) (i.e. business cycle facts).[34]

Before we implement the other part of step (3) – simulating the the-oretical model economy and constructing and computing measures analogous to those constructed in step (2) for the business cycle facts – we must construct and compute the "raw" regularities. For this the strategy is as follows:

• We have time series data on the relevant aggregative variables, for example, GDP, y_t. Let us assume that this variable is the sum of a cyclical component y_t^c and a growth component y_t^g. Now, the conventional, descriptive wisdom of students of business cycles is that fluctuations with a frequency of between 12 and 20 quar-ters around the trend growth path characterizes it – i.e., the busi-ness cycle(s).

• Therefore we take the raw time series of GDP, y_t, and send it through a "filter" so that the filtered time series eliminates the unwanted frequencies. How do we do this, i.e. what sort of filter should we use?

In Real Business Cycle (RBC) empirics, the following filter is used (all variables are in logs):

$$\sum_{t=1}^{T} (y_t^c)^2 + \lambda \sum_{t=1}^{T} [(y_{t-1}^g - y_t^g) - (y_t^g - y_{t-1}^g)]^2, \qquad (9A.7)$$

---

[34] Assuming, of course, a similar, prior exercise for growth theory in terms of (γ) and the external constraints of the stylized facts of growth.

where

$$y_t^c = y_t - y_t^g \qquad (9A.8)$$

and the terms inside the square brackets – the second term – are a rewriting of

$$[y_{t+1}^g - y_{t-1}^g]^2. \qquad (9A.9)$$

Thus:

(a) the first term is simply the sum of the squared deviations from trend – i.e. the cyclical component;
(b) the second term is the variation in the growth rate of the trend component.

Now, choose λ and y_t^g with two criteria in mind: first, to minimise the expression (9A.7); secondly to eliminate irrelevant frequencies. For example, if we choose $\lambda = 0$, then

$$y_t = y_t^g; \qquad (9A.10)$$

i.e., the growth component is the actual series. At the other extreme, as $\lambda \to \infty$, the growth component approaches a linear trend. By trial and error, on the basis of a priori restrictions on frequencies, it has been found that $\lambda = 1400$ does the trick.

Next we implement this procedure for the model (stochastic) growth economy. The broad strategy is as follows:

(1) Simulate the calibrated model stochastic economy or its recursive competitive equilibrium (RCE).
(2) Filter the simulated data exactly as was done for the actual data.
(3) Compute and construct the same statistical measures from the filtered data.
(4) Compare the two sets of measures and try to impute causality to the stochastic productivity shocks.

Summarizing, in the Real Business Cycle scientific enterprise it may be agreed that, for this class of exogenous theories, there is broad consensus on:

(0)   the mode of constructing the evidence;
(00)   the procedure for extracting the structural regularities in the evidence – i.e. the business cycle facts;
(000)   the nature of the theories to be used in encapsulating evidence and encompassing the structural regularities;

(0000) the way the theories are to be used in validating the evidence and its structural regularities.

I do not think the Real Business Cycle scientific enterprise is at either end of the philosophical–methodological divide of instrumentalism or realism: I believe it to be a combination of the two.

Even though such a systematic procedure has not been articulated for the endogenous theories of the business cycle, it is clear that a similar exercise can be devised for these theories, at least in principle. Given, then, this background, we have all the elements necessary to face the main question of this section: can it effectively be decided which is the more "desirable" theory of the business cycle? The framework I suggest is based on those suggested by Chaitin (1979), Bennett (1988), and Koppel (1988).

I will need to modify some of the definitions in previous chapters, particularly those of the Universal Turing Machine (UTM) and complexity – for this exercise.

DEFINITION 9.1 (Koppel 1988: 436). For every partially computable function F, there exists a program P such that, for all data D,

$$U(P, D) = F(D), \qquad (9A.11)$$

where: $U(P, D)$ is the Output of the Universal Turing machine given inputs P and D.

Then, the economic interpretation within the real business cycle scientific enterprise would be as follows.

(I)   The structural regularities in the evidence are represented by the function computed by the program part of the minimal description to the UTM.

(II) The "continuations" (i.e. forecasting) intrinsic to the evidence are those that belong to the range of that program (in (I) above).

(III) The (minimum) measure of the mechanism that generates the structural regularities in the evidence is given by the size of that program; call it *theoretical depth* (Bennett 1988).

From step (III), we get a direct comparative measure for, say, the two theories of the business cycle. The more desirable theory has the shorter program under Definition 9.1 and (I)–(II).

In this framework, the dynamical system I considered earlier, the Rössler system, acts as a "translator" which, given the relevant descriptions, generates the object being described: the "business cycle."

DEFINITION 9.2: COMPLEXITY. The complexity of the evidence E is given by:

$$H(E) = \min \{|P| + |D| \text{ such that } (P, D) \text{ is a description of } E\}.$$

DEFINITION 9.3: THEORETICAL DEPTH (TD). The TD for E, denoted[36] $TD_c(E)$, is given by

$$TD_c(E) = \min \{|P| \text{ such that } \exists\, D \text{ where } (P, D) \text{ is a description of the evidence, } E \text{ and } |P| + |D| \leq H(E) + C\}.$$

Remark 1.

(σ) If $|P| + |D| \leq H(S) + C$ the description (P, D) of E will be called *c-minimal*.

(ρ) If P is the shortest program such that, for some D, (P, D) is a *c-minimal* description of E, then the program P is called a *c-minimal program* for E.

Remark 2. The size of c is a quantitative measure of the amount of ad-hockery in a minimal program (i.e. theory). Thus, we have the c-minimal program for E denoting that part of the description of E which represents the structural regularities in E. On the other hand, the range of this c-minimal program P spans the set of E that encompass the relevant structural regularities. It is because the range is multi-valued that instrumentalist philosophies will differ from the realists; the latter will try to identify the unique c-minimal program so that the range is single-valued.

Remark 3. A final remark may highlight one significant feature of the definition of theoretical depth: it is compatible with evidence that is nonrecursive.

Since all the elements of the Real Business Cycle scientific enterprise are effectively encodable, it is possible to compute the relevant measures defined above. The hard task is to systemize the scientific enterprise that is the endogenous vision of business cycles. I suspect the role of c will be more pronounced in the endogenous theory than in the exogenous theories. A further selection criterion, *ceteris paribus*, could therefore be based on the value of c.

One final question: which of the theories would be compatible with computation universality at the microeconomic level? If, as sug-

---

[35] The role of the parameter c is exactly as in Ch. 5.

gested in earlier chapters, rational behavior in a dynamic sense is encapsulated in a formalism implying computation universality, then which formalism at the macro*dynamic* level would be consistent with it? It seems clear to me, at least within the framework employed in this book, that a nonlinear dynamic formalism at the macro level is the only candidate. This ties up well with the view of Hirsch (cf. fn. 28) on interesting dynamics.

10
Conclusions:
Reflections and Hopes

So the twine unwinds and loosely widens
backward through areas that forwarded
understandings of all I would undertake.

Seamus Heaney, *Unwinding*

All I know is that the hours are long, under these conditions,
and constrain us to beguile them with proceedings which – how
shall I say – which may at first sight seem reasonable, until they
become a habit. You may say it is to prevent our reason from
foundering. No doubt. But has it not long been straying in the
night without end of the abyssal depths? That's what I sometimes wonder. You follow my reasoning?

Vladimir to Estragon, in Beckett's *Waiting for Godot*

"The hours are long," indeed, "under these conditions," and I suspect that readers of this book, expecting a rich harvest of recursion-
theoretic economic propositions, may have felt as if they were
"waiting for Godot." I hope, naturally, that some felt otherwise. In
his characteristically lucid Presidential Address to the Southern
Economic Association, which he titled "Economics as an Inductive
Science," Clower suggested that:

an inductive science of economics must start from explicit recognition that
. . . economies of scale are ubiquitous, and must be accommodated in any
real-time description of economic processes. Neowalrasian analysis is limited strictly to convex economies; so any reconstructed theory must deal with
systems that involve nonconvexities in essential ways. This means, among
other things, that the whole of modern welfare economics must be consigned
to metaphysical oblivion. And that is just a minor casualty, because only
slightly less draconian changes are needed to lend honesty to other con-
strained-optimization branches of economic theory. (Clower 1994: 811)

It is the "draconian changes . . . to lend honesty" to the scientific enterprise in economics that have compromised the main analytical contents of this book. It is my hope that the changes required "to lend honesty to other constrained optimization branches of economic theory" are not as draconian as Clower envisaged, although I am afraid he is inclined to have the correct intuitions about such things.

I have suggested that reformulating the standard economic problem (SEP; cf. Chapter 4) as a decision problem brings integer programming (i.e. nonconvex optimization) problems (for example) quite naturally within its domain. Hence the paradigmatic case of increasing-returns-to-scale economies resulting from indivisibilities is viewed as a decision problem (cf. Chapter 9).

On the other hand, without emphasizing nonconvexities, but by investigating the exact recursion-theoretic content of the Hahn–Banach theorem – i.e. the separating hyperplane theorem – I have suggested, in Chapter 9, that the status of the Second Fundamental Theorem of welfare economics is questionable. I suspect that Clower's pungent conjecture that "the whole of welfare economics must be consigned to metaphysical oblivion" can be rigorously demonstrated with recursion-theoretic tools.

The often implicit – and sometimes explicit – methodological credo of this book has been a plea to (re)inductivize economics. To this end, a whole chapter (Chapter 5) was devoted to a presentation of the modern theory of induction. The "draconian changes . . . to lend honesty" to the scientific enterprise must begin, in my opinion, with a dethroning of the supreme status of deductive logic and the pervasive reliance on set-theoretic foundations. The confident world of determined equilibria and the "super-rational" agent was due to this excessive reliance placed, I think with naive enthusiasm, in the powers of set-theoretic formalisms and their deductive handmaidens (for example the declarative). Perhaps these enthusiasms and the concomitant activities were a sign of the times. Cantor's paradise was the setting, lofty Bourbakianism the methodology, logical positivism the epistemological basis; and Hilbert the Pope with his periodic encyclicals.[1] Brouwer and Gödel cried in the wilderness, at least so far as the odyssey of economic formalism was concerned.

---

[1] But as Wang (and, indeed, many others) observed, " . . . Gödel, in discrediting Hilbert's optimism, opened a new chapter in logic by introducing new concepts and methods which have since been pursued with a more mature enthusiasm" (Wang 1986:

In many senses, this formalistic and deductive dominance of economic analysis is quite surprising. The quantitative impetus to economic analysis was imparted, at the long-ago dawn of the subject, by a Bacon-influenced William Petty. Petty's stated intent was to make and represent the concepts of political economy "in number, weight and measure." Smith and Malthus, surely, were squarely in this Baconian inductive–quantitative tradition. Somewhere along the line, the supreme deductive powers of Ricardo seem to have mesmerized the economic analyst. To that extent, the subject seems to have "made facts fit theories" rather than the other way around.

In another incarnation and context, Clower (with Howitt) pointed out that a class of important problems in monetary economics requires, for their proofs, "the use of number theory – a branch of mathematics unfamiliar to most economists" (Clower and Howitt 1978: 168).[2] However, it is not just for the proofs of certain propositions, but for the realistic and inductive framing of the problems of economics, that there is a need to use number theory and recursion theory – branches of mathematics "unfamiliar to most economists." While this remains true, we will, I am afraid, subvert the framing of problems like increasing returns to scale, decentralization, etc., with the inappropriate tools that were devised for a wholly different class of problems.

Moreover, there is an uncritical faith in the real number system[3] to provide the numerical foundations for quantitative analysis in economics. This faith has also been important in making "facts fit theories" in the vast pseudo-scientific enterprise that is the mathematization of economics. Much hand-waving about approximations is one mode of justifying the use of the (extended) real number system as the domain over which economic entities are defined. That an inductively significant "subset" of these numbers has no numerical meaning or content seems never to have occurred to many economists. This may well be because we have forgotten the following:

We all are familiar with the fascination with impossibility proofs in mathematics: $\sqrt{2}$ is not a rational number, there is no general method to trisect

15). All of this, however, by-passed the derived optimism of the mathematical economists, and their mathematization of economics. They ignored these "new concepts and methods" with princely unconcern.

[2] Almost twenty years later it remains a melancholy fact that it is still a "branch of mathematics unfamiliar to most economists."

[3] Supplemented, with the help of nonstandard analysis, with the infinity and the infinitesimals.

any angle by ruler and compass, arithmetic is incompletable, there are non-computable real numbers, etc. In each case, *we arrive at the negative result by using a clear positive delineation of the original domain.* For example, we give a systematic characterization of the whole range of constructions by ruler and compass, and then we are able to see that for certain angles, to trisect them calls for steps not lying in that range. *It is only after Turing has found a clear characterization of computable real numbers that one sees easily there must also be noncomputable numbers.* (Wang 1986: 138; emphasis added)

Turing's characterization of the computable numbers can be interpreted as distinguishing between numbers that are defined by *pure* existential statements and those that can be algorithmically defined. This is why standard mathematical economics is replete with existential theorems without the slightest concern over their constructive or algorithmic status. A subject whose fundamental entities are defined over the whole of the real number system will, naturally, not worry too much about the subset that is numerically meaningful in a constructive or algorithmic sense. It is also why economic theory has not been a pleasant playing field for those of us who would like to interpret the cardinal aim of the subject to be *problem-solving* and who would, therefore, insist on characterizing rational agents as meaningful problem-solvers and would also indulge in hair-splitting about the importance of *methods* for solving problems.

The skeptical economic theorist might not find the above paragraph particularly convincing. What is the difference between problem-solving on the subset of the computable numbers or constructive numbers and problem-solving on the whole of the real number system (leaving aside the thorny issue of problem-solving on the domain of the nonstandard numbers), the skeptic may ask? There *is* a fundamental and foundational difference, which is best captured in an important theoretical contribution made by Kolmogorov a long time ago:

In addition to theoretical logic, which systemizes the proof schemata of theoretical truths, one can systematize the schemata of solution of problems. . . . *The calculus of problems is formally identical with the Brouwerian intuitionistc logic, which has recently been formulated by Mr Heyting.* . . . it follows that one should consider the solution of problems as the independent goal of mathematics (in addition to the proofs of theoretical propositions). (Kolmogorov 1932: 58–65)

At the very beginning of this book, I pointed out that there was a fourfold division of mathematical logic: set theory, proof theory, recursion theory, and model theory. I also claimed that most, if not all, of standard economic theory was formalized in terms of set theory and model theory. I wondered why it was not possible to try formalizing in terms of recursion theory. However, I did not link this query with my belief – imparted to me by my teacher, mentor, and friend Richard Goodwin – that economic theory should be about problem-solving. I have concentrated, in the whole of this work on characterizing the problem-solvers and the methods recursion-theoretically, but have left out the difficult problem of justifying the basic belief: that *economics is problem-solving*.

I can now round off the whole story. I consider economics as problem-solving because I believe that formalization of economic theory must proceed without relying on dubious logical principles. I do not know whether there is a logic – call it algorithmic logic – lying between classical and intuitionistic logics that would enable me to state, like Kolmogorov above, that problem-solving in the domain of computable numbers is formally identical with such an algorithmic logic.[4] I do not doubt, however, that such a logic can be devised, in the unlikely event that it has not already been done, and that it would be a logic that would not hesitate to leave imaginary paradises, whether sanctioned by Hilbert, Cantor, or Bourbaki. That standard economic theory, in its mathematical mode, is happy to reside in such imaginary paradises is the reason for the somnambulent dominance of existential results.[5]

The dominance of (universal) negative results may not be adequately compensated by the meager algorithmic existential results, at least for the above skeptic. But the strategy followed by Arrow in deriving Impossibility Theorem in social choice theory was no different. The "clear positive delineation of the original domain" of eco-

---

[4] I am aware that much, if not all, of recursion theory relies on classical logic.
[5] They have support for this somnambulence in the majestic words of Auden:

> So, I wish you, first, a sense of theatre.
> Only those who love illusion, and know it,
> Will go far; for, if not, we will spend our time
> In a confusion of what we say and do,
> With who we really are.

> W. H. Auden, *Many Happy Returns*

Mathematical economics has become a theatre whose stage seems to be populated by "those who love illusion"; whether they "know it," I do not know. I consider part of the message of this essay as an attempt to dispel such people of some of their illusions. I do not expect "to go far."

nomics is an activity of the future for which we will, I am sure, find distinguished classes of "Kafka's predecessors," too. When that is done, it will be seen that recursion-theoretic tools will help in the generation of theories that will fit facts, rather than the other way around. At least, that is a message I wish to convey in this work.

On the other hand, I have tried to indicate, in Chapters 6 and 9, that a deft use of computable analysis enables much of the standard framework of economics to be operational in the usual ways. The advantage gained by working within a computable analytic domain rather than the conventional domain of real analysis is that *ad hoc* approximations and undecidable disjunctions are detected quite easily. This detection is faciliated by the (universal) negative results.

I would like to think that the computable approach to economics provides hints on enriching the neoclassical closure in interesting ways. Thus, perhaps it is possible to redefine the closure in terms of decision rules, institutions, and the knowledge base, rather than preferences, endowments, and technology. The former three can be given consistent recursion-theoretic characterizations; the latter three will become special cases.

In Chapter 7 I used the program-card interpretation of a Turing machine. In Scarf's beautiful lecture on "Mathematical Programming and Economic Theory" (Scarf 1989) there is an imaginative interpretation of institutions as algorithms. In Romer's speculative thoughts on understanding growth and development (Romer 1993) there is a fascinating interpretation of modelling production algorithmically (cf. Velupillai 1996). I have suggested that the Rational Man of Economics, by way of Simon's Human Problem Solver and his Thinking Man, could fruitfully be modelled as *Turing's Man of Economics*. Given the program-card interpretation of Turing machines, Turing's Man can also be characterized algorithmically.

These, then, can be the building-blocks for the new closure I am suggesting, a closure that is consistently algorithmic and, hence, intrinsically dynamic and process-oriented. As pointed out earlier, David Ruelle, in his Willard Gibbs Lecture (Ruelle 1988), probed the question of the naturalness of our mathematics: "*How natural is our human 20th-century mathematics?*" (p. 260; cf. also Chapter 1 above). His conclusions were that there was nothing natural about human mathematics: "it could be quite different from what it is" (p. 266).

The laws of economics have been sought by looking for formal structure using a narrow repertoire of mathematical tools. If, as

Ruelle persuasively argues, there is nothing natural about "our human 20th-century mathematics," then could it be the case that we have discovered *unnatural* laws of economics? Perhaps the gods did not lay out a path for the discovery of the laws of economics by human mathematics as we know it today. But, then, we cannot know whether that is the case until we try at least some of the other "human 20th-century mathematics" at our disposal. If all else fails, then that will remain the minimal case for the computable approach to economics.

Appendix
A Child's Guide to Elementary
Aspects of Computability

A1 PREAMBLE

And one might express what [Turing] says also in the form of
games. And the interesting games would be such as brought one
via certain rules to nonsensical instructions.

Wittgenstein (1980: s. 1096)

The following are the contents of a child's toy set, curiously called
"Computable and Uncomputable Games." The game in question is
a game of solitaire, i.e. played by one person:

(a) a tinman with movable joints and sensory organs;
(b) a small box car, big enough for the tinman, on grooved wheels;
(c) a large supply of pieces of rails on which the grooves of the
boxcar fit smoothly; each piece of rail is approximately long
enough to hold the boxcar, but sliding wedges – like in Lego
sets – make it possible to build long railroad lines in both
directions;
(d) a long white board, on stands, that can be placed alongside the
railroad lines – potentially extendable as far as the lines go;
the tinman's vision is constrained, by artificial means, to view
the contents of exactly one square of the white board per unit
of time;
(e) colored chalks, cloth to wipe the board, and an extra boxcar;
also instructions on how to order extra rail pieces and extensions for the white board.

The tinman in action is schematically illustrated in Figure A1.

Like all serious toy sets, this one includes a book of instructions
and rules on how to "play" the game. The boxcar can move to the

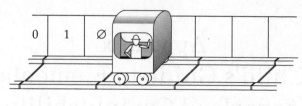

Fig. A1

right or left on the rails, one section of rail at a time; its movement is controlled by a lever which operates the wedges connecting adjacent pieces of rails. The tinman operates the lever. The operation is not unlike that which is done to shunt trains onto different tracks.

The tinman's functions are specified in the book of instructions as follows:

(i)   to write any one symbol at a time in the square on the white board facing the boxcar in which the tinman stands; the instruction book specifies the allowable symbols (usually, 0, 1, and B (for blank, distinguishable from 0));

(ii) to erase the symbol, if any, that is in the square facing the box-car;

(iii) to leave a square without altering its contents, if so wished.

The tinman's sensory organs are connected to a gearing mechanism which can operate at any one of a finite number of states (think of 16 speed gears on a bicycle, for example).

The rules, according to the instruction book, for allowable sequences of symbols with which the tinman can fill the squares are as follows:

(α) The person playing the game begins by filling a finite number of the squares on the white board with the allowable symbols.

(β) The boxcar is placed on the rail facing the leftmost of the squares that the player has filled, with the tinman in the box-car.

(χ) When the tinman's sensory organs sense the scanned symbol – i.e. when the tinman "sees" the square on the white board facing the boxcar in which he is standing – they "instruct" his hand to:

(i)   erase the current symbol and replace it with another one; or,

(ii) leave "as is";

(iii) shift gears to another level depending on the new symbol in the square;

(iv) shift the lever to move the boxcar to the next rail on the left or right.

The above description exhausts the rules of the game as far as playing it is concerned. Games hang by their own bootstraps until some indication of a way to reach a "result" is specified. In "Computable and Uncomputable Games," a play terminates when the gearing mechanism of the tinman's sensory organs reaches a specified position. The result of a game that terminates is a function of the string of symbols appearing on the white board at termination.

Surely, this is a game any child can play?

But, will every play of the game terminate? Does every game of Monopoly end conclusively in finite time? Of course not. In principle, the game of Monopoly can go on for ever. Similarly, in principle, the tinman can keep on working for ever – subject to availability of extension railtracks and white boards!

The above are the ingredients of a machine that can compute anything that is *intuitively* understood and accepted to be *computable*. But, the perceptive child will ask: "Whose intuition," and what does "computable" mean? The second part is relatively easy to answer (cf. next section); the first part is more difficult.

It is in answering the first part of the child's query that one begins to enter the metaphysical zone of computable and uncomputable games. Let us agree, at least *pro tempore*, on the meaning to be attached to "computable" in the everyday sense of arithmetic at the grocery shop. The process of computing a sum, a product, a division, or a subtraction is not universal. The abacus, for example, is still dominant in everyday computing in Japan. But the abacus and the simple calculating machines come to the same answer, when given the same data and asked to perform one of the arithmetic operations. Are there fundamental *irreducible processes* hidden underneath superficially different activities? Turing answered this question by constructing his Turing machine, and its building-blocks are almost exactly those in the above toy set.

We compute not only ordinary sums and the like; we also compute velocities, areas, and so on. Imagine another toy – let us call it "Recursive and Nonrecursive Games," perhaps for slightly older children – which claims to be able to compute all intuitively computable functions! How shall we decide whose intuition is superior? Fortunately, we are spared this difficult decision: it turns out that both games, in their plays, compute exactly the same class of functions. Evidence gathered over the years from different toy sets confirms that all of the games, even while allowing the plays to be different, compute the same class of functions. This "empirical fact" is called the *Church–Turing thesis*. Its origins lie in the deep recesses of mathematical epistemology. I have alluded to these issues, tangentially, in each chapter. A full discussion will appear in the companion book to this one.

But what does it mean "to compute a function"? Surely, any explication would require concepts and a maturity that would be beyond most children? Space and context do not allow me to go into a detailed answer refuting such skeptical thoughts, although an attempt – inadequate, no doubt – will be made in the next section. Suffice it to say that it is much easier to teach and motivate the meaning of a computation and the concomitant computable function than it is to teach much that is commonly taught as mathematics in high schools.

To conclude these elementary observations, consider the following questions posed by a perceptive child:

(1) Since the child learns, by playing, that the result of a terminated game is a function of the final sequence of symbols in the series of squares on the white board, it may wonder as follows: can I specify any pattern I like for the final configuration of a terminating game and ask you to give me the initial configuration that will lead to it? Like most "inverse problems," this one gives a negative answer – unless the final configuration is trivial. This question, and the answer, contain much of the import of Rice's theorem.

(2) The child may also ask, after playing the game many times, if it is possible to "say" beforehand whether any given initial configuration will lead to a terminating game? This, too, leads to a negative answer and contains much of the substance of what I have referred to in the main text as *the undecidability of the halting problem for Turing machines*.

Why, the weary reader may wonder, should an economist try to seek theoretical foundations for economic theory in such simple games? I may happily deflect this reader to the perceptive admonition by

Arrow to economists to seek "more consistent assumptions of computability in the formulation of economic hypotheses" (cf. Chapter 3 above). I could even refer such readers all the way back to Petty's attempts to quantify economics, at its very origin.

But I may also answer by pointing out that it is the mathematization of economics that has caused the subject to become quantitative in a meaningful numerical and constructive sense. The epistemological constraints that mathematicians imposed on their own foundations led to a branch of mathematics that characterized the real number systems into a computable and an uncomputable part. If, therefore, economic entities are to be quantified, then it seems natural that they must be based on the computable numbers. These numbers are algorithmically generated by nothing other than "Computable and Uncomputable Games," "Recursive and Nonrecursive Games," and other games related to this by the Church–Turing thesis. It just so happens that these are almost as simple as children's games to play, and to understand. It is the algorithmic (rule-based) generation that makes the game *playable* (cf. Chapter 7). If, as I have also argued, economics is also problem-solving, then it may be necessary to leave out undecidable disjunctions, uncomputable numbers, and such noneffective methods. There again, the metaphor of the child's toy set is a good example: a toy set with noneffective instructions is useless. The same applies to any formalization. The beauty lies in the fact that a finitely specified effective game for children contains nonterminating plays!

A2 PSEUDO-THEORY

That we *calculate* with some concepts and with others do not, merely shews how different in kind conceptual tools are . . .

Wittgenstein (1980, s. 1095)

A2.1 Description, definitions, and conventions

In preparing this section, I have used Boolos and Jeffrey (1989), Bridges (1994), Davis (1982), Hunter (1971), and Moret (1998) quite freely, and many of the standard classics of computability theory.

DESCRIPTION A.1. *A Turing machine* consists of the following interlinked parts:

(i)   a movable control mechanism which at any given point in time is in one of a finite number of possible *states*;

(ii) a sensor, attached to the movable control mechanism, that can scan the symbols on an infinite tape, interpret the symbols, erase them, and also write symbols on the tape;

(iii) the tape, infinite to the left and right, divided into (scannable) cells, in each one of which one symbol from a fixed alphabet can be written.

One of the many possible ways of depicting the essence of such a machine is shown in Figure A2.

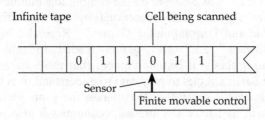

FIG. A2

CONVENTION A1

(a) The sensor can scan exactly one cell at a time.

(b) Only a finite number of cells of the infinite tape are nonempty at any given point in time.

(c) The sensor is placed scanning the leftmost nonempty cell when it is initialized.

(d) The fixed alphabet consists of the three symbols $\langle 0, 1, \varnothing \rangle$ (where $\varnothing$: denotes the symbol "blank" and is different from the numeral 0).

Denote by

Q: finite set of states;

$q_0 \in Q$: a pre-specified initial state;

$q_T \in Q$: a pre-specified terminal state;

δ: a partial function (i.e., not defined over the whole of its domain); i.e.,

$$\delta: \ Q \times \Lambda \to Q \times \Lambda \times \{L, R, \gamma\},$$

where Λ is the symbol set (alphabet): $\langle 0, 1, \varnothing \rangle$ in our case; L is a leftward movement of the movable control; R is a rightward movement of the movable control; γ represents no movement of the movable control; and where (q_T, α) is not defined, $\forall \alpha \in \Lambda$; i.e., if the movable control is in, or reaches, the terminal state T, the actions of the Turing machine cease.

DEFINITION A1. TURING MACHINE. Given the fixed alphabet Λ, a Turing machine (TM) is a quadruple: $\text{TM} \equiv \langle Q, \delta, q_0, q_T \rangle$

Remark. Many elements of the description and the convention have been chosen with a view to making the definition seem "natural." Not all of the elements are necessary. I have not sought a minimal set of elements for the description and the definition.

A2.2 Examples of computation

(a) A general example for the Turing machine

(1) Assume that a finite portion of the infinite tape has written in the corresponding cells the following sequence of symbols:
$1\ 0\ 0\ 1\ \varnothing\ 1\ 0\ 1\ 1\ 0\ \varnothing$,
with empty squares to the left of the leftmost 1 and to the right of the rightmost $\varnothing$.

(2) TM must be set to state q_0 and the sensor places against the leftmost 1.

(3) Then, in general, if the TM senses the symbol α in state q, it will compute $\delta(q, \alpha)$ which may be equal to, say, $\delta(q', \alpha', S)$.

(4) The TM sensors would write α' in place of α, shift to state q', and move one cell to the left (S = L), right (S = R), or not move at all (S = γ).

(5) If the TM ever reaches the state q_T, it will stop its activities.

(6) The sequence of symbols remaining when the TM reaches q_T is the output.

(b) A simple example for TM, i.e. $\langle Q, \delta, q_0, q_T \rangle$

Given $Q = \langle q_0, q_1, q_2, q_T \rangle$, $\Lambda \equiv \langle 0, 1, \varnothing \rangle$ and the following tape input:

0	$\varnothing$	1	1	0	0		

the rules (= "programs") for the activities of TM, i.e. the state transition function δ, can be given in a transition table (Table A1).

TABLE A1

	0	1	∅
q_0	$\langle q_1,1,R\rangle$	$\langle q_2,\varnothing,R\rangle$	$\langle q_T,\varnothing,L\rangle$
q_1	$\langle q_1,1,R\rangle$	$\langle q_1,0,R\rangle$	$\langle q_T,\varnothing,L\rangle$
q_2	$\langle q_1,\varnothing,R\rangle$	$\langle q_2,1,\gamma\rangle$	$\langle q_T,0,L\rangle$
q_T	STOP	STOP	STOP

For example the instructions are read column-by-row; then TM, scanning 0 in state q_0, overwrites 0 with 1, enters state q_1, and shifts to scan the next cell on the right.

Hence, TM_1's activities for the given input and transition table here, Table A1 will be as follows:

Step 1: 0 ∅ 1 1 0 0
Step 2: 1 ∅ 1 1 0 0
Step 3: 1 ∅ 1 1 0 0

This Turing machine's activity consists in replacing the leftmost 0 by a 1.

CONVENTION A2. The natural number $n \in N$ is represented on a Turing machine tape by $n + 1$ symbols of the numeral 1. By courtesy, zero is represented by a single 1.

CONVENTION A3. The transition function δ is represented by a series of program cards, one card for each of the finite states of the relevant Turing machine, each of which specifies, for each symbol of the given alphabet, the computing activity of the machine.

(c) A computation using program cards

Consider the 2-state, 2-symbol Turing machine, TM_2 (Figure A3), whose activities are represented by two program cards (where state 1 corresponds to q_0). On each card we have:

(a) Column 1: scanned symbol
(b) Column 2: the new symbol to be inserted
(c) Column 3: shift left or right instruction
(d) Column 4: next state to enter

Example. Let us start TM_2 on state 1 scanning a blank tape (see Figure A4):

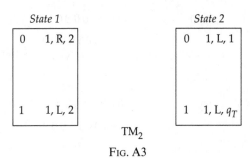

State 1	
0	1, R, 2
1	1, L, 2

State 2	
0	1, L, 1
1	1, L, q_T

TM_2

FIG. A3

(State 1) Step 1: scanning 0; overwrite 1; shift R; enter state 2
(State 2) Step 2: scanning 0; overwrite 1; shift L; enter state 1
(State 1) Step 3: scanning 1; overwrite 1; shift L; enter state 2
(State 2) Step 4: scanning 0; overwrite 1; shift L; enter state 1
(State 1) Step 5: scanning 0; overwrite 1; shift R; enter state 2
(State 2) Step 6: scanning 1; overwrite 1; shift L; stop

The activities of TM_2, started off on a blank tape, can be summarized as follows:

(i) It writes four 1s on a blank tape.
(ii) It is a 2-state machine that shifts 6 times.

DEFINITION A2. TURING MACHINE COMPUTABLE FUNCTIONS. A function f is Turing machine (TM) computable if there exists a Turing machine such that, whenever the TM is started in state 1 ($= q_0$), scanning the leftmost of $x + 1$ consecutive 1s, the TM eventually halts scanning at the leftmost of $f(x) + 1$ consecutive 1s.

(d) An example of a TM that computes $f(x) = 2$

The 5-state, 2 symbol TM depicted in Figure A5 computes $f(x) = 2$ under the above definition (i.e., start in state 1, etc.).
Example of a noncomputable function: cf. Chapter 7.

A2.3 Enumerability, recursive functions, and sets: some definitions and theorems

Consider the following four functions which can be accepted, unambiguously, as intuitively computable in the sense that it is easy to construct Turing machines to compute them:

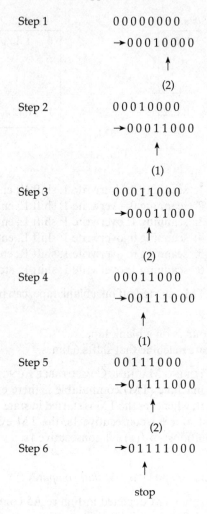

Step 1   0 0 0 0 0 0 0 0
           →0 0 0 1 0 0 0 0
                 ↑
               (2)

Step 2   0 0 0 1 0 0 0 0
           →0 0 0 1 1 0 0 0
                 ↑
               (1)

Step 3   0 0 0 1 1 0 0 0
           →0 0 0 1 1 0 0 0
                 ↑
               (2)

Step 4   0 0 0 1 1 0 0 0
           →0 0 1 1 1 0 0 0
              ↑
              (1)

Step 5   0 0 1 1 1 0 0 0
           →0 1 1 1 1 0 0 0
            ↑
             (2)

Step 6   →0 1 1 1 1 0 0 0
           ↑
         stop

FIG. A4

(i)   *zero function*: $z(x) = 0$, $\forall x \in N$. This function assigns the same value, zero, to each natural number as argument; i.e. $z(0) = z(1) = z(2) = \ldots = 0$;

(ii)   *identity function*: $\text{Id}(x) = (x)$, $\forall x \in N$. This function assigns to each natural number as argument its own value as output; i.e., $\text{Id}(0) = 0$; $\text{Id}(1) = 1$; $\text{Id}(2) = 2$; . . . ;

Card 1	Card 2	Card 3	Card 4	Card 5
State 1	State 2	State 3	State 4	State 5
0 0, R, 4	0 1, R, 3	0 1, R, 1	0 0, L, 4	0 0, R, 0
1 0, L, 2	1 1, L, 2	1 1, R, 3	1 0, L, 5	1 1, L, 5

TM_3

Fig. A5

(iii) *successor function*: $S(x) = x + 1$, $\forall x \in N$;

(iv) *projection function*: Pr_i^k: $N^k \to N$, defined by "projecting" the ith coordinate of a k-dimensional domain as

$$Pr_i^k(x_1, x_2, \ldots, x_i, \ldots, x_k) = x_i \;\; \forall x_1, x_2, \ldots, x_k \in N.$$

DEFINITION A3: THE BASIC FUNCTIONS. The collection of intuitively computable functions given by (i)–(iv) are the *basic functions*.

Next, consider the following two operations that are to be applied to given computable functions – again, in the sense that it is easy to construct Turing machines to perform them.

(α) *Composition of computable functions.* If f and g_i ($i = 1, 2, \ldots, m$) are computable functions of m and n arguments, respectively, then h is obtained by *composition* from f and g_i ($i = 1, 2, \ldots, m$) as follows:

$$h(x_1, \ldots, x_n) = f(g_1(x_1, \ldots, x_n), g_2(x_1, \ldots, x_n) \ldots$$
$$g_m(x_1, \ldots, x_n)).$$

(β) *Primitive recursion of computable functions.* Given the computable functions

$$\phi: N^{n-1} \to N^{n+1} \text{ and } \theta: N^{n+1} \to N,$$

the computable function $\Psi: N^n \to N$ is obtained from ϕ and θ by primitive recursion whenever

$$\psi(0, x_2, \ldots, x_n) = \phi(x_2, \ldots, x_n)$$

and

$$\psi(x + 1, x_2, \ldots, x_n) = \theta(x, \psi(x_1, x_2, \ldots, x_n), x_2, \ldots, x_n).$$

DEFINITION A4: PRIMITIVE RECURSIVE FUNCTIONS. The set $\mathcal{P}$ of primitive recursive functions are those that are closed with respect to (finite applications of) composition and primitive recursion on the basic functions.

Unfortunately, this set does not exhaust the class of intuitively computable functions. The classic intuitively computable function from $N \times N \to N$ defined by Ackerman *grows faster than* any member of $\mathcal{P}$. Recall, from Chapter 7, that the construction of an intuitively uncomputable function used the same principle. Ackerman's famous function is:

$$A(0, n) = n + 1,$$
$$A(m + 1, 0) = A(m, 1),$$
$$A(m + 1, n + 1) = A(m, A(m + 1, n)).$$

The same strategy as used for the Busy Beaver game can be used for the Ackerman function to show monstrous growth rates.

Now, since Ackerman's function is intuitively computable, the class $\mathcal{P}$ of primitive recursive functions will have to be enlarged. On what basis can this enlargement be executed so that exactly the intuitively computable functions are included in it? We have accepted that all the Turing machine computable functions are intuitively computable. Are there, conversely, intuitively computable functions that are not Turing machine computable? Answers to these questions are summarized, as mentioned in earlier sections and chapters, in the Church–Turing thesis. But to get to that, a few more definitions and details are necessary.

DEFINITION A5: PARTIAL FUNCTION AND TOTAL FUNCTION. A function f: $X \to Y$ but where f may not be defined on the entire domain X is called a *partial function*. Correspondingly, a *total function* is defined on its entire domain.

(γ) *Minimalization of computable functions.* The function h of n arguments is obtained by the following operation – called *minimalization* – from the computable total function f of $n + 1$ arguments:

$$h(x_1, \ldots, x_n) = \begin{cases} \text{the smallest } y \text{ for which } f(x_1, \ldots, x_n, y) \\ = 0, \text{if any}; \\ \text{undefined if } f(x_1, \ldots, x_n, y) = 0, \text{ for no } y \end{cases}$$

The qualifications "if any" and "for no y" introduce elements of effective undecidability to elementary computability theory. We may keep on trying, in some definite order, different values of y until $f(x_1, \ldots, x_n, y) = 0$. There is no guarantee, except for trivial functions, that failure to find such a y after a billion or a trillion trials means that it will not be found in the next, say, 18 attempts. The same ambiguity applies to the activity of locating "the smallest y". This operation of minimalization ties up recursive functions with the real activity of computation. A computer (i.e. a Turing machine) may *fail to terminate* for some inputs; a function h may be *undefined*.

DEFINITION A6: PARTIAL RECURSIVE FUNCTIONS. The set of functions PRC that are closed with respect to the (finitely applied) operations of composition, primitive recursion, and minimalization on the basic functions are the partial recursive functions.

CHURCH–TURING THESIS. A partial function is computable if and only if a Turing machine can be constructed to compute it.
    Remark. This is a thesis and not a theorem. It is entirely possible that some future Alan Turing will find a way to tame the monstrous growth rates inherent in a Busy Beaver game. There are distinguished recursion theorists, philosophers, and mathematicians (Laszlo Kalmar, Ludwig Wittgenstein, and Steve Smale, respectively, come immediately to mind) who feel that there is more to be said on these issues.

DEFINITION A7: RECURSIVE SETS. A set $X \subseteq N$ of natural numbers is *recursive* if and only if there is a partial recursive function ϕ such that $\forall n, n \in X$ if and only if $\phi(n) = 0$.

DEFINITION A8: DECIDABLE SETS. A set is *decidable* if and only if there is an effective (i.e. computable) method to characterize any member of the set.

Thus, since every partial recursive function is computable, every recursive set is decidable. In other words, there is an effective method – an algorithm – to decide whether or not an arbitrary n is a member of X.

DEFINITION A9: RECURSIVELY ENUMERABLE SETS. A set $X \subseteq N$ of natural numbers is *recursively enumerable* (r.e.) if and only if it is either empty or describes the range of a partial recursive function.

There is an open-endedness in the definition of r.e. sets that is absent in the definition of recursive sets. The definition of r.e. sets entails the existence of a partial recursive function (or, equivalently – by the Church–Turing thesis – a Turing machine) which can systematically output members of such sets. Thus, the openendedness comes from the fact that an arbitrary $n \in n$ may not, say, till the billionth try be the output of a PRC; but it may well be the next output *after* the billionth try. We can only keep on trying, without any guarantee of a definite answer.

Some elementary and immediate implications of the above three definitions can now be stated.

PROPOSITION A1. If a set is recursive, then its complement is also recursive.

PROPOSITION A2. A recursive set is also recursively enumerable. (In other words, a decidable set is listable (enumerable).)

PROPOSITION A3. If a set and its complement are both recursively enumerable, then the two sets are also recursive.

THEOREM A.1: THE UNDECIDABILITY OF THE HALTING PROBLEM FOR TURING MACHINES. There is no algorithm to decide whether or not any given Turing machine enters the terminal state for arbitrary input configurations on the tape.

Remark. Any standard textbook on recursion theory will normally include a discussion of this theorem and, of course, complete proofs. The reason for stating the theorem at this particular juncture is as follows. According to this theorem, there is no effective method (i.e., again, there is no algorithm) to decide whether or not a Turing machine for an arbitrary program card will enter its terminal state. An immediately relevant question will be: can it be decided whether a Turing machine exhibits some particular input–output behavior? Armed with a knowledge of the undecidability of the halting problem, it will not be surprising that the answer is in the negative. Rice's theorem summarizes the result.

THEOREM A2: RICE'S THEOREM. Denote by $\phi_i: N \rightarrow N$ the partial recursive function computed by Turing machine TM. If $X \subseteq N$ is recursive, then there exists i, j such that $i \in X$ and $j \in N - X$, and $\phi_i = \phi_j$.

In other words, there are distinguishable Turing machines, TM_i and TM_j, that compute the same partial recursive functions. Thus, if D_i is a decidable property possessed by TM_i and not possessed by

TM_j, then it is not possible to tell which is which simply by observing their input–output behavior. Another, and more succinct, way of stating the import of the theorem is as follows:

Any nontrivial input–output property of programs is *undecidable*.

This can be interpreted – exactly – to mean that only the properties of the empty set and the universal set are effectively decidable. Now, Rice's theorem characterizes recursive sets. The natural extension of Rice's theorem would be an analogous result for recursively enumerable sets. Such a result is encapsulated in the following theorem.

THEOREM A3: THE RICE–SHAPIRO THEOREM. Consider the set $\mathscr{C}$ of partial recursive functions such that

$$\mathscr{R} = \{x: \phi_x \in \mathscr{C}\} \text{ is r.e.}$$

Then, for any partial recursive function ψ,

$$\psi \in \mathscr{C} \text{ iff } \exists \theta \subseteq \psi \text{ with finite domain and } \theta \in \mathscr{C}.$$

Now, every finite input–output configuration defines a recursive set. Going, therefore, from Rice's theorem to the Rice–Shapiro theorem would be akin to finding an extension of some finite input–output configuration to define recursively enumerable sets. Thus, according to the Rice–Shapiro theorem, a class of partial recursive functions is recursively enumerable if and only if each member of this class is defined by the extension of some finite input–output configuration in a recursively enumerable set of such configurations.

A3 PARTIAL REFLECTIONS

[T]he importance of the concept of general recursiveness (or Turing's computability) . . . is largely due to the fact that with this concept one has for the first time succeeded in giving an absolute definition of an interesting epistemological notion, i.e., not one depending on the formalism chosen.

Gödel (1946/1965: 84)

Computability and randomness are the two basic epistemological notions I have used as building-blocks to define computable economics. Both of these notions can be put to work to formalize economic theory in effective ways. However, they can be made to work only on the basis of two theses: the Church–Turing thesis, and the Kolmogorov–Chaitin–Solomonoff thesis. Under these theses, we have definitions, independent of any chosen formalism, for computability and randomness.

In this appendix I have given an outline of elementary aspects of computability theory. The building-blocks are simple, intuitively acceptable, and easy to assemble into vast, elegant, and useful structures. A similar outline could be given for the elementary parts of applied computability theory – i.e. algorithmic, computational, and diophantine complexity theories. For reasons of space, I must, reluctantly, refrain from attempting such an outline in this work.

References

Aberth, O. (1980), *Computable Analysis*, McGraw-Hill, New York.

Arrow, K. J. (1959), "Rational Choice Functions and Orderings," *Economica*, 26, 121–7.

——(1962), "The Economic Implications of Learning by Doing," *Review of Economic Studies*, 29: 155–73.

——(1986), "Rationality of Self and Others in an Economic System," *Journal of Business*, 59: S385–S400.

——and Hahn, F. H. (1971), *General Competitive Analysis*, Holden-Day, San Francisco.

Azariadis, C. (1992), "The Problem of Multiple Equilibrium," unpublished manuscript, UCLA, February.

——(1993), *Intertemporal Macroeconomics*, Blackwell, Reading, Mass.

Babbage, C. (1864), "Passages from the Life of a Philosopher," in *Charles Babbage and his Calculating Engines: Selected Writings by Charles Babbage and Others*, ed. with an Introduction by P. Morrison and E. Morrison, Dover, New York, 1961.

Baum, E. (1988), "Discussant's Comments," in P. W.Anderson, K. J. Arrow and D. Pines (eds.),*The Economy as an Evolving Complex System*, Addison-Wesley, Menlo Park, Calif.

Beeson, M. (1978), "Some Relations Between Classical and Constructive Mathematics," *Journal of Symbolic Logic*, 43.

——(1985), *Foundations of Constructive Mathematics*, Springer-Verlag, Heidelberg.

Bennett, C. H. (1982), "The Thermodynamics of Computation: A Review," *International Journal of Theoretical Physics*, 21: 905–40.

——(1988), "Logical Depth and Physical Complexity," in R. Herken (ed.), *The Universal Turing Machine: A Half-Century Survey*, Oxford University Press, Oxford, pp. 227–57.

Berlekamp, E. R, Conway, J. H., and Guy, R. K. (1982*a*), *Winning Ways for your Mathematical Plays*, i, *Games in General*, Academic Press, New York.

————(1982*b*), *Winning Ways for your Mathematical Plays*, ii, *Games in Particular*, Academic Press, London.

Binmore, K. (1987), "Modelling Rational Players, Pt. I," *Economics and Philosophy*, 3: 179–214.

——(1988), "Modelling Rational Players, Pt. II," *Economics and Philosophy*, 4: 9–55.

Bishop, E., and Bridges, D. (1985), *Constructive Analysis*, Springer-Verlag, Heidelberg.

Boehner, P. (1990), *Ockham: Philosophical Writings*, Hackett, Indianapolis.

Boolos, G. S., and Jeffrey, R. C. (1989), *Computability and Logic*, 3rd edn., Cambridge University Press, Cambridge.

Borges, J. L. (1964), *Labyrinths: Selected Stories and Other Writings*, New Directions Publishing Corporation, New York.

Bridges, D. S. (1982), "Preference and Utility: A Constructive Development," *Journal of Mathematical Economics*, 9: 165–85.

——(1994), *Computability: A Mathematical Sketchbook*, Springer-Verlag, New York.

Bronowski, J. (1978), *The Origins of Knowledge and Imagination*, Yale University Press, New Haven, Conn.

Brouwer, L. E. J. (1929/1998), "Mathematics, Science and Language," in P. Mancosu (ed.), *From Brouwer to Hilbert: The Debate on the Foundations of Mathematics in the 1920s*, Oxford University Press, Oxford, pp. 45–53.

Campbell, D. E. (1978), "Realization of Choice Functions," *Econometrica*, 46: 171–80.

Canning, D. (1992), "Rationality, Computability and Nash Equilibrium," *Econometrica*, 60: 877–88.

Caviness, B. F. (1970), "On Canonical Forms and Simplification," *Journal of the Association for Computing Machinery*, 17: 385–96.

Chaitin, G. J. (1979), "Toward a Mathematical Definition of 'Life'", in R. D. Levine and M. Tribus (eds.), *The Maximal Entropy Formalism*, MIT Press, Cambridge, Mass, 477–98.

——(1987), *Algorithmic Information Theory*, Cambridge University Press, Cambridge.

Chipman, J. S. (1960), "The Foundations of Utility," *Econometrica*, 28: 193–224.

——(1971), "On the Lexicographic Representation of Preference Orderings," in J. S. Chipman, L. Hurwicz, M. K. Richter, and H. F. Sonnenschein (eds.), *Preferences, Utility and Demand*, Harcourt, Brace and Jovanovich, New York, pp. 276–88.

Clower, R. W. (1984), *Money and Markets: Essays by Robert W. Clower*, ed. D. Walker, Cambridge University Press, Cambridge.

——(1994), "Economics as an Inductive Science," *Southern Economic Journal*, 60: 805–14.

——(1995), "Axiomatics in Economics," *Southern Economic Journal*, 62: 307–19.

——(1996), "On Truth in Teaching Macroeconomics," in D. Vaz and K. Velupillai (eds.), *Inflation, Institutions and Information: Essays in Honour of Axel Leijonhufvud*, Macmillan, London.

Clower, R. W., and Howitt, P. W. (1978), "The Transactions Theory of the Demand for Money: A Reconsideration," *Journal of Political Economy*, 86: 449–65.

Coddington, E. A. (1961), *Introduction to Ordinary Differential Equations*, Dover, New York.

Condon, A. (1989), *Computational Models of Games*, MIT Press, Cambridge, Mass.

Conway, J. H. (1976), *On Numbers and Games*, Academic Press, New York.

Cook, S. A. (1987), "An Overview of Computational Complexity," in *ACM Turing Award Lectures: The First Twenty Years*, Addison-Wesley (ACM Press), New York, pp. 411–31.

Cooley, T. F., and Prescott, E. C. (1995), "Economic Growth and Business Cycles," in T. F. Cooley (ed.), *Frontiers of Business Cycle Research*, Princeton University Press, Princeton.

Cooper, N. C. (ed.) (1988), *From Cardinals to Chaos*, Cambridge University Press, Cambridge.

David, P. (1975), *Technical Choice, Innovation and Economic Growth*, Cambridge University Press, Cambridge.

——(1993), "Knowledge, Property and the System Dynamics of Technological Change," *Proceedings of the World Bank Annual Conference on Development Economics*, IBRD/World Bank, Washington, DC.

Davis, M. (1982), *Computability and Unsolvability*, Dover, New York.

——Matiyasevic, Y., and Robinson, J. (1976), "Hilbertís Tenth Problem: Diophantine Equations: Positive Aspects of a Negative Solution," in F. E. Browder (ed.), *Mathematical Developments Arising from Hilbert Problems*, American Mathematical Society, Providence, RI.

Day, R. H. (1992), "Models of Business Cycles: A Review Article," *Structural Change and Economic Dynamics*, 3: 177–82.

——(1993), "Nonlinear Dynamics and Evolutionary Economics," in R. H. Day and P. Chen (eds.), *Nonlinear Dynamics and Evolutionary Economics*, by Oxford University Press, Oxford.

de Leeuw, K., Moore, E. F., Shannon, C. E., and Shapiro, N. (1956), "Computability by Probabilistic Machines," in *Automata Studies*, Annals of Mathematics Studies, no. 34, Princeton University Press, 183–212.

De Vany, A. (1996), "Putting a Human Face on Rational Expectations: A Book Review," *Journal of Economic Dynamics and Control*, 20: 811–17.

Debreu, G. (1959), *Theory of Value*, New York: John Wiley.

——(1984), "Economic Theory in the Mathematical Mode," *American Economic Review*, 74: 267–78.

Dresher, M. (1961), *Games of Strategy: Theory and Applications*, Prentice-Hall, Englewood Cliffs, NJ.

Everett, H. (1954), "Recursive Games," mimeo, Princeton University.

Fine, T. L. (1973), *Theories of Probability: An Examination of Foundations*, Academic Press, New York.

Futia, C. (1977), "The Complexity of Economic Decision Rules," *Journal of Mathematical Economics*, 4: 289–99.

Gill, J, (1977), "Computational Complexity of Probabilistic Turing Machines," *SIAM Journal of Computation*, 6: 675–95.

Gödel, K. (1946), "Remarks before the Princeton Bicentennial Conference on Problems in Mathematics,: in M. Davis (ed.), *The Undecidable*, Raven Press, Hewlett, NY.

Gold, E. M. (1965), "Limiting Recursion," *The Journal of Symbolic Logic*, 30(1): 28–48.

——(1967), "Language Identification in the Limit," *Information and Control*, 10: 447–74.

Goldfarb, D., and Todd, M. J. (1982), "Modification and Implementation of the Ellipsoid Algorithm for Linear Programming," *Mathematical Programming*, 23: 1–19.

Gomory, R. E., and Baumol, W. J. (1960), "Integer Programming and Prices," *Econometrica*, 28: 521–50.

Goodwin, R. M. (1950), "A Non-Linear Theory of the Cycle," *The Review of Economics and Statistics*, 32: 316–20.

——(1951), "Iteration, Automatic Computers, and Economic Dynamics," *Metroeconomica*, 3(1): 1–7.

Gottinger, H. W. (1987), "Choice Processes, Computability and Complexity Computable Choice Functions," in *Economics and Artificial Intelligence*, AFCET/IASC/IFIP/IFAC/IFORS, Aix-en-Provence, France, pp. 201–2.

Grandmont, J.-M. (1985), "On Endogenous Competitive Business Cycles," *Econometrica*, 53: 995–1045.

Haavelmo, T. (1944), "The Probability Approach in Economics," *Econometrica*, 12 (Suppl., 118 pp.).

Hacking, I. (1987), "Was there a Probabilistic Revolution: 1800–1930?", in L. Krüger, L. J. Daston, and M. Heidelberger (eds.), *The Probabilistic Revolution*, i, *Ideas in History*, The MIT Press, Cambridge, Mass.

Hahn, F. H. (1994), "An Intellectual Retrospect," *Banca Nazionale del Lavoro-Quarterly Review*, V48: 245–58.

Hamming, R. W. (1991), *The Art of Probability*, Addison-Wesley, Menlo Park, Calif.

Harsanyi, J. C. (1977), *Rational Behaviour and Bargaining Equilibrium in Games and Social Situations*, Cambridge University Press, Cambridge.

Hayek, F. A. (1945), "The Use of Knowledge in Society," *American Economic Review*, 35: 519–30.

Hilbert, D. (1900), "Mathematische Probleme," *Göttinger Nachrichten*, pp. 253-97; trans. M. Winston Newson:"Mathematical Problems," *Bulletin of the American Mathematical Society*, 8 (1902): 437–79.

Hirsch, M. W. (1984), "The Dynamical Systems Approach to Differential Equations," *Bulletin of the American Mathematical Society*, 11 (n.s.): 1–61.

Hodges, A. (1983), *Alan Turing: The Enigma*, Burnett Books, London.

Hoggatt, A. C. (1959), "An Experimental Business Game," *Behavioral Science*, 4: 192–203.

Holland, J. H., and Miller, J. H. (1991), "Artificial Adaptive Agents in Economic Theory," *American Economic Review* (Papers and Proceedings), 81: 365–70.

Holm, J. (1993), *Complexity in Economic Theory: An Automata Theoretical Approach*, Lund Economic Studies, no. 53, University of Lund, Sweden.

Hunter, G. (1971), Metalogic: *An Introduction to the Metatheory of Standard First-Order Logic*, University of California Press, Berkeley and Los Angeles.

Isbell, J. R., and Marlow, W. H. (1956), "Attrition Games," *Naval Research Logistics Quarterly*, 3: 71–94.

Jones, J. (1974), "Recursive Undecidability-An Exposition," *American Mathematical Monthly*, 81: 724–38.

——(1978), "Three Universal Representations of Recursively Enumerable Sets," *Journal of Symbolic Logic*, 43: 335–51.

——(1981), "Classification of Quantifier Prefixes over Diophantine Equations," *Zeitschrift für Mathematische Logik und Grundlagen der Mathematik*, 27: 403–10.

Kalman, R. E. (1994), "Randomness Reexamined," *Modelling, Identification and Control*, 15: 141–51.

Kalmar, L. (1959), "An Argument against the Plausibility of Church's Thesis," in A. Heyting (ed.), *Constructivity in Mathematics*, North-Holland, Amsterdam, pp. 72–80.

Karlin, S. (1959), *Mathematical Methods and Theory in Games, Programming and Economics*, i, Addison-Wesley, Reading, Mass.

Karp, R. M. (1987), "Combinatorics, Complexity, and Randomness," ACM Turing Award Lectures: The First Twenty Years, Addison-Wesley (ACM Press), New York, pp. 433–53.

Kelly, J. S. (1988), "Social Choice and Computational Complexity," *Journal of Mathematical Economics*, 17: 1–8.

Kemeny, J. G. (1953), "The Use of Simplicity in Induction," *Philosophical Review*, 62: 391–408.

Keynes, J. M. (1933), *Essays in Biography*, Macmillan, London.

Khachiyan, L. G. (1979), "A Polynomial Algorithm in Linear Programming," *Soviet Mathematics Doklady*, 20, 191–4.

——(1980), "Polynomial Algorithms in Linear Programming," *Computational Mathematics and Mathematical Physics*, 20: 53–72.

Kleene, S. C. (1952), *Introduction to Metamathematics*, Van Nostrand, Princeton.

Knuth, D. E. (1981), The Art of Computer Programming, ii, *Seminumerical Algorithms*, 2nd edn., Addison-Wesley, Menlo Park, Calif.

Kolmogorov, A. N. (1983), "Combinatorial Foundations of Information

Theory and the Calculus of Probabilities," *Russian Mathematical Surveys*, 38(4): 29–40.

Kolmogorov, A. N. (1932/1998), "On the Interpretation of Institutionistic Logic" in P. Mancosu (ed.), *From Brouwer to Hilbert: The Debate on the Foundations of Mathematics in the 1920s*, Oxford University Press, Oxford, pp. 306–310.

Koppel, M. (1988), "Structure," in R. Herken (ed.), *The Universal Turing Machine: A Half-Century Survey*, Oxford University Press, Oxford, pp. 435–52.

Kozlov, M. K., Tarasov, S. P., and Khachiyan, L. G. (1979), "Polynomial Solvability of Convex Quadratic Programming," *Soviet Mathematics Doklady*, 20:. 1108–11.

Kramer, G. H. (1968), "An Impossibility Result Concerning the Theory of Decision-Making," Cowles Foundation Paper, no. 274, Yale University.

Kreisel, G. (1974), "A Notion of Mechanistic Theory," *Synthese*, 29: 11–26.

Kreps, D. M. (1990), *Game Theory and Economic Modelling*, Clarendon Press, Oxford.

Kuhn, T. S. (1977), *The Essential Tension: Selected Studies in Scientific Tradition*, University of Chicago Press, Chicago.

Kydland, F. E., and Prescott, E. C. (1990), "Business Cycles: Real Facts and a Monetary Myth," *Federal Reserve Bank of Minneapolis Quarterly Review*, Spring: 3–18.

Lakatos, L. (1978), "A Renascence of Empiricism in the Recent Philosophy of Mathematics," in J. Worrall and G. Currie (eds.), *Mathematics, Science and Epistemology: Philosophical Papers*, ii, Cambridge University Press, Cambridge.

Leibniz, G. (1686), "Universal Science: Characteristic XIV, XV," in *Monadology and other Philosophical Essays*, trans. P. Schreker, Bobbs-Merill, Indianapolis, Indiana, 1965.

Leijonhufvud, A. (1974), "Maximization and Marshall: The Marshall Lectures," mimeo, Cambridge and UCLA.

——(1991), "The Uses of the Past," paper delivered at the annual meeting of the History of Economics Society, Boston, 1987.

Lewis, A. A. (1985), "On Effectively Computable Realizations of Choice Functions," *Mathematical Social Sciences*, 10: 43–80.

Li, M., and Vitanyi, P. (1997), *An Introduction to Kolmogorov Complexity and its Applications*, 2nd edn., Springer-Verlag, New York and Heidelberg.

Lin, S., and Rado, T. (1965), "Computer Studies of Turing Machine Problems," *Journal of the Association for Computing Machinery*, 12: 196–212.

Lucas, R. E. Jr (1981), *Studies in Business-Cycle Theory*, Basil Blackwell, Oxford.

——(1986), "Adaptive Behaviour in Economic Theory," *Journal of Business*, 59: S401–S426.

——and Sargent, T. J. (1979), "After Keynesian Macroeconomics," in R. E. Lucas Jr and T. J. Sargent (eds.), *Rational Expectations and Econometric Practice*, George Allen and Unwin, London, 1981: 295–319.

Luce, D. R. (1959), *Individual Choice Behavior: A Theoretical Analysis*, John Wiley, New York.

Machlup, F. (1958), "Structure and Structural Change: Weaselwords and Jargon," *Zeitschrift für Nationalökonomie*, 18: 280–98.

Matiyasevic, Y. (1994), *Hilbert's Tenth Problem*, MIT Press, Cambridge, Mass.

McAfee, R. P. (1984), "Effective Computability in Economic Decisions," unpublished paper, University of Western Ontario, May.

McCulloch, W .S. (1965), *Embodiments of Mind*, MIT Press, Cambridge, Mass.

Megiddo, N., and Wigderson, A (1986), "On Play by Means of Computing Machines," in J. Y. Halpern (ed.), *Theoretical Aspects of Reasoning about Knowledge*, Morgan Kaufman Publishers, Los Altos, Calif.

Metakides, G., and Nerode, A. (1982), "The Introduction of Non-Recursive Methods into Mathematics," in A. S. Troelstra and D. van Dalen (eds.), *The L. E. J. Brouwer Centenary Symposium*, North-Holland, Amsterdam, pp. 319–35.

——Nerode, A., and Shore, R. A. (1985), "Recursive Limits on the Hahn-Banach Theorem," *Contemporary Mathematics*, 39: 85–91.

Minsky, M. (1967), *Computation: Finite and Infinite Machines*, Prentice-Hall, Englewood Cliffs, NJ.

Moore, C. (1995), "Smooth Maps of the Interval and the Real Line Capable of Universal Computation," mimeo, Santa Fe Institute, January 21.

Moret, B. M. (1998), *The Theory of Computation*, Addison-Wesley, Reading, Mass.

Moss, S., and Rae, J. (eds.) (1992), *Artificial Intelligence and Economic Analysis: Prospects and Problems*, Edward Elgar, Aldershot, Hants (UK).

Musgrave, A. (1981), "'Unreal Assumptions' in Economic Theory: The F-Twist Untwisted," *Kyklos*, 34: 377–87.

Myhill, J. (1971), "A Recursive Function Defined on a Compact Interval and Having a Continuous Derivative that is Not Recursive," *Michigan Mathematical Journal*, 18: 97–8.

Myrdal, G. (1939), *Monetary Equilibrium*, Hodge, London.

Nelson, R. R., and Winter, S. G. (1982), *An Evolutionary Theory of Economic Change*, Harvard University Press, Cambridge, Mass.

Newman, P., and Read, R. (1961), "Representation Problems for Preference Orderings," *Journal of Economic Behaviour*, 1: 149–69.

Nozick, R. (1981), *Philosophical Explanations*, Clarendon Press, Oxford.

Osborne, D., and Rubinstein A. (1995), *A Course in Game Theory*, The MIT Press, Cambridge, Massachusetts.

Papadimitriou,C., and Steiglitz, K. (1982), *Combinatorial Optimization: Algorithms and Complexity*, Prentice-Hall, Englewood Cliffs, NJ.

Patinkin, D. (1965), *Money, Interest and Prices*, 2nd edn., Harper and Row, London.

Post, E. L. (1944), "Recursively Enumerable Sets of Positive Integers and their Decision Problems," *Bulletin of the American Mathematical Society*, 50: 284–316.

——(1994), *Solvability, Provability, Definability: The Collected Works of Emil L. Post*, ed. Martin Davis, Birkhäuser, Basel.

Pour-El, M. B., and Richards, J. I. (1979), "A Computable Ordinary Differential Equation which Possesses No Computable Solution," *Annals of Mathematical Logic*, 17: 61–90.

————(1989), *Computability in Analysis and Physics*, Springer-Verlag, Berlin.

Prasad, K. (1991), "Computability and Randomness of Nash Equilibrium in Infinite Games," *Journal of Mathematical Economics*,20: 429–42.

Putnam, H. (1951), *The Meaning of the Concept of Probability in Application to Finite Sequences*, Garland Publishing, New York and London. 1990.

——(1963), "Probability and Confirmation," *Mathematics, Matter and Method:Philosophical Papers*, i, Cambridge University Press, Cambridge, 1975.

——(1967), "The Mental Life of Some Machines," in *Mind, Language and Reality: Philosophical Papers*, ii, Cambridge University Press, Cambridge, 1975.

Rabin, M. O. (1957), "Effective Computability of Winning Strategies," in M. Dresher, A. W. Tucker and P. Wolfe (eds.), *Annals of Mathematics Studies*, Princeton University Press, Princeton.

Rado, T. (1962), "On Non-Computable Functions," *Bell System Technical Journal*, May: 877–84.

Ramsey, F. P. (1978), *Foundations: Essays in Philosophy, Logic, Mathematics and Economics*, ed. D. H. Mellor, Routledge and Kegan Paul, London.

Rice, H. G. (1953), "Classes of Recursively Enumerable Sets and their Decision Problems," *Transactions of the American Mathematical Society*, 89: 25–59.

Richardson, D. (1968), "Some Undecidable Problems involving Elementary Functions of a Real Variable," *The Journal of Symbolic Logic*, 33: 514–20.

Rissanen, J. (1989), *Stochastic Complexity in Statistical Inquiry*, World Scientific, Singapore.

Rogers, H. Jr (1967), *Theory of Recursive Functions and Effective Computability*, MIT Press,Cambridge, Mass.

Romer, P. M. (1993), "Two Strategies for Economic Development: Using Ideas and Producing Ideas," *Proceedings of the World Bank Annual Conference on Development Economics*, IBRD/World Bank, Washington, DC.

Rosenblatt, F. (1962), *Principles of Neurodynamics*, Spartan Books, New York.

Ruelle, D. (1988), "Is Our Mathematics Natural? The Case of Equilibrium Statistical Mechanics," *Bulletin of the American Mathematical Society*, 19 (n.s.): 259–68.

Rustem, B., and Velupillai, K. (1985), "Constructing Objective Functions for Macroeconomic Decision Models: On the Complexity of the Policy Design Process" Memorandum no. 137, Copenhagen University Economic Institute, September.

——and ——(1990), "Rationality, Computability and Complexity," *Journal of Economic Dynamics and Control*, 14: 419–32.

Samuelson, P. A. (1938), "A Note on the Pure Theory of Consumer's Behaviour," *Economica* (n.s), 5: 61–71.

——(1948), "Consumption Theory in Terms of Revealed Preference," *Economica*, 15: 243–53.

Sargent, T. J. (1993), *Bounded Rationality in Macroeconomics*, Oxford University Press, Oxford.

Scarf, H. E. (1981*a*), "Production Sets with Indivisibilities, Part I: Generalities," *Econometrica*, 49: 1–32.

——(1981*b*), "Production Sets with Indivisibilities, Part II: The Case of Two Activities," *Econometrica*, 49: 395–423.

——(1989), "Mathematical Programming and Economic Theory," Cowles Foundation Discussion Paper no. 930, Yale University, New Haven/University Press, Princeton.

——(1994), "The Allocation of Resources in the Presence of Indivisibilities," *Journal of Economic Perspectives*, 8(4): 111–28.

Seidenberg, A. (1954), "A New Decision Method for Elementary Algebra," *Annals of Mathematics*, 60: 365–74.

Sen, A. (1973), "Behaviour and the Concept of Preference," *Economica*, XL: August, 241–59.

Shepherdson, J. C. (1980), "Utility Theory Based on Rational Probabilities," *Journal of Mathematical Economics*, 7: 91–113.

Shubik, M. (1959), *Strategy and Market Structure*, John Wiley, New York.

——(1984), *Game Theory in the Social Sciences*, ii, *A Game-Theoretic Approach to Political Economy*, MIT Press, Cambridge, Mass.

Schrijver, A. (1986), *Theory of Linear and Integer Programming*, John Wiley, New York.

Schwartz, T. (1986), *The Logic of Collective Choice*, Columbia University Press, New York.

Simon, H. A. (1947), *Administrative Behaviour*, Macmillan, New York.

Simon, H. A. (1956), "Rational Choice and the Structure of the Environment," in *Models of Thought*, i, Yale University Press, New Haven, 1979.

——(1957), *Models of Man: Social and Rational*, John Wiley, New York.

——(1969), *The Sciences of the Artificial*, 2nd edn., MIT Press, Cambridge, Mass, 1981.

——(1979), *Models of Thought*, Yale University Press, New Haven.

——(1983), *Reason in Human Affairs*, Basil Blackwell, Oxford.

Solow, R. M. (1954), "The Survival of Mathematical Economics," *Review of Economics and Statistics*, 36: 372–4.

Spear, S. E. (1989), "Learning Rational Expectations under Computability Constraints," *Econometrica*, 57: 889–910.

Spencer, H. (1866), "The Co-operation of the Factors" (ch. XIII, vol. 1, pt. III) in *The Principles of Biology*, in *Adaptive Individuals in Evolving Populations: Models and Algorithms*, ed. R. K. Belew and M. Mitchell, Addison-Wesley, Menlo Park, Calif., 1996.

Stewart, I. (1991), "Deciding the Undecidable," *Nature*, 22 August: 664–5.

Suzumura, K. (1983), *Rational Choice, Collective Decisions, and Social Welfare*, Cambridge University Press, Cambridge.

Swan, T. W. (1956), "Economic Growth and Capital Accumulation," *Economic Record*, 32: 334–61.

Sylos-Labini, P. (1962), *Oligopoly and Technical Progress*, Harvard University Press, Cambridge, Mass.

Tseytin, G. S. (1981), "From Logicism to Proceduralism (an Autobiographical Account)," in A. P. Ershov and D. E. Knuth (eds.), *Algorithms in Modern Mathematics and Computer Science*, Springer-Verlag, Heidelberg, pp. 390–6.

Turing, A. M. (1954), "Solvable and Unsolvable Problems," *Science News*, 31: 7–23.

van der Waerden, B. (1970), *Algebra*, i, Frederick Ungar, New York.

Varian, H. R. (1972), "Complexity of Social Decisions," unpublished paper, UC-Berkeley.

Velupillai, K. (1992), "Implicit Nonlinearities in the Economic Dynamics of 'Impulse and Propagation'," in K. Velupillai (ed.), *Nonlinearities, Disequilibria and Simulation: Essays in Honour of Björn Thalberg*, Macmillan, London.

——(1996), "The Computable Alternative in the Formalization of Economics: A Counterfactual Essay," *Kyklos*, 49: 251–72.

——(1998a), "New Tools for Making Economics on Inductive Science,: forthcoming in P. Howitt, E. di Antoni, and A. Leijonhufvud (eds.), *Money, Markets and Method*, Edward Elgar, Aldershot, Hants (UK).

——(1998b), "Formalization, Rigour, Proof and Existence: Some Subversive Thoughts," forthcoming in *Journal of Economic Methodology*.

——(1999*a*), *An Introduction to Computable Economics*, in preparation for Oxford University Press.

——(1999*b*), "The Effective Content of the Proof of Economic Propositions," forthcoming in *Journal of Economic Behaviour and Organization*.

——and Punzo, L. F. (1996), "Co-ordinating the Not-Too-Rational: Leijonhufvud's Macroeconomic Methodologies," in D. Vaz and K. Velupillai (eds.), *Inflation, Institutions and Information: Essays in Honour of Axel Leijonhufvud*, Macmillan, London, pp. 12–23.

von Neumann, J. (1966), *Theory of Self-Reproducing Automata*, ed. and completed by A. W. Burks, University of Illinois Press, Urbana, Ill.

Wagon, S. (1985), *The Banach–Tarski Paradox*, Cambridge University Press, Cambridge.

Wang, H. (1986), *Beyond Analytic Philosophy: Doing Justice to What We Know*, MIT Press, Cambridge, Mass.

——(1994), *Mathematics, Education and Philosophy: An International Perspective*, ed. by. P. Ernest, Falmer Press, London.

——(1996), *A Logical Journey: From Gödel to Philosophy*, MIT Press, Cambridge, Mass.

Weyl, H. (1917/1994), "Preface," in H. Weyl, *The Continuum: A Critical Examination of the Foundation of Analysis*, trans. S. Pollard and T. Bole, Dover, New York.

Wittgenstein, L. (1980), *Remarks on the Philosophy of Psychology*, i, Basil Blackwell, Oxford.

Author Index

Aberth, O. 201
Anderson, P. W. 201
Anosov, D. V. 105
Arrow, K. J. 29, 31–4, 38, 43, 148, 153, 161–2, 182, 201
Auden, W. H. 144, 150, 163, 182
Aumann, R. J. 13
Azariadis, C. 95, 98, 164, 201

Babbage, C. 16, 107, 201
Bacon, F. 8, 180
Baum, E. 14, 5–9, 201
Baumol, W. J. 18–20, 204
Beckett, S. 178
Beeson, M. 2, 30, 201
Belew, R. K. 210
Bennett, C. H. 6, 175, 201
Berlekamp, E. R. 47, 114, 201
Binmore, K. 22–3, 27, 108, 201
Boehner, P. 78, 202
Bole, T. 211
Boolos, G. S. 122, 189, 202
Borges, J. L. 16, 154, 202
Bourbaki, N. 182
Bowen, R. 105, 179
Bridges, D. S. 96, 105, 189
Bronowski, J. 146, 158, 202
Brouwer, L. E. J. 117, 202, 206
Browder, F. E. 203
Burks, A. W. 211
Burns, A. F. 71

Campbell, D. E. 42, 202
Canning, D. 23, 202
Cantor, G. 179, 182
Carnap, R. 21
Caviness, B. F. 104, 202
Chaitin, G. J. 73–4, 80, 175, 202
Chen, P. 203
Chipman, J. C. 32, 202
Church, A. 1, 7
Clower, R. W. viii, 19, 66, 87, 136, 178–80, 202
Coddington, E. A. 165–8, 203
Condon, A. 127, 131, 203
Conway, J. 114, 116, 131, 201, 203

Cook, S. A. 134, 203
Cooley, T. F. 172, 203
Cooper, N. C. 102, 203
Currie, G. 206

Daston, L. J. 204
David, P. 153, 203
Davis, M. 108, 189, 203–4
Day, R. H. 44, 51, 203
Debreu, G. 2, 13, 18, 148, 150–1, 161, 203
de Finetti, B. 74. 116
de Leeuw, K. 203
De Vany, A. 89, 203
di Antoni, E. 210
Diophantus 107
Dixon, H. 64
Dresher, M. 116, 203, 208

Edgeworth, F. V. 71
Ernest, P. 211
Ershov, A. P. 210
Everett, H. 116, 203

Feyerabend, P. 171
Fine, T. 74, 114, 203
Fisher, R. A. 71
Friedman, M. 37
Fisch, R. 71, 168
Frost, R. 11
Furtwängler, P. 124
Futia, C. 3, 22, 203

Gill, J. 96–7, 203
Gödel, K. 1, 8, 88, 124, 179, 199, 211
Gold, E. M. 83–6, 90, 98, 204
Goldfarb, D. 142, 204
Gomory, R. E. 18–20, 204
Good, I. J. 73
Goodwin, R. M. vi, 2, 52, 59, 169, 182, 204
Gormon, W. M. 137
Gottinger, H. W. 22, 204
Grandmont, J.-M. 169, 204
Guy, R. K. 201

Haavelmo, T. 7, 70–1, 77, 204
Hacking, I. 7–8, 204
Hahn, F. H. 12–13, 161–2, 201, 204
Halpern, J. Y. 207
Hamming, R. W. 103, 204
Harsanyi, J. C. 45–6, 53, 204
Hayek, F. von 19–20, 69, 164, 204
Heaney, S. 90, 101, 178
Heidelberger, M. 204
Herbrand, J. 1
Herken, R. 201, 206
Heyting, A. 181, 205
Hicks, J. R. 169
Hilbert, D. 107, 179, 182, 204, 206
Hirsch, W. M. 168, 177, 204
Hodges, A. 168, 204
Hoggatt, A. C. 112, 205
Holland, J. H. 45, 205
Holm, J. 22, 205
Howitt, P. W. 19, 180, 202, 210
Hume, D. 6, 87
Hunter, G. 189, 205
Hurwicz, L. 202

Isbell, J. R. 116, 205

Jacobsen, N. 104
Jeffrey, R. C. 122, 189, 202
Jevons, W. S. 6, 8
Johansson, M. viii
Jones, J. 4, 109, 120–1, 124–30, 205

Kaldor, N. 172–3
Kalman, R. E. 71–2, 77–8, 205
Kalmar, L. 197, 205
Karlin, S. 116, 205
Karp, R. M. 10, 128, 134, 205
Kelly, J. S. 22, 205
Kelvin, Lord 12
Kemeny, J. G. 66, 205
Keynes, J. M. 6, 8, 71, 74, 87, 205
Khachiyan, L. G. 4, 14, 20, 205–6
Klee, V. 134, 145
Kleene, S. C. 8, 101, 156, 205
Knight, F. 74
Knuth, D. E. 74, 206, 210
Kolmogorov, A. N. 72–3, 77, 80, 82, 181–2, 206
Koopmans, T. C. 71–2
Koppel, M. 175, 206
Kozlov, M. K. 141, 206
Kreisel, G. 167, 206
Kreps, D. M. 110–12, 206

Krüger, L. 204
Kuhn, T. 8, 24, 206
Kydland, F. 71–2, 172, 206

Lakatos, I. 6, 206
Lange, O. 164
Latsis, S. viii
Leibniz, G. W. 10, 16, 206
Leijonhufvud, A. viii, 12, 15, 25–6, 136–8, 145, 202, 206, 210–11
Leontief, W. 6
Levine, R. D. 202
Lewis, A. 3, 11, 17–18, 35, 39, 42–3, 96, 100, 114, 206
Li, M. 97, 206
Lin, S. 121, 206
Löfgren, L. 73
Lorenz, E. 169
Lucas, R. E. jr. 46–8, 51, 70, 168, 172, 206–7
Luce, D. 32, 207
Luna, F. viii
Lundberg, E. 153

McAfee, R. P. 17–18, 100, 207
McCall, J. J. viii, 69
McCulloch, W. 89, 156, 207
Machlup, R. 37, 44, 207
Malthus, T. R. 87, 180
Mancosu, P. 202, 206
Mantel, R. 161
Marlow, W. H. 116, 205
Matiyasevich, Y. 107–8, 124, 130, 203, 207
Megiddo, N. 108, 207
Mellor, D. H. 208
Menger, K. 19
Metakides, G. 150, 207
Mill, J. S. 6, 8, 12, 87
Miller, J. H. 45, 205
Minsky, M. 47–9, 207
Minty, G. J. 134, 145
Mises, von L. 19, 164
Mises, von R. 76
Mitchell, M. 210
Mitchell, W. C. 71
Molière (Jean Baptiste Poquelin) 7, 159
Moore, C. 47–9, 207
Moore, E. F. 203
Moret, B. M. 189, 207
Morgenstern, O. 11, 116
Morrison, E. 201
Morrison, P. 201

Moss, S. 64, 207
Musgrave, A. 37, 101, 207
Myhill, J. 96, 207
Myrdal, G. 5, 87, 207

Nelson, R. R. 46, 158–60, 207
Nerode, A. 150, 207
Newell, A. 23–4
Newman, P. 32, 207
Nozick, R. 32, 36, 207

Osborne, D. 22, 63, 207

Papadimitriou, C. 61, 208
Pareto, V. 164
Patinkin, D. 33, 208
Peano, G. 1
Petty, W. 6, 8, 16, 87, 180
Phelps, E. S. 70
Pines, D. 201
Pitts, W. 156, 167
Pollard, S. 211
Polya, G. 2, 25, 43
Post, E. 1, 7, 29–30, 88, 120, 208
Pour-El, M. B. 96, 167, 208
Prasad, K. 20, 208
Prescott, E. C. 71–2, 172, 203, 206
Punzo, L. F. 1, 25, 211
Putnam, H. 3, 21, 23, 40–2, 66–7, 73, 78, 83, 87, 208

Rabin, M. 1, 3–4, 17, 96, 108–9, 117–21, 123–4, 127, 129–30, 208
Rado, T. 88, 121–2, 206, 208
Rae, J. 64, 207
Ramsey, F. 32, 116, 208
Read, R. 32, 207
Reichenbach, H. 21
Ricardo, D. 2, 6, 8, 180
Rice, H. G. 93, 208
Richards, I. 96, 167, 208
Richardson, D. 104, 208
Richter, M. 202
Rissanen, J. 100, 170, 208
Robbins, L. 19, 164
Robinson, A. 13
Robinson, J. 203
Robinson, J. V. 153
Rogers, H. jr. 34, 208
Romer, R. 147, 151–60, 183, 208
Rosenblatt, F. 25, 209
Rössler, O. 170
Rubinstein, A. 22, 63, 207

Ruelle, D. 2, 183–4, 209
Rustem, B. viii, 3, 17–18, 20, 42–3, 99, 142, 144, 209

Samuelson, P. A. 37, 209
Sargent, T. J. 68, 75, 89, 100, 168, 207, 209
Savage, L. J. 74, 116
Scarf, H. 2–3, 11, 14–15, 18, 20, 22–3, 148, 183, 209
Schreker, P. 206
Schriver, A. 141, 209
Schwartz, T. 30–1, 209
Seidenberg, A. 104–5, 209
Sen, A. K. 37–8, 209
Shannon, C. 203
Shapiro, N. 203
Shepherdson, J. C. 96, 209
Shore, R. A. 207
Shubik, M. 110, 113, 117, 209
Simon, H. A. 3, 6, 11, 17–18, 20–3, 25–6, 28, 43, 60, 87, 89, 160, 183, 209–10
Slutsky, E. 168
Smale, S. 197
Smith, A. 6, 8, 23, 87, 180
Smith, V. 22
Solomonoff, R. J. 73, 79–80, 84, 86
Solow, R. M. 1, 12, 173, 210
Sonnenschein, H. 161, 202
Spear, S. 3, 17–18, 87–91, 94, 101–6, 114, 210
Spencer, H. 44, 210
Spencer, J. viii
Steiglitz, K. 61
Stewart, I. 52, 160, 210
Stigler, G. 69
Strotz, R. H. 137
Swan, T. 153, 210
Swift, J. 16
Suzumura, K. 30, 34–5, 43, 210
Sylos-Labini, P. 110, 210

Tarasov, S. P. 206
Taylor, R. 164
Thalberg, B. vii, 210
Todd, M. J. 142, 204
Tribus, M. 202
Troelstra, A. S. 207
Tseytin, G. S. 26, 210
Tucker, A. W. 208
Turing, A. M. 1, 7 32, 116, 118, 146, 168, 181, 197, 204, 210

Ulam, S. 102

van Dalen, D. 207
van der Waerden, B. 105, 210
Varian, H. R. 22, 210
Vaz, D. 202, 211
Velupillai, K. 2, 11–12, 17–18, 20–1, 25,
    42–3, 99, 142, 144, 154, 168, 183,
    202, 209–11
von Neumann, J. 11, 47, 116, 211

Wagon, S. 148, 211
Wald, A. 13

Walker, D. 202
Walras, L. 13
Wang, H. 124, 179, 181, 211
Weyl, H. 146, 211
Wigderson, A. 108, 207
Winston Newson, M. 204
Winter, S. G. 46, 158–60, 207
Wittgenstein, L. 28, 185, 189, 197, 211
Wolfe, P. 208
Wood, J. 7
Worrall, J. 206

Zambelli, S. viii

Subject Index

Academy of Lagado 16
adaptive:
  behavior 4, 44–6, 49, 51, 60, 150;
    steady states of 46–7, 50
  process 47, 50, 58–9
adaptively rational agents 45
ad-hoc shockeries 51, 65
algebraic theory of automata 22
algorithmic complexity theory 4, 20, 69,
  75, 77, 80–2, 97, 144, 156
algorithmic economics 22
algorithmic information theory, *see*
  algorithmic complexity theory
algorithmic knowledge 26
algorithmic logic 182
algorithm(s) 2, 15, 27, 62
  efficiency of viii, 6
  Khachiyan's 4, 20, 141–4
  simplex 7, 134–5, 145, 149
  Sturm's 103–5
alternating diophantine machines 130
ambiguity ix
American institutionalists 8
arithmetical games 3, 18, 109, 116, 124,
  127–9
  diophantine complexity of 18
Arrow's impossibility theorem 43, 182
artificially adaptive agents 45
"as if" 37, 101–2
  logic of 37
axiom of choice 38, 112, 154

backward-induction 108
Bayesian 74, 85, 98
  learning 90
Bayes's:
  formula 79
  rule 83
  theorem 82
behavioral economics 22, 24
black-body radiation 12
binary:
  sequences 75, 76, 79
  strings 79, 80
Boolean:
  propositions 54
  expression 115, 128, 130

Book of Blueprints 154, 156
boundedly rational expectations 79
Bourbakianism, *see* formalism; formal-
  ist-school of mathematics
business cycle theories 5, 51, 147, 164,
  168–9, 171, 173, 176–7
busy beaver 88, 156
  function 104
  game 109, 121–2, 197
  number 121–3

capital:
  human 152, 156–8
  physical 155
Cantor's paradise 179
Cauchy–Peano theorem 164–5
cellular automata 49, 64
Centre for Computable Economics viii
Chaitin's Ω 74
chance:
  taming of 7
choice:
  binary 31
  functions 28–32, 37, 39, 40
  process 30–1
  theory 32, 34, 96, 102
Church's thesis, *see* Church–Turing
  thesis
Church–Turing thesis 1, 19, 25, 30, 37,
  43, 46, 73, 78, 88, 101, 144–5, 158,
  161, 188–9, 196–8, 200
classical analysis 96, 144, 146
classical mechanisms 167
classical recursion theory 5–6, 29, 98,
  120
Coddington's S-machine 166–8
cognitive science 23, 25
combinatorial optimization 6–7, 19
complexity 68, 128
  algorithmic 6, 10, 118, 164, 200
  average-case 145
  computational viii, 3, 6, 10, 17, 20,
    100, 200, 108–9, 118, 128, 130,
    134–5, 144, 164
  descriptive 75
  diophantine 6, 10, 18, 100, 108–9,
    129–30, 200

complexity (*cont.*):
  information-based 145
  polynomial-time 4
  stochastic 6, 10
computable analysis 4, 6, 94, 100,
    102–3, 114, 144, 150, 162, 167, 183
computable approximation 86, 103–4
computable economics vii, 1–4, 10–11,
    14, 16–17, 22, 25–6, 40, 144, 146
computable functions 1, 76, 104, 119,
    120, 122–3
  intuitively 188, 193
computable general equilibrium 4, 15,
    17, 22
computable numbers 94, 114, 159, 181–2
computable probability density func-
    tions 74, 96
computable rationality 25
computable real function 96
computable real numbers 96, 158, 167
computable winning strategy 121,
    123–4, 126–7, 129
computability 1, 81, 89, 108, 199
  theory 10
computation universality vii, 47, 49,
    50–1, 59, 64–5, 69, 105, 158, 176–7
computationally viable 42–3
conjunctive normal form 128, 130
conservation principles 64–5
constructive:
  analysis 6, 13, 103, 144
  numbers 181
  proof 122
countable infinity 32–3, 116, 118–19
curse of dimensionality 112, 153

decentralization 164, 180
  effective 148
  efficient 149
decidable 38, 89, 102, 115
  effectively 35, 39–40
  property 35
  proposition 38
  set 197
decision problems 7, 15, 18, 63, 107,
    145
Delphic oracle 148
demand curve 110
Dharmapada vii, ix
diagonalization 29, 86
difference equations:
  linear 170
  nonlinear 169

stochastic linear 5, 168
differential equations:
  initial value problem for 165–6
  nonlinear 168–9
  ordinary 165
  partial 168
diophantine 115
  equation 59–60, 107–9, 124, 130
  formalism 55
  nature of recursively enumerable sets
    109, 116, 124, 127, 129, 159, 163
dynamic programming 7, 135
dynamical system(s) 47, 52, 158, 168,
    175
  attractors of 59
  basins of attraction of 50
  capable of computation universality
    49, 53, 59
  computable 165
  differential 161–2
  evolutionary 158
  hyperbolic 105
  limit sets of 44, 49
  measurable 161–2
  stochastic 105
  universal 49–50, 53

economic theory:
  mathematization of 3, 6, 8, 11–12,
    151
economic dynamics 5
economics:
  computable approach to 8, 68, 88,
    183–4
  as a deductive discipline 6
  as an inductive science 66, 178
  inductive tradition in 87
  probability approach to 7, 70
  as problem-solving 182
effective:
  calculability 1, 101, 108, 144
  decidability 35
  encodability 33–6, 38, 40
  instructions 1
  process 79, 95, 108, 189
  procedure 38–9, 40, 51, 100, 104, 122,
    163, 169
  undecidability 4, 115, 124, 161
effectivizing 36
enumerability 98, 193
epistemology 2, 8, 48, 199
equilibrium:
  existence of 11, 13, 15, 91, 103

stability of 11, 15
uncomputable 18
uniqueness 11, 15
Euler's number 15
evolutionary:
    agents 45
    development 160
    economics 44, 136, 159
existential:
    quantifiers 113, 115, 123–5, 129, 131
    results 108
existence proofs 14, 162
expected utility maximization 114

finite automata 21, 41–2, 100, 118
fix-points 91–4, 103, 162
    computable 167
formalism 11, 27, 69
formalist school of mathematics 13, 87,
    157, 179
formalization:
    of economics 2
four colour map problem 19
frequency stability 76–7
function(s):
    Akerman's 146
    computable 1, 76, 104, 119, 120,
        122–3, 193, 195
    excess-demand 33, 103–4, 161–2
    identity 194
    non-recursive 40, 78
    partial 196
    partial recursive 39, 88, 98, 144,
        162–3, 197–8
    primitive recursive 83, 196
    projection 195
    propositional 34
    recursive 83, 85–6, 193
    semi-computable 81
    successor 195
    total 86, 196

games 16–17
    alternating 113
    arithmetic 3, 18, 109, 116, 124, 127–8
    attrition 115
    busy beaver 109, 121–2, 197
    computable 185, 187, 189
    determined 115–16, 125, 130, 133
    diophantine complexity of 18
    of economic survival 109, 113, 116
    effectively playable 18, 107–9,
        115–16, 119, 121, 130, 150, 189

effectively undecidable 18, 115
effectively unplayable 18
extensive form of 110, 113
Gale–Stewart 90, 96, 108–9, 118, 121,
    124–5, 127, 131
nonrecursive 187, 189
recursive 116, 187, 189
silver dollar 114–15, 121
uncomputable 185, 187, 189
generalized recursion theory 120
(Gödel–Herbrand) general recursiveness
    1, 101, 199
Gödel numbering 29, 33, 171
Gold's model of learning 83, 90, 98–9
growth theory 5, 51, 157, 164, 173
    endogenous 147, 159
    evolutionary models of 159–60
    models 89, 152, 159–60
    production sub-model of 157

Hahn–Banach theorem 103, 148, 150,
    164, 179
    recursive version of 150
halting problem for Turing machines
    49–50, 100, 115, 159, 198
Heine–Borel theorem 105
Hilbert's tenth problem 6, 59–60, 104,
    107, 109, 123–4, 126
human mathematics 183–4
Hume's problem 88

ideas:
    as bit strings 156, 158
    excludable 152
    in growth models 151–2, 155
    nonrival 152
    as programs 158
identification:
    by enumeration 83–4, 86, 99
    in the limit 83–4, 99
incompleteness 3, 8, 73, 154–5
    of reasoning processes 9
incompressibility 81
increasing returns to scale 180
    due to indivisibilities 15, 17, 179
indeterminism 7, 8
induction 4, 8, 72, 100, 106, 147
    modern theory of 4, 21, 66–8, 71–2,
        79, 83, 90, 179; theorem of the 82
    process 68, 135
    recursion theoretic vii, 68, 135
inductive:
    inference 67–8, 83–4, 86–7

inductive (*cont.*):
  logic 21, 66–7, 87
  methods 66
  ontology 8
  reasoning 67
infinite divisibility 112
infinitesimals 14
information 69, 70, 79, 97, 109, 138, 170
  as bit strings 155–6
  as an economic good 70
  economics 136
  recursion-theoretic 114
  theory 72
integer programming 19, 62, 148–9
interesting dynamics 50, 168, 177
intuitionistic logic 181–2

Jones's modified Rabin game 109, 120–1, 123, 129

kinked-oligopoly-curve 110
Kolmogorov–Chaitin–Solomonoff thesis 88, 144–5, 200
Kraft's inequality 82

Lagrange multiplier 143
λ-calculus 1, 30, 88
law of the excluded middle 3, 34, 103, 125
learning 3, 7, 16–17, 79, 83, 89, 150
  as induction 4, 6, 72, 79, 90, 100, 106
  machines 66
  rational expectations equilibria 89, 90–1, 93, 98, 105
  under computability constraints 89, 90
"Library of Babel" 154
LIFE 47, 49
linear programming 7, 134–5, 141, 148–9
Lipshitz condition 164
logic:
  algorithmic 182
  classical 182
  intuitionistic 181–2
  mathematical 2, 12, 181
  theoretical 181
Lorenz equations 169

McCulloch–Pitts neurons 53–4, 57
marginal revolution 12
Marshallian consumer 136–9, 141
Marshallian consumer's algorithm 140–1

Marshallian consumer's decision process 141
martingales 114
mathematical logic 2, 12, 181
Maxwell's demon 64
maximum principle 135
measurement without theory 71
meccano sets 5, 151
Methodology of Scientific Research Programs (MSRP) 14
Michaelson–Morley experiment 12
minimum description length (MDL) 6, 100, 170
model theory 2, 10, 12–13, 26, 181
modern theory of induction 4, 21, 66–8, 71–2, 79, 83, 90, 179
  theorem of 82
monopolist 110, 112
Monopoly (game of) 116–17, 187
multiple equilibria 5, 164, 168

Nash equilibrium 110, 118
natural numbers 167
neoclassical closure 70, 114
newclassical 70, 168
NIM 114–15, 121
no-arbitrage hypothesis 51, 65, 68–9, 75
nonalgorithmic:
  knowledge 167
  machine 166
nonconstructive 108
  existence proofs 162
nonconvexity 19
nondeterministic diophantine machines 130
nondeterministic Turing machine 31, 130
noneffective 96, 108
  existence proofs 164
  processes 41
nonlinear deterministic formalisms 5
nonlinear programming 7
nonrecursive:
  functions 40, 78
  reals 95
nonstandard:
  analysis 2, 13, 103, 180
  numbers 187
NP-complete 128

Occam's razor 78, 80, 83, 86–7, 98
oligopoly 110, 113
operations research:

classical 7
modern 7
optimization 17, 178–9
  combinatorial 6, 19
  problems 7, 18, 150
oracle computation 80
overlapping generations model 88, 94–5

partial differential equations 168
partial recursive functions 39, 88, 98,
  162–3, 197–8
phenomenological thermodynamics 76
place-selection function 74, 76–7
political arithmetic 8, 16
positive aspects of negative solutions
  18, 40, 42, 51
Post's machine 88
predicate:
  calculus 52–3
  logic 26
prefix:
  code 81–2
  complexity 81, 99
  machine 81
prenex normal form 113, 125–6, 128,
  172
price-taking behavior 13
primitive recursion 195
primitive recursive function 83, 196
prisoner's dilemma 108, 118
probability 68–73, 103, 113–14, 172
  frequency theory of 71, 74, 76
  Kolmogorov 77, 82
  logical 116
  subjective 118
problem:
  analogical 25
  heuristic 25
  human 24
  inductive 25
  recursion-theoretic characterization
    of 3
  solvers 2, 3, 149, 181–3
  solving 24–5, 61, 181–2
procedural decision making 4
  knowledge 26–7
program machine 47–8
  see also register machine
proof theory 2, 12, 181
PSPACE-complete 128–9

QSAT 128–9
quantum mechanics 167

Rabin-type games 108–9, 124, 126–7,
  129
random numbers 73–4
randomness:
  of finite sequences 74–6
rational behaviour 21, 43–4, 47, 51, 114
  normative theories of 45
rational choice 28–9, 36, 47, 52, 63, 100
  function 29, 35
rational economic agent 4, 21, 23, 29,
  30–1, 36–7, 42, 48, 58, 60, 74–7
rational expectations 17, 79
rational expectations equilibrium 4, 83,
  88, 90–1, 93–4, 98–9, 103, 105, 114,
  135, 150
  computable identifiability of 4
  learning 88, 90, 93
rational numbers 10
rationality 3, 4, 16, 18, 23, 31, 49, 50,
  88, 150
  bounded, *see* boundedly rational
    expectations
  ε-approximate 45
  global 23
  limited, *see* boundedly rational expec-
    tations
  principle of 9
  procedural 17, 63, 137
  recursion-theoretic characterization
    of 17
  substantive 63, 64
rationalizable choice function 37, 40
real analysis 94, 183
real numbers 94, 96, 98, 131, 167, 180
real business cycles 147, 171–6
reasoning processes:
  formalisms underlying 9
  incompleteness of 9
recursion theoretic:
  formalism 2, 10, 14–15
  learning 90
  mathematics viii
  randomness 74, 114
recursion theory 2, 6, 7, 12, 18, 181
  applied 4, 16, 20, 109
recursive 50, 65, 81, 96, 100, 123, 126,
  129
  functions 83, 85–6, 193; *see also* com-
    putable functions; partial recursive
    functions; primitive recursive func-
    tions
  hypotheses 78
  measure 83

recursive (*cont.*):
  real numbers 97–8
  rule 30
  real number 167
  sets 29, 115, 119, 123, 197, 198
recursive competitive equilibrium 174
recursively enumberable 50, 65, 81, 109,
  160, 162, 197–8
  sets 29, 115, 120, 197–8
reductio ad absurdum 108
register machine 47–8
Rice–Shapiro theorem 87, 102, 159,
  163, 199
Rice's theorem 40, 50, 87, 93–4, 102,
  159, 163, 188, 198–9
Rössler system 170, 175

satisfiable 128, 130
satisficing 17–18, 25
S–D–M theorem 161
second fundamental theorem of welfare
  economics 5, 146–7, 149, 164, 179
semicomputable:
  from above 82
  from below 82–3
  function 82
  measure 83
sensitive dependence on initial conditions 49
set theory 2, 10, 12–13, 18, 26, 151, 181
shadowing lemma 105
Shannon code 72
signal processor 33
simple set 120, 124
socialist calculation debate 5, 19, 164
Solomonoff–Levin distribution 82
strange attractors 59, 60
stylized facts 172
supporting hyperplane theorem 150
surreal numbers 131

tâtonnement 5, 15, 147, 161
thinking man 23–5, 28, 155, 183
Thirukkural v, viii, ix

theoretical depth 175–6
theory of value 12–13
travelling salesman problem 19
Turing machines 4, 19, 21, 23, 25, 28–9,
  30–1, 33–9, 40–2, 46–9, 50, 52, 56,
  62, 64, 65, 69, 73, 77, 79 80, 88, 98,
  100, 115, 121–3, 127–9, 130–1, 146,
  156, 158, 162–3, 166–7, 183, 189,
  191–3, 196, 198
  alternating 129–30
  nondeterministic 31, 130
  universal 39, 47, 49, 50, 80, 83, 175
Turing's man of economics 183

uncomputable (real) numbers 96, 181
uncomputability 3, 38, 69, 72, 81
uncountable infinity 112, 118
undecidability 3, 8, 39, 52, 73, 108–9,
  126, 198–9
  of the limit sets of dynamical systems
  49
undecidable disjunction 183, 189
universal:
  computation 14
  dynamical system 49, 50, 52
  language 84
  measure 81–2
  prior 74, 79, 80, 99
  proposition 52, 59
  quantifiers 113, 115, 123–5, 129, 131
  Turing machine 39, 47, 49, 50, 80, 83,
  175
  see also computation universality
utility computer 33

Voyage to Laputa 16

Waiting for Godot 178
Walrasian:
  consumer 136
  equilibria 161
welfare economics 13–15, 178–9
well formed formula (w.f.f.) 33